D0863108

_____ *Aboard Air Force One*

Aboard
Air Force One

200,000 MILES WITH A
WHITE HOUSE AIDE

Ken Chitester

FITHIAN PRESS, SANTA BARBARA, CALIFORNIA, 1997

Back cover photo: One of two specially configured Boeing 747-200Bs that serve the President, Air Force One flies over Mount Rushmore. The planes, which entered service in 1990, each carry 73 passengers, cruise at speeds up to 630 miles per hour, can reach a maximum altitude of 45,100 feet and have a range of 9,600 statute miles. (U.S. Air Force photo)

Published by Fithian Press
A division of Daniel and Daniel, Publishers, Inc.
Post Office Box 1525
Santa Barbara, CA 93102

Book design: Eric Larson
Front cover design: Kath Christensen

LIBRARY OF CONGRESS CATALOGING-IN-PUBLICATION DATA
Chitester, Ken, [date]
    Aboard Air Force One : 200,000 miles with a White House aide ; Ken Chitester.
       p.   cm.
    ISBN 1-56474-234-2 (alk. paper)
    1. United States—Politics and government—1933–   2. Clinton, Bill, 1946–   .
3. Chitester, Ken.   I. Title.
E885.C48   1997
973.929—dc21
                                        97-12389
                                          CIP

Contents

Preface

A COLUMNIST for *The Indianapolis News* once wrote, "Outside of the CIA, Hoosier Ken Chitester probably knows more about what's going on in the universe than just about anybody."

That's probably a bit of an exaggeration. But in my job as White House Director of the Office of News Analysis, I constantly monitored the news and reported it to the White House staff. Our office of more than thirty-five staffers, interns and volunteers produced nearly forty news reports each week, summarizing coverage from newspapers, magazines, wire services and television. We produced an estimated 5.7 *million* pages of news reports annually.

To keep President Clinton and his aides in touch with breaking news, I brought a laptop computer aboard Air Force One to monitor the wire services. I traveled 201,197 miles to 22 countries, 36 states and 137 cities with the President (in 65 trips, 162 days and 225 flights) during my nearly two years at the White House.

When I went to Washington, I didn't expect to travel with the President. I was just a junior staffer who ended up being afforded a remarkable opportunity. I didn't come to Washington as a political insider; I was just along for the ride. But along the way I experienced once-in-a-lifetime chances to see people and places across our country and around the world.

I guess I had a lot of naiveté about Washington when I arrived. I was expecting *Mr. Smith Goes to Washington,* but it turned out to be more like *Alice in Wonderland.* Never had I encountered an entire culture where logic and reason and common sense were so routinely ignored. The convoluted rumormongering and backstabbing and distrust along the banks of the Potomac River hung in the air like the August humidity. The obsession with power made me realize that power is to Washington what fame is to Hollywood or money is to Wall Street.

The chasm between the Beltway and the rest of the country seemed almost surreal. Salvador Dalí would be right in home in Washington. Some days I half expected to see a melting watch draped over the Washington Monument. I sometimes thought of that scene in *JFK* in which Kevin Costner, portraying prosecuting attorney Jim Garrison, says, "We're through the looking-glass here, people."

Some of this was readily apparent in our early days at the White House. Political appointees serve "at the pleasure of the President," meaning they can be replaced at any time for any reason. That alone is enough to make one feel insecure. But when the titanic egos of political operatives, the uncertainty of establishing one's role in a new administration and the bright glare of media attention are added, the mixture can be explosive. The highs are dizzying, the lows are crushing, and there is little in between.

All this partially led to the early press hostility toward the Clinton White House (and vice versa). One day I ran into fellow communications aide Bob Boorstin in the first-floor Old Executive Office Building men's room, around the corner from our offices. I was complaining to him about the utter arrogance of the Washington media. "Well," Boorstin said, "there's been a lot of that on both sides."

That combative attitude was apparent not just between the Administration and the press but between the White House and Congress and between Democrats and Republicans. The polarization and divisiveness manifested themselves in political debate that focused on personalities instead of policies and which gave off a lot of heat but shed very little light. In Washington, I thought, there was an insecurity and defensiveness from political aides that bordered on paranoia. Their brash, abrasive arrogance was in fact, I thought, a defense mechanism against a pervasive uncertainty.

In terms of the White House's early dealings with the media, certainly we were hurt by an unfamiliarity with the ways of Washington. Many of us were stunned by the daily buzz, a focus on who's up/who's down, who's in/who's out, who's hot/who's not. Some of us were also taken aback by the constant, overwhelming drumbeat of cynicism and negativity.

One of the most surprising aspects of working as a White House political appointee was what a miserable existence it could be. The hours were horrendous, the stress was palpable and the pay (compared to the private sector) was paltry. In my case, there were other factors (a promised pay raise that never materialized, losing my office, having my staff cut) that didn't help. Many of us felt a deadening, overwhelming sense of constant exhaustion. All of those conditions eventually took their toll, until I was physically, mentally and emotionally drained. When I left, it was largely because I was simply tired of being tired.

By the time I boarded Air Force One for my last trip with the President, I was just going through the motions. I'd become a hollow-eyed drone, devoid of the passion needed for the job. I found myself silently repeating a mantra to remind myself of how lucky I was, even if I didn't feel that way: "I am honored to have the opportunity to serve the President of the United States. I am honored to have the opportunity...."

I came to realize that working at the White House is like eating chocolate cake. No matter how much you like chocolate cake, no matter how delicious you think it is, if you eat it for breakfast, lunch and dinner, seven days a week, 365 days a year, you *will* get sick of it. In fact, eventually you'll get to the point where you dread sitting down at the kitchen table because you know that no matter what, you have to eat more chocolate cake. After two years in Washington, that was the way I'd begun to feel about serving as a White House aide.

After my first year in Washington, I realized that MTV's Beavis and Butthead had taught us that life could be divided into two categories: stuff that's cool, and stuff that sucks. With that in mind, I listed elements of what life—or at least, my life—was like there.

Stuff that's cool:

Working for the President of the United States. Walking past the Oval Office every day. The Marine Band playing "Hail to the Chief" at Rose Garden ceremonies.

Flying on Air Force One. Interacting with the President occasionally. Riding in motorcades. Flying in helicopters. Getting to see America in ways I'd never otherwise be able to.

Traveling overseas. Getting to see Tokyo and Seoul. Spending three days on the beach in Hawaii.

Driving down the U.S. Route 50 hill near Arlington National Cemetery and into Washington across the Potomac River as the sun rose behind the Lincoln, Washington and Jefferson monuments. The view out of the Diplomatic Room on the White House ground floor, with the Jefferson framed in the distance, across the South Lawn, through the double doors. The view of the White House out my Old Executive Office Building window.

Passing and signing of the Family and Medical Leave Act, national service, motor voter registration, the budget, North American Free Trade Agreement and the Brady Bill. Trying to change the country.

All the cool high-tech communications toys at the White House, on Air Force One and at trip sites.

Stuff that sucks:

Washington, the world's most corrupt city. The self-important, condescending, rude, abrasive, self-centered people. The traffic. The weather. The parking, or lack thereof. The expense.

The entrenched bureaucracy, from Congress to career White House employees. ("This is the way we've always done it.") The hierarchy at the White House. The almost military atmosphere.

Occasionally taking for granted what I was fortunate enough to be a part of.

Congress. Bob Dole. Newt Gingrich. Filibusters. Anti-change elements. Weak, visionless, gutless members of Congress.

The Washington press corps. Whining, pampered, spoiled national correspondents. Inside-the-Beltway, out-of-touch, closed-minded, cynical, pompous know-it-alls.

Routine fourteen-hour days. Weekend travel. Red-eye flights. Seeing sunlight only out the office window. Not knowing anyone there except the people I worked with. Not having a real life.

It wasn't an easy time. But perhaps the worst part was that it was easy to lose track of how incredibly, implausibly lucky I was to be working for the President and to be serving my country, not to mention traveling across the United States and around the world aboard Air Force One. It's easy to lose perspective when you're inside the fish bowl.

I fought against it, but it was hard. One day in May I took a long walk to the Vietnam Memorial, the Lincoln Memorial and the Washington Monument for a view of Capitol Hill. I stood at each site a while, reflecting on what I drove past every day and had been taking for granted. Then I tucked the staff ID card around my neck into my shirt pocket and roamed outside the south fence of the White House, along E Street, mingling with the tourists to get a renewed perspective of where I worked.

But such reaffirming efforts didn't always work. One Wednesday evening, after we'd been at the White House about five months, Keith Boykin (news analysis) and I were watching "NBC Nightly News" in our office. I said that I'd had two prevailing emotions since coming to Washington: frustration/anger/depression on one hand and apathy/failure/resignation on the other. "Plus confusion," Boykin said. "That's pervasive. It encompasses everything."

The only sense of accomplishment or involvement I'd had was...well, never. Boykin said his high point had been attending an Oval Office meeting he'd arranged between gay leaders and the President. As the month of June ended, I was hoping my upcoming first Presidential trip to Japan, Korea and Hawaii would be my high point.

In fact, it was only the beginning.

Aboard Air Force One

▶Introduction: Welcome Aboard

IT WAS JULY 4, 1993. I was riding in a taxi from my rented condominium in Arlington, Virginia, across the Potomac River to the White House on a hot, sunny Sunday morning. In a few hours I'd be leaving on my first trip with President Bill Clinton, an eleven-day jaunt to Japan, South Korea and Hawaii, beginning with first-day stops in Philadelphia, the Quad Cities of Illinois/Iowa, and San Francisco.

After perusing the stack of newspapers on my desk (*The New York Times, The Washington Post, The Washington Times*), I dropped off my three bags long before baggage call. Military staff were in charge of collecting staff luggage at a designated time outside Room 89½ of the Old Executive Office Building, located next to the White House, and transporting it to Air Force One. They also unloaded it, delivered it to the hotel, collected it the next morning and loaded it onto Air Force One again. It was like that scene on the bus in *Bull Durham*, in which Kevin Costner tells his minor-league baseball teammates about life in the major leagues: "In the Show, you never handle your own bags."

Later I boarded a staff van, portable computer bags slung over each shoulder, and we headed out the White House gates to Andrews Air Force Base. We were detoured at Morningside, Maryland, by a classic small-town Independence Day parade—convertible Corvettes, fire engines, a marching band, Uncle Sam on stilts…pure Americana.

17

Somehow it seemed fitting to see that as I headed out on my first trip with the President.

On the Andrews tarmac, fellow White House aides and I boarded Nighthawk 3, a huge green Marine helicopter, with the press pool. It was a bright, sweltering day, and we were blasted by hot exhaust, smelling fumes as we entered through the tail. A Marine crew member gave us soft yellow ear plugs, and we settled onto the benches, with plastic green cushions, lining the walls. We lifted off for a one-hour, fifteen-minute flight to Philadelphia. Upon arrival, we swept in at an angle over the water, and I was reminded of *Apocalypse Now*. As we exited the tail and headed toward our vans, a couple of the photographers said the heat and the exhaust fumes had made them nauseated. Me, I kind of liked it.

Then it was through the cleared streets of Philadelphia in the motorcade. I once had read in Timothy Crouse's *The Boys on the Bus* that being in a motorcade is kind of like riding a fire engine with the siren blaring, and it was. People standing on sidewalks pointed at us and waved. When we got to the Liberty Bell Pavilion, the press pool scrambled to get to the President, who was shaking hands along a ropeline. And I didn't get hit in the head by a TV camera until we'd been there, oh, five minutes at least. Actually, it was my fault. I didn't know where to go and just followed the pool and ended up getting too close.

The first person I saw was Ernie Gibble (media affairs). I worked with Gibble in the campaign and the transition, and his familiar face was a welcome sight. I saw the Liberty Bell and Independence Hall (both for the first time, and on the Fourth of July!) before heading to the press office to dial in and monitor wire coverage of the first event. Later, my boss, Director of Media Affairs Jeff Eller, called from the staff office and suggested I work there. So I checked my trip book, found a map, figured out where he was, walked through the police barricades and ducked into a nearby bookstore that was serving as a staff hold.

It was a small, old store with wooden floors, and food was set up on tables. I found a phone jack and an electrical outlet and sat down, my modem squealing as I dialed in to the White House wire service computer system, downloaded stories and then printed them on a nearby laser printer before handing them to Eller and Bruce Lindsey (senior adviser).

The President came in a little later, and I was struck that I was seeing an American President in person. I'd seen him since the Inauguration, of course, but not often and not in a long while.

Julius Erving ("Doctor J"), the former star of the Philadelphia 76ers, was there, too. He came over and chatted with a couple of the non-uniformed military personnel from the White House Communications Agency, which handled all technical communications for the President and his aides. I told Doctor J that I remembered him playing against my hometown Indiana Pacers at the old State Fairgrounds Coliseum when I was a kid, back in the early 1970s. "Oh, man, you're not *that* old," he said, adding, "Yeah, I remember those Fairgrounds games."

Then we went outside for the event in front of Independence Hall, and the President presented the Liberty Medal to South Africa's President de Klerk and Nelson Mandela. Afterward, it was back to the motorcade, on to the helicopters and to the airport, where we boarded Air Force One for Iowa.

Once we were airborne, I took a look around. There was hardly anyone on board: Lindsey, Eller, Steve Rabinowitz (communications/advance), Jeff Watson (political affairs), Andrew Friendly (President's personal aide) and Kelly Craighead (First Lady's trip director) were virtually the only aides aboard besides the usual medical, military and Secret Service staff. I sat in the staff section, facing the rear of the plane, with Eller seated across a table from me. "Not bad, huh?" he said.

I nodded and soaked it all in. In fact, I was overwhelmed. I was so wound up it was all I could do to sit still, but I worked hard to be cool and act professionally. Inside, I felt like a little kid on Christmas morning.

In the staff section were two side-by-side wooden tables with four adjustable seats (two facing forward, two backward). There was another, smaller table by the starboard-side windows, with one seat facing forward and one backward. And then there were four identical blue leather seats without tables, facing forward, in the rear of the staff section, with the walled, four-desk office beside them. (The office included four computers, two laser printers and a typewriter, with a copier just outside each doorway.) The conference room was on the other side of a bulkhead in front of the staff section, with the guest section located behind a bulkhead behind the staff section. In front of the conference room was a four-seat senior staff area, galley, medical compartment and the President's suite. Behind the guest section was the off-duty crew and the fourteen-member press pool, who had their own typewriter. Upstairs was the cockpit and communications center, with fax machine. Downstairs was the luggage compartment.

The two identical, specially configured Boeing 747-200Bs (tail numbers 28000 and 29000) commonly known as Air Force One came into service in 1990. Tail number 28000 made the first trip September 6, 1990, when President Bush flew to Kansas, Florida and back to Washington. Whenever the President is aboard either (or any other Air Force aircraft), the radio call sign is "Air Force One."

According to a U.S. Air Force fact sheet, 28000 and 29000 cruise at speeds up to 630 mph (.92 Mach, or just shy of the speed of sound) at a maximum altitude of 45,100 feet. The maximum passenger load is 73 (plus 22 crew), and each aircraft has a range of 9,600 statute miles. Four General Electric engines each provide 56,700 pounds of thrust, and each plane has a maximum gross weight of 836,000 pounds.

Unlike a normal 747, Air Force One includes sophisticated electronic and communications equipment, a self-contained baggage loader, front and aft air-stairs and the capability for in-flight refueling. Also on board, in the plane's nose, are the President's executive suite, consisting of a dressing room (including two couches which fold out into beds), lavatory (including shower) and office. There is a conference/dining room, about a dozen TVs and VCRs, six lavatories and a fully equipped medical compartment. The two galleys can provide up to 100 meals at one sitting.

A little later, I was settling in as my adrenaline subsided for the first time all day. The President came back to our section, and he wasn't happy. Apparently he'd learned something he didn't like about the event in Iowa we were about to do. In fact, he threw a major temper tantrum. "This is the worst! *The* worst! Whose idea was this?" He was yelling and swearing. Jeff Watson had the misfortune to be standing in front of him, and Eller went over to lend support.

Even above the noise of the plane's four engines, the President's tirade was audible. And within the confines of even a 747, there was no escape. He stood venting his anger by the port-side windows, maybe fifteen feet from me. Finally, after about ten minutes, his tirade subsided and he headed back to the front of the plane. Eller slipped into a chair next to me. "Welcome to the big leagues," he said to me under his breath with a tight grin. I swallowed a smile.

We landed in Moline, Illinois, and headed via motorcade across the swollen Mississippi River to a farm in flooded Iowa, stopping along the way to gaze at the damage from a bridge in downtown Davenport. Water had completely submerged a street and was halfway up the outfield fence at the minor league baseball stadium. At the farm in Eldridge, the President and Agriculture Secretary Mike Espy, both wearing jeans, sat on hay bales under a backyard tent and held a town hall meeting with local farmers. Afterward, over the miles of flat cornfields, a distant Fourth of July fireworks display exploded just over the horizon. Then it was back into the vans, back to the airport and back aboard the plane for the three-hour, forty-minute flight to San Francisco.

I was again sitting in the staff section when the President came back to chat with us. Some aides had their feet up on tables and were sipping soft drinks. Still dressed in his boots, jeans and short-sleeved casual shirt and clearly in a much better mood, he said, "Good job, everybody. Those were real people. You've gotta get out of Washington to meet them."

Later the President poked through a plastic shopping bag full of videotapes brought on board by Andrew Friendly. The President pulled out several, one at a time, and made brief comments: "This is a good one…. Oh, this is a classic…." Then he came to Mel Brooks' 1967 film, *The Producers*, and began to sing, on key but slightly hoarsely, a song from the movie: "It's springtime for Hitler and Germany…." We all laughed.

Not long after that, though, we got word that there had been an explosion at the Seoul, South Korea, hotel where our advance team was staying. We were scheduled to stay there after finishing the upcoming Group of Seven economic summit in Tokyo. White House Communications Agency personnel were trying to make contact with our team there to get updated information. "You have him call me as soon as he knows anything," Army Colonel Tom Hawes (WHCA commander) said into the phone. The lead person of the advance team was Bev Lindsey, Bruce's wife. For several minutes that seemed like an eternity, Bruce stood silently by the windows, waiting for news about his wife. I felt awful for him. I wanted to go over and say something, but at the time I didn't know him very well.

Lindsey had been a friend of the President's since the mid-1960s. A graduate of what is now Rhodes College in Memphis, Lindsey went on to join his father at Little Rock's Wright Lindsey Jennings law firm, where Clinton worked after losing the 1980 gubernatorial election. In addition to directing the Office of Personnel (and later serving as Deputy Counsel to the President), Lindsey's most important role was that of long-time confidant and adviser to the President. He was a short guy who wore button-down collar shirts and striped ties, who was quiet and yet approachable, with a wry sense of humor. Asked by a *Time* reporter during the transition what the biggest difference was after winning the election, Lindsey replied, "Having to shave on Saturday."

Finally we got word that everyone in Seoul was fine, that the hotel's basement furnace had exploded but that our people didn't know the cause. In any case, our advance team was okay and was being taken care of by U.S. Embassy and military staff, and we'd have to find another hotel for the President's visit. Later I finally relaxed enough to sleep a little bit on the way to San Francisco.

We touched down about 12:30 A.M. local time (3:30 A.M. our time), and the motorcade took us to the hotel, bounding through the hilly, empty streets on a ride out of a "Starsky and Hutch" chase scene. At the Fairmont Hotel, we headed to the staff room, where Kim Hopper (media affairs) greeted us. She'd joined the campaign not long after I had, and it was great to see another familiar face in another unfamiliar city. I stayed up late to get a head start on producing the next day's news clippings.

Later, as I lay in bed, my mind raced. I thought back to how I'd gotten to this hotel room, just down the hall from the President of the United States. The past several days had been hectic.

Jeff Eller had taken the laptop on the road with the President for a couple months on several trial runs. He dialed into the wires and got instant coverage of the President's events, helping aides plot communications strategy. It was becoming clear that soon the system would be in place and that I would take over. Having taken my paperwork to a State Department office at 14th and K streets to get my passport a few weeks previously, I found out I needed shots to travel overseas. So

I went to the first-floor Old Executive Office Building medical unit (run by the military) and got a gamma globulin shot, capsules for ty-phoid and a tetanus shot.

Then I had photos taken downstairs in the travel office for my visas. I was issued an Official passport (as opposed to Diplomatic, which went to members of the official party—basically senior staff— or a Tourist passport.) The Office of Scheduling and Advance handled all passports for us. In fact, I ended up traveling to twenty-two coun-tries and saw my passport only once—near the end of the first trip. When I left the White House, the State Department kept my pass-port, since it was for official travel only.

Three days before we left, I tracked down Captain Mike Curry of the White House Communications Agency, on site in Tokyo. I could dial a regular five-digit extension, same as if I were dialing anywhere on the White House grounds, and reach the temporary WHCA office in Tokyo. Curry was helping set up the phone operations on site. "Well, y'all must've done a good job," I told him, "because it sounds as if you're in the next room."

Nobody had ever taken a White House laptop computer halfway around the world and tried to dial in and monitor the news in real time.

I went in to the office the day before we left for some last-minute details, including a final briefing from Eller. I stood by his desk as he chewed on a cigar and clicked on his computer keyboard. He ran through last-minute information on staff pins, motorcades, trip sites, hotels, luggage, technical equipment, Air Force One dial tone...all sorts of stuff. I tried to remember everything. "And never get in the front seat of Staff 1," he said of our motorcade vehicle. "That would be (trip director) Wendy (Smith)'s seat. I made that mistake once."

I glanced over the aircraft manifests to see where I was supposed to be and who else would be there. Looking at the manifests of all the various aircraft, Eller said, "There's gonna be a lot of hardware in the air tomorrow," adding, "Once you get on the plane, you can wear whatever you want. But tomorrow you'd better wear a coat and tie."

I could hardly get to sleep that night, I was so keyed up. I won-dered what it would be like. I hoped I wouldn't screw up or get lost. And I kept realizing I was about to become a part of the traveling White House staff, that I'd be representing my country overseas. Me?

On Air Force One? I couldn't believe it.

Still awake in that first night in San Francisco, my mind wouldn't stop spinning. I thought about my first—and only—trip to Washington before I moved there. I was eight years old, and my mom, dad, cousin and I drove there from our home in Indiana. We visited the White House one hot weekday with fellow tourists in shorts and sunglasses, cameras around their necks and strolling the sidewalks with maps in hand. We stood in line for what seemed (to a little kid) to be a really long time. Richard Nixon was President, and I was mad when I found out we'd waited in line all that time and he wasn't even there. I thought, what's the "Western White House?" I thought there was only one White House. And if the President is in San Clemente, California, why didn't we go there? I don't remember very much about the White House tour itself.

I grew up in Indianapolis, surrounded by cornfields and Republicans. I never thought much about politics. As a kid, I loved sports. I knew at an early age that the odds of a professional athletic career were slim, so I focused on sports writing. In high school, I developed a passing interest in politics, basic 1960s-bleeding-heart-liberal-stuff, completely out of place in early 1980s Indiana.

After graduating with a journalism degree from Indiana University in 1985, I worked in Danville, Illinois, as assistant sports editor of the *Commercial-News*. It was four years of slow death. Danville is a Rust Belt hellhole, a tiny, backward, blue-collar town in the middle of nowhere with ancient factories and an ugly, abandoned downtown. It was probably a nice little place back when railroads were the major method of transportation. I used to compare being there to being a prisoner of war. If I were a soldier, I thought, at least I could do my tour of duty and move on. But I never knew when that evac chopper would swoop in and take me to a new job and a new city.

I used to think about doing something else, and a political campaign sounded fascinating. But the idea of giving up a job where you got paid every week to try for one where you'd get paid less, and infrequently (if at all), not to mention one that in the best scenario would end in a few months, just didn't make sense. Instead, I watched the 1988 Democratic National Convention on television at Fatman's Warehouse Saloon. There was some guy at the podium who was the Governor of Arkansas, supposedly some young hotshot on his way up the political ladder. Every time I looked up at the TV, the guy was still jabbering.

I finally got an offer to join the *Arkansas Gazette* as a sports copy editor in early 1990. I was excited about moving to a city I'd at least heard of. "You want to live in *Arkansas?*" my friends asked. "No, I want to live in Little Rock, and it happens to be in Arkansas," I said. (Later, I'd come to fall in love with both the city and the state.)

The *Gazette* was in the midst of a newspaper war with its cross-town rival, the *Arkansas Democrat*. Both produced morning editions, but that was where the similarities ended. The liberal *Gazette*, owned by Gannett Co., Inc., had changed from family ownership and the paper of record (known as "The Old Gray Lady") to a color-laden, headline-blaring, tabloid-news, *USA Today* wannabe. The conservative *Democrat*, with its decaying newsroom and tiny salaries, was the hungry up-and-comer, owned by a local millionaire.

Eventually, the *Democrat* won the war. Gannett, losing an estimated $15 to $20 million on the *Gazette* that final year, pulled the plug on October 18, 1991. The *Democrat* bought its assets (the printing presses, the building, the name, even the *Gazette's* two Pulitzer Prizes from coverage of the 1957 Central High School desegregation crisis) and renamed itself the *Arkansas Democrat-Gazette*.

In fact, the reason I ended up working for the Clinton campaign in the first place was that, basically, nobody else wanted me. After two months of using severance pay to job hunt, it became obvious nobody in Little Rock had an opening for a former newspaper sports writer/ editor who wanted to do communications work. I was reminded of President Kennedy, who rescued his PT-109 crew in World War II after the boat was cut in two by a Japanese destroyer. He was often asked how he became a war hero. "They sank my boat," he'd reply, deadpan. Well, that's how I ended up on the campaign: they sank my newspaper.

As I lie in bed, exhausted from following the President across the country, that quiet night in San Francisco seemed a long time removed from a memorable sunny October day in Arkansas almost two years earlier, when this adventure began.

1▶Rock the Vote

IT WAS A SUNNY, WARM THURSDAY at lunchtime in downtown Little Rock. An overflow crowd in business attire, estimated by police at 4,500, was surrounded by red, white and blue bunting and signs. They gathered on the grounds of the Old State House for an event many of them had awaited for years.

It was October 3, 1991, and Arkansas Governor Bill Clinton was announcing his candidacy for President of the United States.

Clinton, in a dark gray suit, light blue shirt and dark blue striped tie, talked for thirty-five minutes about personal responsibility, welfare as a second chance and not a way of life, bringing people together instead of tearing them apart, tax fairness for the middle class, an end to '80s greed and preventing this generation from becoming the first to do worse than its parents. Standing on the Markham Street sidewalk outside a black iron fence, I found myself nodding and applauding.

My liberalism had started to become shaky as early as 1988. As hard as I tried, I could never make myself like Michael Dukakis. And when he lost, I vowed never to vote for another liberal loser. Winning was what mattered. You can't change things if you don't govern, and you can't govern if you don't win. It was better to vote for somebody you only partially agreed with and have them win than to vote for somebody you completely agreed with and have them lose.

And by fall 1991, I'd moved to the South, bought a house, gotten a

27

dog and grown up a little. I'd watched Bill Clinton for a year and a half by the time I heard him speak that day and had voted for him for governor in 1990. He'd made all the right moves to position himself for the nomination. At the time, I didn't think anybody could beat George Bush, who had an approval rating of more than 70 percent. But I thought Clinton would make a good candidate. And he was the hometown boy.

The circus had come to town, and I love circuses. So one day I went to Clinton for President Committee headquarters at Third and Pulaski streets and met the volunteer coordinator. He escorted me to the press office, where I met Dee Dee Myers, the recently hired press secretary.

Myers was just coming back from lunch and was wearing a long black leather coat. She was in her early thirties (although, knowing a little about her vast experience, I'd assumed she was older). She had short blond hair and wore a dark blue suit. A southern California native, her father was a Naval aviator who had flown combat missions in Vietnam. Her given name was Margaret Jane, but she was dubbed "Dee Dee" by her sister, who as a toddler was trying to say "baby." A Catholic graduate of the University of Santa Clara, Myers had gotten her start in national politics working for longtime Clinton ally Mickey Kantor on the 1984 Mondale presidential campaign in California. She then worked on Dianne Feinstein's unsuccessful 1990 California gubernatorial bid and had just finished a winning mayoral campaign for Frank Jordan in San Francisco. During the campaign, she became a favorite of the press corps. Once, during one in a seemingly endless series of long campaign events, she literally turned a cartwheel to amuse the reporters.

We chatted briefly in her office, and she said to call back in a few days. After a couple weeks of trying to reach her, I got a call from Matt Smith of the press department. He was in charge of monitoring news coverage and needed help. I went down to talk with him on a Friday and began work the following Monday.

Smith was about thirty years old, a Chicago native who had worked on Mayor Richard Daley's campaign and then in his administration. A balding guy who favored dark shirts and wild ties, he liked sports and pop culture and was funny and friendly and great to work with. We started in a windowless room that previously had been a storage shed for gas cans and a snow blower and quickly began covering the brick walls with goofy newspaper photos and clippings. We had a file cabinet, a desk, a table, a pair of scissors, a ruler and a roll of tape. With those meager supplies and a tiny copier, we produced morning and afternoon editions of news clips. There were about sixty people in the national headquarters then, with most of the staff supporting the candidate on site in New Hampshire.

One day in late January, George Stephanopoulos and David Wilhelm, who were running the campaign, addressed the staff in the largest room we had, shared by the press and scheduling departments. It was the day after the *Star* tabloid had run a front-page story on Gennifer Flowers' alleged twelve-year affair with Governor Clinton. Now I know how Gary Hart's staff felt, I thought. Instead, Wilhelm vowed we'd stay and fight. "We have the message, and we have the candidate," he said. Then Stephanopoulos told us that Governor and Mrs. Clinton would appear on "60 Minutes" after the Super Bowl that Sunday.

Smith left for a few weeks in March to work on the primary in his home state of Illinois. I filled in, and a few weeks after he got back, I started to get paid on a part-time basis. One spring afternoon Smith and I were in the parking lot, throwing a Nerf football as we often did during the mid-day lull between news cycles, when senior staffer Jeff Eller walked by with George Stephanopoulos. They were talking about installing a wire service computer system in the new headquarters. Later, I told Eller I'd been a copy editor in the *Arkansas Gazette* building, where we'd be moving

"I didn't know that," he said.

"Well, when you go to find somebody to monitor that system, keep me in my mind," I told him, and he said he would.

During the primaries, Tuesdays were game days. It was like the National Football League, where teams play once a week. Which primary is it this week—New York? Vermont? We'd have pizza or chicken or ribs or catfish or Mexican food delivered, with cans of soft drinks and beer nearby in huge ice-filled tubs, on pleasant spring evenings. We'd eat dinner outside, with the setting sun casting an orange glow behind the nearby state capitol dome and train station clock. Then we'd go inside and monitor the results and count up the delegates we'd won.

A couple months after that, we'd all but sewn up the 2,145 delegates needed for nomination. The headquarters were moving...back to the *Gazette* building, of all places. It was vacant and perfect for a national campaign. (There had been talk of moving the campaign to Washington.) Even better, I'd been hired for a paid, full-time position and would be in charge of the wire system when it was installed.

Our first week in the new building, Clinton clinched the nomination with a victory in the California primary. We watched his appearance on "The Arsenio Hall Show." Thanks to our new satellite dish, we got to see it hours before it aired nationwide. After a celebration party, we drove to the airport and greeted the candidate's plane, woofing and waving our fists as the laughing candidate descended the stairs. He was wearing the same wildly colorful tie he had on TV. David Wilhelm grabbed me on the tarmac and asked me to drive consultant Paul Begala, James Carville's less-publicized partner, to the hotel. Begala turned out to be a great guy, really nice and down to earth.

On a hot, sunny June weekday afternoon not long afterward, a few hundred campaign staffers and other supporters stood on the back lawn of the Governor's Mansion as Governor Clinton announced that Senator Al Gore of Tennessee would be his running mate. "I didn't seek this," Gore said. "I didn't expect it."

That rang a chord with me. Unlike many of the folks I'd end up working with in Washington, I didn't grow up eating and breathing politics. In fact, I never thought about working in the White House. It was just too remote, too unreal. As a kid, I dreamed more about playing in the Super Bowl or the World Series, and that was unrealistic enough.

In July, we headed to New York for the convention. Money was in short supply since we hadn't yet received our Federal Election Commission matching funds for the general campaign. So Matt Smith and I were among those who had to stay at the YMCA. The Manhattan YMCA looked pretty much like you'd expect it to...kind of like Dan Aykroyd's rented room in *The Blues Brothers*, minus the El train running outside the window. But we were rarely there anyway.

We spent our days in the chilly, air-conditioned Intercontinental Hotel (where each morning at a press office meeting we learned the "message of the day") and our evenings at Madison Square Garden. I stood on the floor when Ohio put us over the top ("Madam Secretary, Ohio casts 144 votes for the next President of the United States...."), soaking in the atmosphere as music played and confetti fell and delegates cheered. Backstage we hugged and shook hands and high-fived near our trailers, where fellow Clinton/Gore staffers had tracked delegate counts on the floor. Governor and Mrs. Clinton and Chelsea made an historic, televised walk down Seventh Avenue to appear before the convention.

The next night I heard Clinton's nearly hour-long acceptance speech ("I still believe in a place called Hope") and sang along to Fleetwood Mac's "Don't Stop," which also had been played at his announcement speech. It was a wild time. All week we saw political, journalistic and entertainment celebrities everywhere. ("Hey, that was Jackie Kennedy!") The final night Clinton staffers joined 1,500 other Democrats at the Palladium, where Bo Diddley performed, singing, "*Push* Bush out the door/Push *Bush* out the door."

Back in Little Rock, the three-story headquarters building, erected in 1908, got crowded as new staffers flooded in. Smith went upstairs to work for James Carville's famed "war room." I stayed on the second floor and worked for Eller. Every two hours, I compiled a collection of relevant wire stories and transmitted them around the building via e-mail. Four times a day I did the same thing for the Clinton traveling party, so they could dial in to an electronic mailbox and download the most recent stories. I did the same thing four times a day for the Gore traveling party, and three times a day for all fifty or so state offices. It went on seven days a week, twelve to fourteen hours a day, ninety-plus hours a week from the convention until Election Day.

But it was an exciting atmosphere. The young, energetic, casually dressed staff was trying to change the country. I was usually the first one in the press department each morning, e-mailing the first batch of news stories to the candidates' traveling parties. Gore's was usually the first to leave the hotel and often was on Eastern time, an hour ahead of us. Soon afterward, the sun would stream through the blinds as the morning talk shows aired on the three elevated television sets near my desk, and a box of muffins from Solar Cafe would arrive ("The muffins are in the house!").

Later the candidate's first event of the day would air via satellite on our in-house channel, which we called BCTV. As Gore introduced Clinton, he would launch into soundbites so familiar to the staff that we'd all say them along with him: "When Bush and Quayle say 'Four more years,' it sounds more like a threat than a promise!" Then at 3:30 P.M., every TV would tune to CNN so we could watch "Inside Politics."

The staff at the national headquarters swelled to about 450, including about 80 full-time volunteers. We had about 300 computers, 60 fax machines, 30 copiers and 45 TV sets. Each day eight receptionists handled about 10,000 incoming phone calls, and about 15,000 outgoing calls were made, making Clinton/Gore '92 one of the state's largest phone users. Every day 8,000 letters arrived, and we spent $5,000 on outgoing mail. The campaign spent about $8,000 on travel expenses daily. Each week we recycled 2,500 pounds of white paper, 600 pounds of newspaper and 100 pounds of aluminum cans. There were people all over: vendors roaming the building selling sandwiches to those who couldn't leave for lunch, electricians on ladders pulling cables, tour groups. We had more than 7,000 students tour the headquarters. Among the staff, there were pregnancies, births and deaths.

Campaign workers from more than forty states across the country ate lunch at Your Mama's Good Food and dinner at Doe's Eat Place. They flocked to staff parties at Solar Cafe, where we watched the World Series one Saturday night in October. The Toronto Blue Jays beat the Atlanta Braves, and somehow it seemed a harbinger. Things were so bad under George Bush, we said, that we can't even keep the championship trophy to the American game in our own country. (The following year in the White House, I found myself cheering for the Philadelphia Phillies against Toronto.)

Election Day, of course, was the culmination. For those of us ready to drop from exhaustion, it was welcome relief. For one night, Little Rock was the center of the universe, and downtown was jammed with satellite trucks beaming signals around the world. By that night, the day-long rain had halted and the streets were so crowded with tens of thousands of people that it was difficult to walk on the chilly evening.

At the Old State House, where Clinton would make his speech, a half-dozen fellow press staffers and I squeezed onto the lawn and into a reserved spot right in front. I was fifteen feet from the stage when the governor thanked "my brilliant, aggressive, unconventional but always winning campaign staff. They were unbelievable. And they have earned this." We all yelled and cheered, and he looked at me and returned my thumbs-up with an identical gesture. But it didn't seem real until later at a campaign staff get-together at the Arkansas Repertory Theater, when I saw taped coverage of President Bush's concession speech. We did it, I thought. We really did it.

It was a strange evening: walking down Main Street (closed to traffic) with fellow press staffers, carrying an enormous American flag and singing "Battle Hymn of the Republic"; leaving a late-night party with a drunken, incoherent Hunter S. Thompson; watching on TV in the staff food tent as state after state turned blue on the maps, indicating Clinton/Gore victories; earlier in the day, greeting the governor's plane at the airport and driving back with fellow staffers, "Don't Stop" blaring out the car speakers.

A couple weeks later, we moved two blocks down Louisiana Street to the Atkins Building, where the Little Rock transition office would be established. A Washington office was set up, too, and a lot of campaign staff also went to the Presidential Inaugural Committee in Washington. The President-Elect, many key staffers and the press operation stayed in Little Rock. I collected all the wire service computers, wiring and other hardware from the *Gazette* building, loaded them in the back of my car, drove to the new office, carried them upstairs and plugged them in. My hiring consisted of Dee Dee Myers telling us in a press staff meeting to let her know if we were interested, my telling her I'd like to go and her saying, "You should count on going with us."

Compared to the campaign, the transition was a breeze: only twelve hours a day, with little to do on the weekends. But underneath it all was the uneasiness over who would be hired by the administration and who wouldn't. At first, I wasn't sure I even wanted to go to Washington. But eventually I realized it was too rare an opportunity to pass up. One wet, windy, gray afternoon, Jeff Eller and I stood outside the main entrance of the Atkins Building. As he smoked a cigar, I told him I definitely wanted to be included. "If I get to do what I want," he said, there would be a White House department much like ours had been in the campaign, and I'd be in charge of monitoring the wire services.

Appointments came agonizingly slowly. The White House staff were the last to be announced, just days before the President-Elect left for Washington. One day in mid-January, Eller walked behind me on the way to his desk. "I can officially offer you a job now," he said.

"Congratulations," I said, knowing that meant he'd been hired. "Can I tell anybody?"

"Sure," he said.

And that was it. We started to box up our office supplies Friday to take to Washington. The staff plane would leave on Sunday.

I couldn't wait.

2▶1600 Pennsylvania Avenue

CRAIG SMITH STOOD AT THE FRONT of the chartered airplane carrying transition staffers from Little Rock, Arkansas, to Washington, D.C. Smith, a long-time Clinton gubernatorial aide, was the first staffer hired at the presidential campaign's exploratory committee a year and a half earlier. He took the public address system microphone and made sure everyone had a glass of champagne. Then he toasted our success.

It was Sunday, January 17, 1993. In three days, Bill Clinton would become the forty-second President of the United States. Shortly after Smith's toast, the sights of Washington were visible from the plane's windows. We could see the Lincoln Memorial, the Washington Monument...and the White House. "Ladies and gentlemen, welcome to Washington," our pilot said over the public address system, and we all applauded and cheered.

A couple days later, I was sitting in our press office at George Washington University, temporary headquarters until we could move into our offices at the White House a few blocks away. We were watching morning news coverage of events around town leading up to the Inauguration in a few hours. "This is it, Kenny," Press Aide Dave Seldin said, "the day we take over and run the country."

"Yeah, yeah—so when's lunch?" I said, and we both laughed. Actually, up to that point I'd been in a bit of a foul mood because I hadn't been able to contribute that week and felt in the way. And it wasn't at all clear who would be doing what once we moved in. Only a few senior-level White House staff had even been officially hired.

After attending the Inauguration swearing-in ceremony, four of us in the press office shared a taxi from Capitol Hill to near Lafayette Park ("where Bush bought the crack," I said, citing virtually my only knowledge of the site, which was an anti-drug Oval Office address President Bush had delivered in which he displayed a bag of crack cocaine federal agents had purchased in Lafayette Park, across the street from the White House).

Once inside the White House, everything seemed smaller than I'd expected, especially the press briefing room. Near the press office, I saw a package addressed to former Press Secretary Marlin Fitzwater, with "Trash" written on it. One of our press staffers said she'd taken a phone call for Fitzwater that day. How could somebody not know he was gone?

Later, a half-dozen of us on the communications staff checked out our offices on the first floor of the Old Executive Office Building, across one-lane West Executive Drive and within the White House complex. We got prime real estate—first-floor offices with views of the West Wing across the driveway. We high-fived and took a group photo. Sir Edmund Hillary's men were no more glad to reach the pinnacle of Mount Everest.

The Old Executive Office Building, completed in January 1888 at a cost of slightly more than $10 million, was originally known as the State, Navy and War Building. An enormous, haunting structure in the Second Empire style, its architect committed suicide two and a half years after it was completed. It was renamed the Executive Office Building in 1949 and then the Old Executive Office Building when the New Executive Office Building a block away was completed in the 1960s. The OEOB was designated a National Historic Landmark in 1969 and has provided offices for two Presidents, a host of Vice Presidents, twenty-five Secretaries of State, twenty-one Secretaries of War and fifteen Secretaries of the Navy.

That night we all put on our tuxedos and gowns and attended Inaugural balls around town. I got tickets to the Midwestern ball, the last of the evening to be attended by the President and First Lady. Frankly, it was lame, full of stuffy people in formal wear. Besides, I was exhausted from the move to Washington and the hectic week.

It's hard to explain the thrill of being part of a new administration in Washington. And when the staff is younger than any in memory, when there's a change of the party in power for the first time in twelve years, when your guy was elected as the candidate of change, that's especially true. Suddenly you're important simply because of what you're a part of. Even low-level staff are treated as special. That honeymoon period is an incredible rush.

Unfortunately, it doesn't last long. In our case, the honeymoon was particularly brief. And even during that period—when everything you do seems outwardly so new and fresh and exciting—in fact, on the inside it's horribly frustrating. That first Sunday, I clipped a "Doonesbury" cartoon, in which the last panel was the familiar South Portico, with a voice from inside saying, "Anyone figured out the phones yet?"

When we moved into the White House, the hard drives of our computers had been removed in compliance with a court order related to an old campaign issue. There were typewriters (!) all over the place. The lack of modern equipment was striking. All the file cabinets were empty, as were the desks. No office supplies...nothing.

After we'd been there a few days, I found out officially that I'd be the Deputy Director of News Analysis. Director of Media Affairs Jeff Eller said there were to be three aides in our office, which would be in charge of monitoring all the news coverage of the President and summarizing it for the White House staff. We'd create a set of newspaper clippings and write a news summary each morning, in addition to creating weekly magazine summaries and weekly editorial cartoon compilations.

In the previous administration, the Office of News Summary was located in four offices up in the corner of the Old Executive Office Building fourth floor. We were told they had five full-time staff and three full-time interns and worked in various shifts twenty-four hours a day. Our three-person office was in OEOB 162, near the corner of the first floor, overlooking the North Lawn where the TV reporters did their stand-ups. (One of the early oddities in those days was looking out the window and seeing CNN's Wolf Blitzer talking to a camera, and then looking at the TV in our office and seeing the same thing.)

In addition to me (primarily in charge of monitoring the wire services), we had Director of News Analysis Keith Boykin. He came to the campaign after the convention from a San Francisco law firm and had been in charge of media affairs for the Midwest region, one of six regions under Jeff Eller. A Dartmouth graduate who earned his law degree at Harvard, Boykin was tall, soft-spoken, intelligent, articulate and polite. A former college track and field athlete, he also was one of only two openly gay African-American men on the White House staff. In addition to his title, Boykin was a Special Assistant to the President. (An Assistant to the President outranked a Deputy Assistant, who outranked a Special Assistant. But few White House staff were an Assistant to the President of any type. Basically, it meant that you could eat in the White House Mess and park inside the gate.)

Also in our office, as Assistant Director of News Analysis, was Julie Oppenheimer, a Chicago native who had worked in field operations for the campaign, starting in the early primaries. Our full-time, overnight volunteer would be Larry Sampas, a former Maryland campaign office staffer, whose parents were career State Department diplomats.

Our office had ornately detailed molding, old wooden furniture, dark blue carpeting, a twenty-foot-high ceiling, a TV set, two desks, two tall windows with beige drapes, two computers, a round table with four chairs and wooden file cabinets. Fortunately, we had some volunteers to help with the early-morning clipping of papers. But that was about all we did have.

Oppenheimer worked next door in an enormous conference room (which would become the "war room" for the budget bill and later for health care reform). To monitor the wires, I had to go upstairs to a fourth-floor walk-in closet, where five dot-matrix printers spit out hundreds of feet of text from the wire services. No wonder we blitzkrieged these guys during the campaign, I thought. When it came to quick retrieval and immediate internal dissemination of news coverage, they never had a chance. Granted, I didn't know what Bush/Quayle campaign headquarters had, but surely it wasn't any better than what the White House had.

Those early weeks for me in News Analysis usually began at 6:30 A.M. and didn't end until after 8:30 P.M. They were full of frustration over insufficient resources and our ignorance of how the White House ran and who was in charge of what. The news we were monitoring quickly turned from the Inauguration to the raging controversy over gays in the military, overrunning our agenda.

One of the surprising things about those early days was what I called the "ghosts." After all I'd read and studied about the White House, and especially about the Kennedy Administration, I thought that when I saw sites like the Oval Office and the Cabinet Room in person for the first time, I'd visualize Kennedy's men, or maybe FDR and his staff. (The West Wing had been constructed in 1902, so other favorite Presidents like Jackson and Lincoln wouldn't have worked there.) But instead, the only feel I got was for Bush and his staff. I guess that's because they'd been there only days before we moved in, and those were the television images I'd most recently been inundated with.

In addition to the many changes facing the new staff, there were some similarities with the campaign. For the State of the Union address, the "war room" next to our News Analysis office was jammed as several dozen of us watched on TV, following along in the prepared texts in front of us. Afterward, several of us each tuned in a network to monitor reaction and then wrote quick summaries. Pizzas were delivered for us afterward.

Paperwork, of course, was a pervasive element as we adjusted to life at the White House. "Ken, do you know why the FBI came to my house today?" a friend from Little Rock said on the phone. Oh, yeah, I said, I forgot to tell you about that.

The SF-86 ("Questionnaire for Sensitive Positions") is the standard form for prospective White House political appointees. Among other things, it requests would-be staffers to list their addresses and someone there who knows them—for the past fifteen years. It's extensive, delving into many areas. But when I put down friends' names for verification, sometimes I forgot to tell them the FBI would be contacting them.

There were so many of us going through the process at the same time that to speed things along, the FBI agents (who had an Old Executive Office Building fifth-floor office for that purpose) sometimes asked us to vouch for each other. Upon seeing that I was in the Office of Communications, the agent interviewing me (Gary Aldrich, who went on to write a much-ridiculed book that ripped the Clinton White

House) asked how well I knew fellow communications aide Heather Beckel (assistant to George Stephanopoulos). Well, I've never seen her naked, if that's what you mean, I thought.

When I later told Beckel that, she said, "You didn't really say that, did you?" No, I said, the FBI doesn't joke around much. (Aldrich, who in his book shows himself to be straight-laced even for an FBI agent, probably would have had a stroke.)

I also heard one story, undoubtedly apocryphal, about one of our prospective appointees who was asked the inevitable question about drug use.

"Yeah," he said, "but only four, five...hundred times."

"Son," the agent supposedly told him, "that's not experimentation. That's abuse."

I didn't have a White House parking pass when we first got to Washington. Most of that time I rode the Metro. Sometimes I'd get Keith Boykin's parking pass (he didn't have a car) from our full-time volunteer, Larry Sampas, as he completed the overnight shift, and then park inside the gates. The first time I did that, I pulled up to the southwest gate and showed my pass to the uniformed Secret Service officer. Then the black iron gates with gold stars slowly opened, and I wished I'd had a video camera to capture the view as I carefully pulled onto West Executive Drive, Old Executive Office Building on the left and West Wing on the right. This is just like riding the tour bus into Graceland, I thought...except the gates of Graceland have musical notes and not stars on them.

Not long afterward, Jeff Eller hosted a few meetings in his office with myself and staff from the White House Communications Agency. They were in charge of pagers, cellular phones, satellites, television reception, secure communications, the public address system at events, phone lines at trip sites...everything. Also in attendance at one meeting was Mike Bennett of Generation Technologies, the software vendor who designed the system we used to monitor the wire services during the campaign. Generation also provided the same service for the House of Representatives, the Senate, CBS and WGN radio in Chicago, among others.

It was at one of those meetings that Eller happened to mention that I'd be issued a laptop computer and would go on all Presidential trips to monitor the wire services. He'd never told me that. I was shocked. And I was thrilled. "You will be on the permanent manifest," he said.

I tried to be low-key in case it didn't work out, but plans for a wire service computer system like we had in the campaign were rolling along, on everything from who would pay for it to how it would be installed. Among the complications was the fact that the White House and the Old Executive Office Building aren't places you can just go drilling holes and pulling cables any place you want. Aside from security concerns, the buildings are National Historic Landmarks. But I had faith in Eller.

Jeff Eller was, ironically, a fellow Hoosier. Born and raised in rural Arcadia (about twenty-five miles north of Indianapolis), he was the first in six generations to leave the family farm. A former local television reporter, he'd worked for about half a dozen years on Capitol Hill in several political capacities, most recently at the Democratic Senatorial Campaign Committee. He joined the Clinton campaign in November 1991 and was sent to Florida. Clinton won a December straw poll there and then won the state's primary in March. Eller then reported to Little Rock, where he headed up what became the state press operation, similar to the White House's Office of Media Affairs.

Eller was a workaholic and a technological wizard, always pushing the edge of the envelope, finding new ways to use communications technology to advance the candidate and the message. A sign on his White House office door said, "When entering this room, do NOT say: 'We're never done it that way before.'" An idiosyncratic sort, he'd alienated his fair share of people during his career. But even more marveled at his drive and his resourcefulness. Wearing glasses, a mustache (and later a beard) and usually dressed in penny loafers, khakis and a tieless oxford shirt with the sleeves rolled up, Eller was in his late thirties. A cigar connoisseur, he also was known to randomly call out prayer chants in Arabic and imitate barnyard animals' noises. During the transition in Little Rock, he proudly tended to a chia pet, for which he had a staff ID card made. White House Deputy Director of Legislative Affairs Susan Brophy used to say, "It's a full-time job being Eller."

Eller was always full of ideas. One morning he burst into my office, and, pulling up a chair beside my desk, said, "All right, Chitester. I got ten hours sleep last night and I've got plenty of ideas."

"So grab a pen," I said, notepad in hand.

"So grab a pen," he agreed, and we chatted about ways to get more out of the wire service computer system.

A test set-up from Generation arrived the last weekend of March. ("The toys are here," Eller told me.) Technicians installed a phone line at my desk, and Mike Bennett of Generation hooked up a modem and a computer loaded with software to access the wire services. It was a piggyback from another feed, so it was only a temporary solution. But we tied it in to our printer and were on our way.

The final four workstations of the wire service computer system were connected the following December. That made fifteen, scattered throughout the White House and Old Executive Office Building. It took a long time, but it was a tremendous achievement, especially considering what was (or wasn't) there when we started. The goal was for Presidential aides or their assistants to be able to check for wire stories in their area of responsibility and hopefully take some of the load off our understaffed Office of News Analysis.

About three weeks later, I was able to e-mail the four daily compilations of relevant wire stories directly to a bulletin board on our computer system so everybody at the White House could scroll through them. That was a huge step forward. (One afternoon I took a bunch of data the White House computer staff provided for me and created a one-page report on the electronic readership of what our office produced. I was pleasantly surprised that so many staffers—an average of more than 168 each day one month—read what we created.) We finally had all the wire service feeds coming in, all the workstations were in place, everyone could print and I could e-mail compilations not just to selected individuals, but could post them so everyone could see them.

To take advantage of all this technology at the White House when I traveled with the President, I was issued a laptop computer made by GRiD, which provides the military with computers. (GRiD laptops have flown on the space shuttle.)

I also got a SecurID card, which had a digital readout that changed every sixty seconds, synchronically with the code at the main computer in the New Executive Office Building. Combined with my pager and the cell phone, portable printer and two-way radio I was later issued, I was loaded with high-tech toys to take on the road.

Our Motorola Bravo pagers accepted alpha-numeric messages. So in addition to punching in a number from a phone, White House aides could send text messages via our computer system. What some aides didn't know in the early days of the Administration was that those messages were read and relayed by White House Communications Agency personnel. Army Colonel Tom Hawes (WHCA commander) laughingly told some of us a story of a romantic couple on staff who sent each other extremely ribald messages. When a WHCA officer informed the female aide that her messages were being read by people other than her boyfriend, she was aghast, to say the least.

We each also were issued a "hard pass," a blue-bordered plastic badge with photo worn on a chain around one's neck. To enter the White House grounds, staffers had to wave their passes over a red electronic eye, which activated a keyboard (the numbers appearing in a random pattern), and then punch in an individualized identification number, which released the turnstile for entry.

In addition to such high-tech matters, a more substantive highlight of those early days was passing legislation. Our daily legislative/communications morning meeting in the conference room adjacent to the News Analysis office was particularly uplifting the day after the Family and Medical Leave Act reached the President's desk. Congress had been trying for years to pass it, and enacting it had been a Clinton campaign promise.

Later that February morning, on an unseasonably warm and sunny Friday, the President signed the bill in a Rose Garden ceremony. I stood off to the side with other applauding staffers. As I told Keith Boykin later, "This is it. This is why we're here. It was important to kick Bush out, it was fun to win and move in, but this is it—we can actually improve people's lives." It was a thrill to be part of doing the public good, to be working with those engaged in public service. All those months of the campaign were worth it. But that evening, the top story on the TV news was Attorney General nominee Zoe Baird withdrawing her name because she hadn't paid Social Security tax for her housekeeper (more "Nannygate").

We as a staff often seemed to be among the top Washington stories. That was true the first week of June 1993. David Gergen, a PBS commentator and former *U.S. News and World Report* editor who had worked at the White House for Nixon, Ford and Reagan, was hired to turn around our foundering communications efforts. The President made the announcement at a Saturday morning Rose Garden ceremony. George Stephanopoulos was in effect kicked upstairs, moving into an office adjacent to the Oval Office, where he'd serve as a senior adviser.

Stephanopoulos had been one of Clinton's earliest hires in the campaign. The son of a Greek Orthodox priest, he was a former high school wrestler from Cleveland who became a Rhodes Scholar. He'd worked as Missouri Congressman Richard Gephardt's legislative director before taking one of the Clinton campaign's top positions in October 1991. By the time we got to the White House, Stephanopoulos was virtually a pop culture icon, his smallish frame, bushy dark hair and youthful countenance regularly appearing on television. Aside from his political astuteness and his obvious intelligence (as James Carville used to say, "If IQ were Fahrenheit, that boy could boil water"), the thing that most impressed me about Stephanopoulos was his articulateness. He could be more succinctly expressive off the top of his head than most people could if they had a week to write it.

I couldn't believe Gergen's hiring. A *Republican* is my boss? A *Reaganite?* I thought, I got into this partly because I wanted to fight against everything they did in the '80s. I had a bad feeling about it, and I wasn't alone. At the end of Gergen's first week, we held a communications staff meeting in Room 180 of the Old Executive Office Building. (Ironically, Nixon had used that office as a study when he was President.)

Gergen seemed pleasant enough, but there was a real uneasiness from all of us. He told us we seemed a lot nicer to each other than previous White House staffs. With Reagan's staff, he said, "you had to sit in meetings with your back to the wall or somebody would stick a knife in it." One of the topics was leaking to the press. Ironically, two and a half hours later, Reuters ran a five-paragraph wire story describing what happened at the meeting.

The following Monday, I walked into Stephanopoulos' office for the regular 7:45 A.M. meeting, and his personal effects were gone. Deputy Chief of Staff Mark Gearan's staff and belongings were there. Then Gearan walked in, wearing a preppy green striped tie and a monogrammed oxford shirt, and we knew the story in that morning's *Washington Post* was true. Gearan became Director of Communications, and we were all thrilled. There had been rumors that if Gergen would in fact work at a more senior level, an outsider would be hired to run the Office of Communications.

With Gearan sitting behind his new desk, I stood by the fireplace and opened my daily news briefing by saying, "The top story this morning: Mark Gearan is the new White House Director of Communications." Some folks applauded, some laughed and at least one jokingly said I was sucking up already.

I hadn't met Gearan previously, but people who I knew and trusted and respected and liked thought the world of him, and that was good enough for me. I'd heard Governor Clinton originally sought him to be his campaign manager, but Gearan's wife was pregnant at the time, and he turned down the job. He later became Senator Gore's campaign Chief of Staff. At the time, I read that an anonymous staffer had told a reporter, "This is proof that Leo Durocher was wrong." Gearan was indeed a nice guy who didn't finish last.

The former executive director of the Democratic Governors Association, he was a preppy, soft-spoken, charming political insider from Gardner, Massachusetts, with wire-rim glasses and short, neat hair. He was witty with a terrifically wry sense of humor and was proud of his wife and infant daughter. His appointment was widely popular among the staff and did wonders to boost morale in the wake of Gergen's hiring. At the 8:30 A.M. staff meeting his first day, he was greeted with applause. Even the reporters were friendly at his first briefing.

Gearan opened the hallway between lower press and the communications director's office that had been a "no-fly zone" from which reporters had been banned, unlike the policy in previous administrations. As another make-nice with the press, we hosted a party for them on the South Lawn. The memo I received said, "All communications staff are strongly encouraged to attend."

So on a warm late Sunday afternoon in June, I strolled from my office through the West Wing to the Rose Garden, where fellow communications staffers were munching hors d'oeuvres and sipping drinks from a portable bar manned by bartenders in white jackets and black bow ties. An enormous tent had been erected on the South Lawn, in addition to a volleyball net. We ate a chicken and roast beef buffet, and the evening was kind of an odd mix of 4-H county fair and state dinner. A couple TV sets were tuned to the Chicago Bulls-Phoenix

Suns NBA Finals game. There were about 800 guests.

The high point of the evening was a parody of Jimmy Buffet's "Margaritaville," sung by a couple dozen communications staffers. Mark Gearan played piano and George Stephanopoulos turned the sheet music pages. Deputy Communications Director David Dreyer, in a baggy beige suit, wild tie and sunglasses, sang the lead vocals. The chorus was: "Spinnin' away again in the press briefing room/Lookin' for the last question today/Some people say President Clinton's to blame/But I know…it's Helen Thomas' fault," changing the reporter's name for each chorus. A casually dressed President and First Lady later spoke briefly to the crowd.

There were other events on the South Lawn that were memorable. One Sunday afternoon in September, Vicki Rivas-Vasquez (assistant press secretary) called me at home and said she needed help for the next day's Mideast peace treaty signing ceremony with Israeli Prime Minister Yitzhak Rabin and PLO Chairman Yasser Arafat. So I went in to the office and we ran through what needed to be done. Although I was less than thrilled with all the extra work involved, it was exciting to be a part of something so important and historic. National Park Service employees were busy setting up 3,000 chairs on the South Lawn, and labor crews from the networks, all of which planned live coverage of the ceremony, were constructing sets. The hammering of nails into lumber echoed across the South Lawn in the late afternoon sun.

On Monday, I was on the South Lawn before 5:00 A.M., when crews from the networks began arriving to set up for the morning news shows. It was still dark, and the First Lady had requested no lights be turned on in her backyard until 6:00 A.M. I nearly broke my neck in the dark, stumbling over all the cables and TV gear out there.

My assignment was to serve as White House liaison to CBS, escorting their staff wherever they needed to go and generally helping them get things done at the White House. I worked primarily with the morning and evening shows' producers. Timing for the morning show was particularly important, with commercial breaks set in stone so that everything had to be on time down to the minute. I walked over to the NBC set on the east side of the South Lawn and talked to Secretary of State Warren Christopher's security agent, advancing our route back to the CBS set (located near President Eisenhower's putting green), through the other sets and cables and equipment.

As Christopher waited to be interviewed by Paula Zahn, I mentioned to Christopher's Secret Service agent that Zahn (tall, thin, beautiful, pleasant-natured and wearing a flowing, pleated red dress) was actually eight months pregnant. "With what?" he asked. "A tadpole?"

Later that morning, a former aide to President Carter, who had worked for Carter Press Secretary Jody Powell, and I advanced Carter's route from the NBC set over to CBS. About halfway, the former President stopped suddenly. He turned to a companion, pointed to a nearby tree and said in that familiar Georgia accent, "That's where Amy's treehouse was."

At 9 A.M., the floor manager called "Clear!" and "CBS This Morning" was off the air. After all the scrambling about, that was a relief. I walked with one of the morning show's producers to the White House Mess, where we got tea and a sandwich for Zahn. Later, Dan Rather arrived an hour or two before the ceremony was scheduled to begin. He sat in a director's chair and got a haircut under a tree, a towel around his neck. Later, Connie Chung showed up and they did the showbiz huggy-kissy thing and seemed genuinely glad to see each other. Later, on the air, I noticed even in person how awfully stiff they seemed together on camera. Talk about a shotgun marriage, I thought. Chung, by the way, furiously puffed cigarettes when she was off camera.

Meanwhile, all sorts of famous names and faces were arriving to take their seats in the crowd on the sunny day. The event was the hottest ticket in town, and I even got thrown into the mix. A State Department aide, a former co-worker from the transition staff, at the last minute had somebody who just *had* to get in, and I got on the phone with our already hassled staff. But we got it done.

While Rather and Chung were on the air, I was working on setting up CBS' post-coverage interviews. CBS wanted Vice President Gore and Assistant Secretary of State Dennis Ross. But the White House two-way radio I'd been issued (a heavy high-tech walkie-talkie that clips onto one's belt and is very cumbersome) didn't work. I could transmit but could receive only sporadically. I tried to reach fellow former campaign staffer Julia Payne of the Vice President's staff ("Payne, Payne—Chitester") but couldn't. I ran around and finally found her.

"Why didn't you answer me?" I asked.

"I called you," she said. "I said, 'Go ahead, Ken.'"

We arranged for the Vice President to appear on CBS. But as it turned out, CBS went back to its regular programming right after the ceremony and didn't conduct any interviews.

I didn't see much of the event itself on a hot, sunny day because I was working. But maybe the strangest thing was seeing former President Bush in person for the first time. He was clear across the crowd, but it stopped me cold. He had been the focus of everything I'd reacted to the previous year in the campaign, and now he was no longer the enemy. He was harmless, even at the White House. As Bush headed toward his seat, an advance staffer leading the way tried to clear a path, calling out, "Make way for the President." And Bush just said, "Ex, ex, ex."

There wasn't much down time after the event ended. After the crowd cleared, CBS (which was the pool network that day) was to provide technical support for the Israeli and Palestinian networks during an Oval Office interview. So I did what I could to help before Steve Rabinowitz (communications/advance) took over. I was glad to be relieved, and went back to my office to eat a late lunch at my desk in the air conditioning and return phone calls. I was tired, sunburned, hungry, leg-weary and dehydrated.

I went back to the South Lawn a couple hours later as the "CBS Evening News" team started preparations for its show. The producer asked if I could get the sprinklers behind Rather and Chung shut off so it wouldn't look as if water were squirting out of their ears. Although secretly wanting to see that on TV, I checked with the National Park Service workers, who said they were planning to turn off the sprinklers half an hour before air time anyway. Of course, I took credit when reporting to one of the producers that I'd taken care of their problem. As with everybody from CBS all day, they were grateful.

In fact, everybody was terrific to work with all day, from the morning crew to the evening staff, from the on-air talent to the union labor. I think largely they were just happy to have somebody from the White House assigned specifically to them to help them out. And by the end of the day, I was practically part of the CBS crew from being with them so long.

Afterward, I hung out for a few hours as the crew broke down its set and equipment, rolled up the cables and began the long, slow process of loading everything into the trucks, which took seemingly forever to arrive. Meanwhile, dinner guests were arriving on the South Lawn driveway. Limos and dark sedans would park outside the Diplomatic Room, under the famous South Portico, and men in tuxedos and women in long dresses would emerge. We could hear and see them upstairs on the Truman Balcony. Their view was even better than ours as I gazed over the White House fountain with lights and flowers, to the Washington Monument and the Jefferson Memorial, soft lights illuminating them on a pleasantly warm evening. Rivas-Vasquez took over for me after my fifteen-and-a-half-hour day, and I practically limped to my car parked on the Ellipse.

We also celebrated birthday parties on the South Lawn. The President's and Tipper Gore's birthdays both are August 19, and our first summer at the White House we celebrated outside near the Oval Office. The Clintons were headed to Martha's Vineyard, and the President noted his family hadn't taken a vacation in years. "And that was dumb," he said.

The Vice President, who normally stood stiffly in the background when the President spoke, gave the President a lifesize cardboard cut-out of himself, to make the President feel at home when they were separated. Then the Four Tops, in town to perform elsewhere that evening, lip-synched a couple of their songs for the President. The staff gave the President a book of Abraham Lincoln's writings. (A memo had been sent to all staff seeking voluntary contributions to buy it, which I thought was a bit odd, especially since some senior aides were millionaires. They have more money in their wallets than I have in my bank account, I thought.)

The following year, I cut through the West Wing on my way to the South Lawn for the President's and Tipper Gore's birthday party. I passed a guy in the hall who looked familiar, but it wasn't until I was a couple dozen steps past him that it clicked: Stephen Stills. Soon afterward, I strolled onto the South Lawn, where a tent was set up east of the South Portico on that perfectly-sculpted grass, north of the fountain and beautiful flowers on a warm, sunny Friday afternoon. Sure enough, Crosby, Stills and Nash were performing for the assembled staff with a keyboard and two acoustic guitars. When the President, First Lady, Vice President and Mrs. Gore emerged from the Diplomatic Room, Crosby, Stills and Nash began an *a cappella* version of "Happy Birthday, Mr. President" to staff applause.

Chief of Staff Leon Panetta spoke first. (I found myself beginning to dislike him. He'd been hanging a potential staff shakeup over everybody's heads for months. It wasn't fair, especially to people like Mark Gearan and Dee Dee Myers. And that "I'm gonna kick some ass" comment on Capitol Hill, just before we got our clocks cleaned on a health care vote—a clip which then began airing seemingly hourly on CNN—made us look ridiculous.)

Then the First Lady spoke. She joked that, with the President and Mrs. Gore sharing a birthday, she and the Vice President felt left out. "Al's the stiff one, and I'm the stern taskmaster," compared to the fun-loving Bill and Tipper, she said of public perception. "Come on up here, Mr. Vice President," she said, and she and Gore stood arm-in-arm. The President, meanwhile, stutter-stepped around the back of the stage in a circle, arms straight at his sides, stiff-necked and looking straight ahead, in an absolutely hysterical impersonation of the Veep's reputation. Gore laughed as loudly as anybody.

The Vice President then introduced Tipper, saying, "I love her with all my heart," to which much of the staff responded, "Awww...." She then introduced the President.

Like the other three, the President thanked us for our work. He told us to "keep your spirits up" and reminded us that "when public service becomes easy, it's no longer service. If it's easy, let someone else do it." And he encouraged us not to rest on the perks of office but to continue to fight for change. It was nothing new, but it always meant something to hear it directly from him. It was invigorating and reaffirming.

Crosby, Stills and Nash then played a couple songs, including "Our House." We ate slices of two enormous birthday cakes—one for the President and one for Mrs. Gore—carried out by members of the White House Mess staff.

South Lawn arrival ceremonies were always big deals, too. Formal ceremonies for official state visits took place on the South Lawn. Premiers, prime ministers and presidents appearing at less formal, "working" visits arrived at the West Wing through the VIP reception area on the north side of the White House. The first time we had a visiting head of state or government was when Canada's Brian Mulroney visited. The multi-branch military corps holding flags of all fifty states lined the north driveway, a sight especially impressive for those of us new to Washington.

I attended my first formal arrival ceremony on the South Lawn one early fall day. Russian President Boris Yeltsin appeared with the President amid all the standard pomp and pageantry. All the formally dressed military bands, including some in Revolutionary War-era garb, along with a large military multi-service contingent bearing all fifty state flags, filled much of the lawn. Hundreds of people, probably Administration types, were invited, and they took pictures like tourists on a warm, sunny day. We were handed U.S. and Russian flags and impressive programs. To be honest, it was neat to see, but kind of boring. I decided I'd been there too long if those types of things were starting to seem routine.

More interesting was a South Lawn departure in the first weeks of the Administration. One morning, one of our News Analysis volunteers and I walked over to the South Lawn to watch the President depart for a trip to St. Louis, where he planned to rally support for his economic plan. We watched as he shook hands along the rope line and then boarded Marine One, Marine guards saluting him at the steps. (Those helicopter blades really kick up the wind when you're that close.) Like many other events and places I'd seen the first few weeks, it reminded me of television coverage I'd watched over the years from hundreds of miles away. Of course, a South Lawn takeoff of Marine One made me think of Richard Nixon's final departure on August 9, 1974.

But if I thought that history flashback was odd, there were plenty more oddities to come.

3▶Behind Closed Doors

"KEN—THANKS, BILL" · GALLOWS HUMOR IN THE
MORNING COMMUNICATIONS MEETINGS · A WHITE HOUSE
CHRISTMAS PARTY · BIRTHDAY CAKE AND CHAMPAGNE IN
THE ROOSEVELT ROOM · "HI, I'M CINDY CRAWFORD"

ONE OF THE MOST EXCITING THINGS about working for the President is the opportunity to help shape public policy, to play a role in key decisions. And even if that doesn't happen, even junior-level White House aides can have some opportunity to get information to the President.

During the Southeastern Conference basketball tournament, I prepared "talking points" for the President. Aides generally provide talking points for the President whenever he has a meeting or an event. The one-page fact sheets provide basic background information quickly and simply. Since the President is such a big Hogs fan, I thought he might appreciate something similar for Arkansas' games in the SEC Tournament.

After the televised tournament, I asked Appointments Secretary Nancy Hernreich, a longtime Clinton gubernatorial aide, who told me, "He thought it was great." So I prepared another set for the Hogs' second-round game against St. John in the NCAA Tournament. A few days after the game, an inter-office mail envelope with a red dot (meaning "for immediate delivery") arrived at my desk. What now, I thought. But when I opened it, I found a copy of my memo and talking points for the President. And scrawled at the top with a black felt-tip pen was: "Ken—Thanks. These are great—as was the game. Bill." I was alone in the office at the time, and I laughed out loud.

Then one morning not long afterward, I stopped by a small office adjoining the Oval Office and handed Nancy Hernreich a set of Presidential talking points for the baseball season opener. She later handed it to him as he left with staff, security and the press pool for Opening Day at Camden Yards in Baltimore.

The President threw out the first pitch—a high looper—from the mound and then joined the local television broadcasting crew in the booth. When one of the commentators mentioned the home-run hitting power of the visiting Texas Rangers' Ivan Rodriguez, the President said, "Led the league [last year], didn't he?" Indeed he did. That was one of the factoids I'd included in my talking points.

Adjusting to the ways of the White House wasn't always so easy, of course. In addition to bad news beyond our control, the staff's inexperience in Washington manifested itself often in the early months of the Administration. The Waco/Branch Davidian fiasco, the World Trade Center bombing, the economic stimulus package's failure, the travel office imbroglio, the President's haircut aboard Air Force One, Lani Guinier's doomed nomination…spring 1993 was not a good time for us. The White House staff was called "amateurish," "ham-fisted" and worse. It was like the campaign primaries all over again, when we had to deal with so-called scandals on a seemingly weekly basis.

The daily 7:45 A.M. communications meetings in Communications Director George Stephanopoulos' office became real downers. Gallows humor prevailed. In *The New York Times* one day in May, an unidentified senior staffer said a guillotine was being installed on the South Lawn by the tennis court. There was talk in one communications meeting of Jim Jones' cult suicide Kool-Aid for the staff. Someone else suggested cyanide margaritas instead. After one morning meeting, Media Affairs Director Jeff Eller walked into our News Analysis office and said, "Boy, those 7:45 meetings used to be fun. I wouldn't get depressed and want to go home until 9 or 9:30. But *now….*"

In fact, the morning communications meetings were, at least initially, important parts of the day. (By late 1994, for whatever reason, they had lost their sense of urgency.) At their best, the meetings provided a chance to hear what was going on in various areas and to know what was happening before it was made public. My responsibility was to open each meeting with a brief summary of the top news stories and to indicate how they were playing in various media.

The meetings could be fun. Sometimes we'd overdose on C-SPAN. Once, when I was still Deputy Director of News Analysis and Keith Boykin was Director, I concluded my report and told Mark Gearan (who replaced Stephanopoulos as Communications Director), "Mr. Speaker, I yield the floor and yield back the remainder of my time to the gentleman from News Analysis." With mock seriousness, Gearan said, "The chair recognizes Mr. Boykin."

During a discussion about the Senate Whitewater hearings, Michael Waldman (communications) said, "You know, if you close your eyes, [Senator] Al D'Amato sounds just like Steve Richetti" of our legislative affairs staff. We laughed and decided he was right.

Another time, during a discussion about an upcoming trip to the United Nations, UN Secretary General Boutros Boutros-Ghali's name came up. After a couple joking comments about his name, Press Secretary Dee Dee Myers said her first name actually was Dee and her last name was Dee-Myers. "His name's not so strange," she said, straightfaced.

Other staff events were more social, such as our first White House Christmas party. The first weekend in December, Christmas decorations were hung throughout the White House and Old Executive Office Building. It really looked warm, homey and festive—if a little odd—to see an office building, especially an historic government building, decorated throughout with trees, wreaths and lights.

Then about two weeks before Christmas, the First Family participated in the annual lighting of the national Christmas tree on the Ellipse, between the White House and the Washington Monument. I had half a dozen tickets but gave them away to interns and volunteers. Keith Boykin and I watched on TV in our first-floor Old Executive Office Building office. It was festive, but hokey. It struck me as what a show at one of those clubs in Branson, Missouri, is probably like. Who'd guess lighting the tree was such a big production?

The President and the First Lady greet thousands of guests each holiday season. Our first Christmas, that task was made less festive by bad news. One Sunday, CNN broke a story about to run in *American Spectator* magazine in which Arkansas state troopers accused then-Governor Clinton of using them to set up and then cover up his extramarital affairs. Combined with the Whitewater/Madison Guaranty Savings and Loan fiasco, Secretary of Defense-designate Bobby Ray

Inman not paying Social Security taxes and Surgeon General Joycelyn Elders' son being arrested for selling drugs, it was not a happy holiday season at the White House.

The next night was the White House staff Christmas party. Around 6:30 P.M. I ambled over from my Old Executive Office Building office with fellow ex-campaign staffers Kim Hopper (media affairs) and Morrie Goodman (Federal Emergency Management Agency) to the East Wing on a cold, dry evening. Military aides in formal uniforms directed us upstairs to the second-floor East Room, where we enjoyed cocktails and hors d'oeuvres. There was no furniture in the room, but a large Christmas tree and decorations made for a festive atmosphere. There were hundreds of people there.

The East Room has been used over the years for everything from Abigail Adams' laundry to Susan Ford's senior prom to Presidents' daughters' weddings to a Harlem Globetrotters' basketball exhibition to boxing and wrestling matches during the Theodore Roosevelt Administration. Seven Presidents have lain in state there. Usually the East Room is used for news conferences, bill signings and award presentations.

We were then ushered into the hallway, where we roamed the French-influenced, oval-shaped Blue Room (site of the official Christmas tree), the Green Room (reflecting the 1800–1810 American Federal Style and featuring American art) and the Red Room (in the 1810–1830 American Empire style), all of which visitors see on the public tour.

Next we were escorted—herded—into the State Dining Room, with ivory-painted walls and gold curtains. (Theodore Roosevelt once hung a moose head over the fireplace and placed other big-game trophies on paneled walls.) A portable bar stood in one corner, a roast beef carving table in another and, in the middle, a long table full of shrimp, salmon, spinach-filled mini-pastries and lots of other delicious food. I wore a black suit and festive red Scotch-plaid tie. (At the previous year's staff Christmas party at the Governor's Mansion in Little Rock, the President-Elect pointed to my holiday neckwear and said with a smile, "Nice tie.")

Aides sipped white wine, munched tasty food and chatted among themselves. On one side of the room was a seventy-five-pound gingerbread replica of the White House. I was told Socks had been banned from the room because the First Cat couldn't resist the delicious, enormous would-be treat. On the other side of the room was a view of the South Lawn with glowing, flowing fountain and, past that, the Washington Monument and Jefferson Memorial. The President and First Lady stood in the hallway and briefly addressed the crowd, wishing everyone a merry Christmas.

It was over all too quickly, as the military aides hustled our large group out of there so another group could come in behind us. For the President and First Lady, it was just another night during the holiday season. They did the same thing two or three times a night, every night, for weeks on end.

In addition to the Christmas party, on occasion we also held all-staff meetings in the East Room. Our first came at the end of our first full week in the White House. The President, First Lady, Vice President, Mrs. Gore and Chief of Staff Mack McLarty spoke to us late on a Friday afternoon. The President warned us not to leak information to reporters and talked about what Washington is like. The First Lady made a great speech, reminding us why we were there and who sent us. And the Vice President spoke. After a tough week in the news about issues not high on our agenda, he said, the President wanted to bring us together, seriously, for just a moment, to discuss…gays in the military. We all laughed and applauded. It was a good way to end the week, and the President, cabinet officials and senior staff spent the weekend at Camp David.

Unfortunately, the state troopers' allegations and controversy over gays in the military weren't the only difficulties we faced. During the presidential campaign, Whitewater allegations (about the Clintons' real estate investment years ago in Arkansas) had haunted the President and First Lady. The story again topped the news in March 1994.

Late one Friday afternoon, the first subpoenas were handed down for information on Whitewater that the White House had in its possession. Also, six White House aides—Bernie Nussbaum (chief counsel), Harold Ickes (Deputy Chief of Staff), Bruce Lindsey (senior adviser), Mark Gearan, Maggie Williams (First Lady's Chief of Staff) and Lisa Caputo (First Lady's press secretary)—and three Treasury officials were subpoenaed. Of course, the independent counsel was just looking for information, and those people weren't indicted. Still, that isn't the way you want your name to appear in *The Washington Post*.

I was at first concerned about Lindsey and Gearan because I knew them the best and worked with them and liked them so much. But they were lawyers; they knew how to deal with such matters. It was Caputo's subpoena that bothered me the most. I knew her from the campaign and from the transition in Little Rock, when not many staffers were there. While I was sure that she could take care of herself, it seemed to me she was just doing her job.

The next day, White House Counsel Bernie Nussbaum resigned. He'd been blamed for lots of other mistakes before Whitewater and ended up taking the fall for the recent Whitewater problems.

The following Monday, Rahm Emanuel (deputy communications director) came by our office and told Keith Boykin and me to search our trash cans, burn bags (where classified material was deposited to be destroyed), recycling bins, hard drives, e-mail and diskettes for anything related to Whitewater fitting the criteria in the subpoena. Then we were to fill out the form he gave us indicating whether we'd found anything and return it to him by that afternoon. As expected, we didn't have anything but public information—newspaper and magazine clippings, wire stories and so forth.

But we couldn't get the trash emptied by the housekeeping staff, and stuff was piling up. All day CNN showed video of overflowing trash cans around the White House, and Wolf Blitzer kept talking about how the subpoenas and the search for information had totally disrupted activity at the White House. The President, unsurprisingly, was hounded by Whitewater questions every time he emerged in public.

Even those of us having nothing to do with it were hounded by Whitewater. The following September, on my first day back from vacation, I found out independent counsel Kenneth Starr's office wanted to talk to me. Alexis Suggs, the lawyer in Starr's office who called, said she wanted to know if I, or anybody on my staff, had seen anyone in or around Vince Foster's office the morning after he committed suicide. The next day two FBI agents, who began by showing me their badges, asked me about the morning after Foster's death. They were interested in my office because we would have had interns delivering the clips at 6:30 to 7:00 A.M., when some files allegedly were removed. Suggs said they weren't investigating me or anyone in my office; they were just looking for witnesses. "If that was on your mind, just put it out," she said.

The day after Vince Foster died was, unsurprisingly, a sad one at the White House. When I came in to work that day at my usual time of 6:30 A.M., Julie Oppenheimer (assistant director of news analysis) in our office told me that Foster had committed suicide the previous night. I was embarrassed to admit I wasn't positive who he was before she reminded me he was White House deputy counsel. A meeting for all White House staff was called for 11:30 A.M. in a small fourth-floor auditorium in the Old Executive Office Building.

Foster was a lifelong Friend of Bill (FOB). I didn't know him, but it hurt to see how his death affected people like the President and Mack McLarty, especially since we couldn't help. They'd known him all their lives, since they were kids in Hope, Arkansas. The President spoke to us almost as a father figure. "No one can ever know why this happened," he told the hushed room. "And I hope all of you will always understand that."

The whole experience was kind of like having an uncle you didn't know die; you hurt not for yourself but how it hits your dad. We'd all do anything for the President. The emotion in the crowded room, where people stood along the walls and sat in the aisle, was overwhelming.

The day after the White House search for subpoenaed Whitewater records, we had a meeting in the East Room for all aides. The President introduced former Carter White House counsel Lloyd Cutler as Bernie Nussbaum's replacement in a thirty- or forty-minute televised appearance in the press briefing room. About 350 of us watched it on a TV set temporarily rolled into the East Room. Then the President, Vice President, First Lady, McLarty and Cutler arrived, and each spoke.

The President said he'd never do anything to hurt the office held by Lincoln, Jefferson, Washington and Teddy Roosevelt. Then he said: "They want to know, 'What did you know and when did you know it?' I want to ask, 'What planet am I on and who are these people?'" And he quoted from a children's book he and the First Lady used to read to Chelsea that went, "I was minding my own business/As happy as could be/When a big ol' ugly man came up/And tied a horse to me." We all laughed, and he added, "That story had a happy ending, and so will this."

That evening I got a phone call at home from a longtime friend, a

Republican. "Hello?" I said. And the first words I heard were, "Mr. Chairman, I refuse to answer on the grounds that it may incriminate me." Thanks, dude.

The day after the meeting, Jeff Eller returned from his three-week vacation wearing a new beard. I ran into him in the first-floor Old Executive Office Building copier room near my office, and he asked how things were going. "Well, I don't hate it *all* the time," I said. He laughed loudly.

Eller was responsible for my promotion to Director from Deputy Director of News Analysis. With my car being repaired, I was walking home from the Metro stop on a pleasant Thursday evening in April 1994 when my pager went off. "Call Eller," the message said. So as soon as I walked in, I phoned him. "How'd you like to be director of news analysis?" he asked. Well, sure. Keith Boykin was going down the hall to join the Office of Media Affairs. After asking about Boykin, my first question was whether I'd be able to hire someone to fill the opening, and I was told yes.

About a week later, Eller told the communications staff at the morning meeting in Mark Gearan's office that Boykin was going to Media Affairs and that I was the new Director of News Analysis. None of the details had been worked out, but it would've leaked anyway, so I figured it was probably just as well it was announced.

Boykin moved a few days afterward to an office down the hall in the Old Executive Office Building. So our News Analysis staff became just me and Larry Sampas, our overnight guy. Sampas had black hair and glasses and graduated from Carlton College in Minnesota. As a kid, he spent a few years in China, when his parents worked at the U.S. Embassy in Beijing. His parents were career foreign service officers (his father was retired, and in 1994 the Senate confirmed his mother as ambassador to Mauritania) and he was probably one of the brightest people around there. But he was also the most quiet. ("Does he ever *talk?*" staffers and interns sometimes asked me.)

A computer whiz, Sampas also was a skilled writer. He worked overnight and was in charge of producing the 150- to 200-page sets of clips. He and interns delivered the clips to about 125 aides around the White House on weekdays, and to several dozen staffers on weekends, by 8 A.M. He also wrote a summary of all that news and electronically distributed it every weekday morning.

I still had no word on what would happen with my staff, salary, title or anything else. I spent much of that day on the phone trying to find replacements for the equipment and furniture Boykin took with him when he moved out.

In early May, Al Kamen's "In the Loop" column on the Federal page of *The Washington Post* included a brief mention of my and Keith Boykin's job changes. *Everybody* in government reads that column. I figured it must have been Eller's doing that got that in.

In mid-May, I got my pay stub in the mail, and I still hadn't received the raise I'd been promised, despite having the new job and title a month. This is ridiculous, I thought. I'm making two-thirds of what my predecessor did, but I'm doing more work—with less staff, without volunteers or interns, without the supplies, equipment and resources I need. I've been asked to do the job but not given the tools to do it. Who needs this? After the two upcoming trips to Europe this summer, I decided, it would be time to start looking to leave.

A couple weeks later, I walked across West Executive Drive from the West Wing to the Old Executive Office Building, where I ran into Jeff Eller on the outdoor steps. He said the health care reform staff (located next door to my office in the war room) was taking over my office: effective immediately. My department was being moved across the hall into a smaller office already being used by someone in Media Affairs. I just sat in my office all afternoon, stunned and silent.

Around noon the next day, I began the hassle of getting together the Office of Administration (OA), General Services Administration (GSA), White House Communications Agency (WHCA), AT&T and all the other acronym organizations involved to get the computers, phones, fax, printers, desks, chairs, lamps, furniture and files in my office moved across the hall to a smaller office already occupied by media affairs and interns. What a pain. It wasn't just the move. It was the loss of autonomy, control, responsibility, it was the budget and salary and staffing and it was the resources we were supposed to have but didn't.

I was even told I'd get my office back after health care passed. I almost laughed out loud. First, you never got anything back around there. When it was gone, it was gone. Second, and I hoped I was wrong, but I just knew Congress wasn't going to pass our health care reform plan. Debate went on and on and there was never any progress on it. I felt lied to, cheated and betrayed. About a month later, I stopped by Mark Gearan's office and told him about all the ways my office had been mistreated. He sympathized but said there was little he could do about it.

After the next day's morning communications meeting, Jeff Eller stopped me outside the White House Mess. He told me there was an opening for a writer at NASA and that he'd recommend me if I wanted it. I didn't (figuring that when I left the White House, I'd leave Washington), but it was great of him to offer to help.

I stood with Eller on the balcony outside his office one morning about a week later, looking at the West Wing across West Executive Drive. He was smoking a cigar and told me he'd demanded an answer on my raise, which I never did receive. He said he'd told Mark Gearan he'd resign if it didn't come through. "Man, it's up to you, but, I mean, don't do anything like that because of me," I said.

But he said I wasn't the only one being mistreated, that others in his Office of Media Affairs were in the same situation. "You don't do that," he said. "That's not the way you run a business. That's not the way you treat people." Boy, I thought, is this place screwed up. I grew up thinking the White House was a time-honored bastion of order and professionalism. Surely the White House, of all places, was well-orga-nized. How different the view was from the inside.

Hassles like that were not uncommon. Security red tape was a constant nightmare. It was amazing how much time I spent dealing with it. Just getting volunteers into the White House fortress was a monumental headache. Some days it seemed I spent as much time on getting them cleared and approved and on file as I did doing every-thing else. With just two staffers in our office, we relied on about three dozen interns and volunteers to get everything done. Without volunteers, we'd have had to slash the number of reports we produced and ignore vast amounts of news. I understood the need for security there, of course, but some of the rules seemed completely capricious and arbitrary. It was frustrating for the volunteers...and for me.

On top of that, there was always the matter of fellow staffers want-ing the clips our office produced. It was amazing how seriously people took the packages of news clippings we produced each morning. A lot of folks who got them didn't even need them—they just wanted to be on the distribution list because somebody else with a similar title was, and they didn't want to be left out. The insecurity people had there, their defensiveness and addiction to perks and perceived power, never ceased to amaze me. I often was disappointed that some aides took themselves more seriously than they took their jobs.

I became so tired of getting phone calls from whiny assistants to self-important "senior" staffers from ancillary departments who demanded to get on the clips list. Sorry, I'd tell them, we can only produce and distribute so many copies. Between us, it seemed Keith Boykin and I got several calls a week.

And, of course, there were the impossible requests by well-meaning aides. One day David Dreyer (deputy communications director) said, at our regular morning meeting in Mark Gearan's office, that a report from independent counsel Robert Fiske was coming out at 11:00 A.M. Dreyer asked me to compile all the relevant quotes about Whitewater from all television coverage for the past several months. That way, we'd be able to compare those Republican and media accusations with what was in the fact-finding report.

It was a good idea. But it was also a huge project—way too big for one person in one day. It should've gone to Research, with all their on-line search services and huge staff. But at the White House you can't pawn off your assignments on another department unless you outrank them. So I muddled through. I asked the third-floor Old Executive Office Building library staff (who were career employees, not political appointees) at 8:00 A.M. to get me everything they could, as soon as they could. At 1:30 P.M. they gave me transcripts on diskette. Then I pulled the relevant material. But it wasn't good enough or particularly useful, I don't think. It was frustrating not being able to do the job right due to factors beyond my control.

The next day, Dave Leavy (administrative assistant to Dee Dee Myers), called about 10:00 A.M. and said Myers wanted to know how all the Whitewater stories had originally played so she could use the information in her briefing that afternoon. I only had three hours, working by myself, to pull together an enormous amount of information that would have taken several people several days. I put a summary together, but I'm sure it wasn't exactly what she needed.

Other times, however, when no one else was around, there were special moments. As I was leaving work one perfect fall evening, I stopped at the top of the Old Executive Office steps, just outside the double wooden doors, under the second-floor balcony. It was a clear, black evening, and I stood looking across West Executive Drive at the West Wing. Over the White House was a nearly full moon, bright and brilliant and shining in the darkness. The American flag flying over the north entrance flapped in the breeze as spotlights shone on the gleaming White House. I stood there by myself for a moment in the quiet and soaked it all in. I had to remind myself that I knew how Lou Gehrig felt about being "the luckiest man on the face of the earth."

On my trips around the White House complex delivering reports from our office, sometimes I ran into fellow aides I didn't see often and got to chat with them. News Analysis was on the first floor of the Old Executive Office building, in the northeast corner. Halfway down the hall was the main hallway. Then I'd walk through the doors and down a couple dozen outdoor stairs and across West Executive Drive to the West Wing ground floor entrance. A few offices (including the National Security Council Situation Room and the White House Mess) were on the ground floor. Then it was upstairs to Upper Press, where Mark Gearan and Dee Dee Myers were located.

Sometimes I'd stop by Lower Press nearby to check in with the press assistants, and often I'd swing past the Oval Office (when delivering material to George Stephanopoulos and Mack McLarty). When I helped the interns deliver the morning clips, we also had to go upstairs and also all the way to the East Wing. Even though it was a pain to have to accompany the interns when they delivered, it was still exciting to see the off-limits areas of the White House. Unfortunately, I never had time to enjoy it.

One day I was making one of my regular trips around the West Wing, hand-delivering wire reports, when I stopped by George Stephanopoulos' office, two doors from the Oval Office. I was chatting briefly with Heather Beckel (Stephanopoulos' assistant) when I noticed *Rolling Stone*, with Janet Jackson on the cover, on her desk. It was the cover where Jackson is topless, her arms over her head, with a man's hands reaching around her from behind, covering her breasts.

Beckel said the President had stopped by and, after looking at the magazine cover, said with a grin, "I've got pretty good hands." She had gestured to a nearby large, framed photo that was a closeup of the President's hand reaching to shake dozens of hands and had said, "I know." I told her that was a clever, diplomatic response, and she said,

"Well, I was *going* to say, 'And I've got pretty good....'"

Although I didn't have a lot of contact with fellow Clinton Administration aides working in the agencies around Washington, I did keep in touch with some of my former campaign co-workers. One November Wednesday evening, I went to Washington's Hard Rock Cafe for the one-year anniversary celebration of Election Night 1992. There were plenty of fellow former campaign staffers I hadn't seen since our victory, and we reminisced and caught up on what was new.

Then the week after our election anniversary party, we attended the premiere of *The War Room*, a documentary about the campaign filmed at the national headquarters with microphones on James Carville and George Stephanopoulos. A building full of ex-campaign staffers watched on several screens at the Key Theater in Georgetown. My perspective was much different from Carville's and Stephanopoulos', of course, and watching it made me recall my mindset at the time. I had expected to be done with politics after the election.

A reception afterward at the Dixie Grill, across the street from Ford's Theater, was jammed with familiar faces. Everyone was working their way through the crowded bar, excitedly greeting former co-workers and joyfully retelling campaign stories. "Did you see yourself in the movie?" we asked each other.

I was again at the Dixie Grill one autumn night when I ran into a guy I'd met at the President's birthday party during the campaign. He was working in the Pentagon press office. He said he really liked it, that the career and military staff were terrific. I swear, I thought, it seems all the political appointees at the agencies love their jobs, and everybody at the White House is miserable.

I also occasionally ran into fellow Administration aides on Presidential trips. Ellen Berlin, who worked in public affairs for the Department of Transportation, joined the advance teams on some of our trips. I'd met her on the Tokyo-Seoul trip during the Administration's first summer. The following spring, we strolled Pennsylvania Avenue in front of the White House on a comfortable, partly sunny day. We went to lunch at Old Ebbitt Grill on 15th Street, across the street from Treasury, which is on the east side of the White House. Established in 1856, Old Ebbitt (featured in *In the Line of Fire* with Clint Eastwood) is full of dark wood, brass railings and white men in gray suits, power-lunching Washington-style.

We talked about the differences between political appointees and career government employees, about how nerdy some of the latter are. She said a fellow appointee in her office one day had a pen leak in his shirt pocket, and a career employee noticed. "Don't you hate it when that happens?" the career person said, adding, "Here, I've got something for you." Whereupon he opened his desk and pulled a plastic pocket protector from a stack in his drawer. The appointee later pinned it to his bulletin board.

I thought of that not long afterward when I sat outside in a lawn chair at home one Saturday morning, jotting in my notebook on the patio. It had been a couple years since I'd had a suntan. Ever since I'd joined the campaign, I realized, I'd had the pasty, fluorescent-lit, white-collar pallor of a Washington govern-nerd…you know, the geeks with the slicked-back hair, pens in the pocket, short-sleeve shirts, casual slacks and rubber-soled dress shoes who inhabit every bureaucratic nook and cranny of the federal government.

Not all of the events we experienced as a staff took place in the West Wing, or even inside the White House. Some took place in the Rose Garden, the Roosevelt Room, Room 450 of the Old Executive Office Building and on the North Lawn.

On a sunny, cool, spring day, I attended a Rose Garden ceremony honoring the North Carolina and Texas Tech men's and women's national champion basketball teams. The President interrupted an emergency meeting on Bosnia with Capitol Hill leaders so he could attend. Afterward, as the Marine Corps Band played, he strolled back to the residence with George Stephanopoulos and National Security Adviser Tony Lake, swinging his arms, clapping his hands and grinning. And I thought, This guy clearly loves his job. He really enjoys this. We all get down, I thought, but it's great to see him so up, especially when things hadn't gone that well since we'd arrived.

Our first Thanksgiving in Washington, I attended a Rose Garden event that included the biggest live turkey I'd ever seen. The President stood behind it and spoke about Thanksgiving, and the huge bird clucked a couple times during his brief remarks. I was worried the big white bird would snap at him. The President gave it a Presidential reprieve so it wouldn't get cooked for somebody's dinner the next day. And then a group of area school children came up and petted it and posed for photos with the President and the turkey. A few of us on staff stood to the side and chuckled throughout the event.

One hot summer day, fellow Arkansans in the Administration and I sat in an enclosed tent in the Rose Garden, sweating and sipping lemonade and iced tea as the President and First Lady welcomed Coach Nolan Richardson and his national champion Arkansas Razorbacks basketball team. "You did your state proud," the President told the team. "You made the President happy. But more importantly, you showed America the best about what college athletics should be. And we are all very, very proud of you." The Marine Band played the school song, and we all called the Hogs ("Woo! Pig! Sooey!").

Sometimes we'd use the Roosevelt Room for events. It is a large room, located perhaps four steps across the hall from the Oval Office, with a fireplace and a long, dark wooden conference table and paintings of Presidents Theodore and Franklin D. Roosevelt. One afternoon, we gathered in the Roosevelt Room to honor Dave Seldin (press assistant). He was leaving to become press secretary for unannounced Maryland gubernatorial candidate Parris Glendening (who ended up winning). It was also Deputy Press Secretary Arthur Jones' birthday, so we had birthday cake along with champagne. Seldin took plenty of kidding about his notorious spelling and was given a dictionary as a going-away gift.

"How many R's in 'Parris'?" Mark Gearan quizzed him.

"Three," Seldin answered with a laugh.

Another time, I attended a communications staff meeting in the Roosevelt Room. One winter Saturday morning we talked about a few immediate and long-term issues, but I'm not sure we settled anything. Then one summer evening, Jake Siewert (communications) came by my office and, at 6:05 P.M., told me of a 6:00 P.M. meeting in the Roosevelt Room.

"Didn't anybody tell you?" he said. "You're on the agenda."

He showed it to me. Sure enough, I was.

"No," I sighed, "nobody told me anything."

So I ambled across West Executive Drive, up the stairs and into the Roosevelt Room. There were representatives from the Treasury and State departments there as well, discussing the upcoming trip to

Naples, Italy, for the annual Group of Seven economic summit. Mark Gearan said he wanted me to coordinate with Treasury and State to get more clips in the morning package on the road. It figures, I thought. They cut my staff, cut my office space, freeze my budget and salary, and yet they expect more.

Located on the other end of the White House from the Roosevelt Room, the East Room is (along with the State Dining Room) the largest room in the White House. Its roof collapsed in 1803, only three years after President John Adams moved in, due to water leaking through poorly fitting slate roof tiles. It has elegant classic white woodwork and an oak parquet floor. Hanging on the east wall is Gilbert Stuart's famous full-length portrait of George Washington, the only object that has remained since the White House first was occupied in 1800. As British troops approached during the War of 1812, First Lady Dolley Madison refused to leave the White House until she had Stuart's painting in her possession.

One autumn afternoon, I took our office's intern to a news conference in the crowded East Room, where the President and Russian President Boris Yeltsin fielded questions from the enormous White House press corps. We wore headphones connected to devices like a Walkman, tuning in the correct channel so we could hear the questions and answers translated from Russian to English. Yeltsin was his usual jolly self. We stood off to the side by the door, and out of camera range, with some other Office of Communications staff.

Located upstairs in the Old Executive Office Building across West Executive Drive from the White House is Room 450. It is an auditorium with soft chairs and armrests and is used for Presidential events. One spring day I attended a security briefing classified as "secret." (The White House director of security told me that all White House appointees with permanent passes have "top secret as needed" security clearance.) A National Security Agency staffer presented a slide show and lecture about the threats to our communications, both at the White House and especially when we traveled.

There were all sorts of anecdotal examples of ways the President's, and his staff's, communications have been compromised in the past. The President's schedule is often a target of those seeking information. Some of the advice was common sense: never discuss sensitive material on a cell phone, use the secure phones and faxes whenever necessary. One of the most interesting pieces of information was not just that the Russians are still in the intelligence game but that they—and others—have equipment in their embassies in Washington that can monitor our phone calls. We were told about devices, for example, that will automatically record any phone call made to a number with a 456 (White House) prefix.

Unlike OEOB 450, the North Lawn, facing Pennsylvania Avenue, isn't generally used for official events. One spring day, Ralph Alswang (staff photographer) took a color photo of fellow Indiana University graduate Ann Walley (scheduling and advance) and me for *Indiana Alumni* magazine. I asked the White House Ushers Office if we could take the photo on the more picturesque South Lawn but was told the South Lawn is "the purview of the First Family." In other words, it was their back yard, and we couldn't go tromping around there. So we took the photo on the North Lawn "triangle," where all the TV news crews set up. That's why all the backdrops behind the TV reporters look alike…it's the only place they're allowed to set up.

One of the great things about working at the White House is you never know who will drop by. I don't mean the official state visits of various foreign dignitaries. I mean the American pop culture celebrities straight off your television set or movie screen.

One early spring afternoon Vicki Rivas-Vasquez (assistant press secretary) asked if she could use my office as a holding room for a TV crew that would be taping in the Old Executive Office Building the next day. "Sure, if you have to," I said, unenthused about being overrun but trying to be helpful.

"Good. Now do you want to know who the on-air talent is?" she asked.

"Who?"

"Cindy Crawford."

"As in, the supermodel?"

"That's the one."

"Oh, *this* should be interesting."

So the next day Larry Sampas, who usually worked about 9:00 P.M. to 9:00 A.M., hung around our office another hour or so to meet Cindy Crawford. She walked in, and Rivas-Vasquez introduced us to her. "Hi, I'm Cindy Crawford," she said, leaning over my desk to shake hands. She was wearing an untucked sleeveless white shirt and tight black stretch pants, looking somewhat like Mary Tyler Moore (circa "The Dick Van Dyke Show").

At lunch, I went to McDonald's and picked up a brown bag of fast food. When I walked back in to my office to eat at my desk (thinking to myself that supermodels surely never eat such stuff), Crawford was sitting there reading *People* magazine. (How weird must it be to pick up *People* and know there's at least a 50-50 chance you'll be in it any given week?) An intern from another office came in and asked for an autograph, and Crawford sat and talked with her very politely for several minutes. I thought that was very cool for her to do.

Mark Gearan had said in a communications meeting the previous week that Chevy Chase recently had walked into Gearan's office, looked up at the ceiling, said, "Nice chandelier" and walked out. Said Gearan: "Sometimes it's like a Fellini film around here."

Sometimes the visitors were even more unusual. The day after Easter is the date of the traditional Easter Egg Roll on the South Lawn for all the kids and parents who can get in the gate. I saw the line forming already as I arrived for work shortly after dawn. In fact, going through the gate with me were half a dozen clowns from the Ringling Brothers circus on hand for the festivities. It would've made a great photo, I told Jeff Eller. "That's okay," he quipped, "I come to work with clowns every morning." The previous Friday, a staffer in an eight-foot Easter bunny costume was standing outside George Stephanopoulos' office, literally taking aback the wide-eyed communications director, cracking us all up.

Other times, faces from the past would show up. Politicians of all types were regularly seen in the West Wing's VIP reception area. One Saturday morning I strolled from my office to Stephanopoulos' office so I could drop off news reports. Political consultants Paul Begala, Mandy Grunwald and a few other folks were in there. And there, sitting on a couch, was Michael Dukakis.

He was looking tanned and relaxed and was wearing a red sweater. He walked out into the adjacent reception area and said hello to a bunch of us, including Kathy McKiernan (press assistant), who is from Massachusetts. We addressed him as "Governor" and chatted briefly. I couldn't get over how much better he looked in person, apparently how much happier, than the TV images I'd seen of him in 1988. And he looked at the twentysomething staffers before him. "You're all so *young*," he said.

Instead of politics, sometimes our famous visitors were from the world of entertainment. One spring day, I was walking out the West Wing ground floor exit, when who should enter the door but John Ritter, Billy Crystal and Lindsay Wagner. Last in line was Christopher Reeve (more than a year before his crippling accident), to whom I said, "Hello, Mr. Vice President." (Not really...but they did look a lot alike.)

And sometimes our visitors combined politics and pop culture celebrity. I was shopping for compact discs at Serenade Records at 17th and Pennsylvania, next door to the Old Executive Office Building, when I looked over and saw a guy who looked familiar. Then his friend called him "John," and I knew for sure it was John F. Kennedy, Jr. He was looking for CDs by a group from Colorado that neither I nor the guy working there had heard of. When I later told them who I'd seen, the girls at work were insanely jealous.

Perhaps among the most important, and certainly most impressed, visitors were our volunteers in the Office of News Analysis. One Saturday afternoon, I took five of the evening TV news volunteers on a tour of the White House West Wing. Some of them had worked for us for a year or more and never actually had been in the White House.

Meetings in preparation for the upcoming Group of Seven economic summit trip to Latvia, Poland, Italy and Germany were in progress around the White House. We ran into Mack McLarty, Bruce Lindsey, Mark Gearan and George Stephanopoulos during our tour. I think the volunteers might have been a little overwhelmed.

In fact, it was funny to see people's faces when they realized they were looking up-close at the Oval Office. You'd expect them to say something, and they wouldn't. You'd kind of be disappointed that they weren't impressed, but it wasn't that at all. They'd just be overwhelmed. It wasn't until they were out of the White House, sometimes until they were almost to the outside gate, that they'd start talking about it and seem to fully realize what they'd seen.

Those of us inside the gate often wanted to be on the outside. And when the President traveled, even if it was only for the day, I went with him.

4▸Day Tripper

ONE OF THE GREAT BENEFITS Air Force One provides the President is the ability to conduct business in the morning at the White House, fly to some city in the United States for an event and fly back to Washington that evening, where he can attend yet another event.

As other Presidents before him, President Clinton often took advantage of that opportunity. He could visit two or even three states in one day and still return home to sleep in his own bed. It was more convenient for the White House staff as well. (But that was an afterthought, I'm sure.)

Sometimes sampling local food was a highlight of those day trips. Just after 8:00 A.M. one pleasant spring morning, the staff van headed from West Executive Drive to Andrews Air Force Base. Ralph Alswang (staff photographer) turned on WARW-FM, a Bethesda/Washington classic rock station. Jeff Eller (media affairs) covered his ear as he tried to talk on a cellular phone in the front seat. The opening strains of Lynyrd Skynyrd's "Sweet Home Alabama" came over the speakers, and Linda Moore (political affairs) said to Alswang, "Turn it up" about the same time that Ronnie Van Zandt said the same thing in the song.

Breakfast aboard Air Force One was French toast, fruit and orange juice. Upon arrival, Milwaukee was cool and sunny as we motorcaded to the Italian Community Center for a health care speech to Ameritech employees. I stayed in the staff room all day, dialing in and watching the event on TV. A couple Wisconsin congressmen were in the room with us. "I can't make my calls with these guys here," Amy Zisook (intergovernmental affairs) whispered to me.

The President entered the room and ate lunch, looking over a table of food set up for the staff before Wendy Smith (trip director) said, "Here's your lunch, sir," holding a plastic-covered plate prepared by White House stewards. (The Secret Service was pretty strict about where the food the President ate came from.) He sat at a table behind me and was briefed by a few aides. Just before heading out the door to conduct TV interviews, he said, "All right—let's do it."

The weather was warm—the wind off Lake Michigan had shifted, our local volunteer van driver told us—as we boarded the motorcade again. We made an unscheduled stop at a frozen custard stand owned by a Republican. The President had asked one of the Wisconsin congressmen, "Are there going to be stories in the paper after we leave talking to this guy about 'Clinton's a no-good so-and-so'?"

But we stopped at Leon's, featured in "Laverne and Shirley," we were told by our advance team, where a decent-sized crowd was kept at a distance by police. The President shook some hands and then headed to the window as some of the staff tried to get out of the way.

Bruce Lindsey (senior adviser) got some frozen custard, and it looked good. So after the President walked across the parking lot to shake more hands, I scooted over to get a ninety-five-cent cup of chocolate. I rejoined the others and said to Linda Moore, "Okay, Moore—here you go," pointing a plastic spoonful toward her. She tasted it and said, "Mmmmm" before I ate the rest of it.

Moore used to work at the Democratic Leadership Council, a policy group of centrist Democrats, which Clinton headed when he was Governor of Arkansas. She was short, with short blond hair and short skirts, and was dating a guy at the Democratic National Committee whom I worked with in the campaign. Moore was from a small town in Texas. One time on the plane she told us about high school football games and Frito pies. She explained that you open a bag of Fritos and pour in chili and then spoon it up.

Across the parking lot, the President stopped shaking hands and chatted with Lindsey.

"What do you think they're talking about?" Moore asked.

"Well," I said, "you always assume it's something substantive, like Bosnia, but sometimes they're just talking."

Jeff Eller came over later and said it was about the Federal Reserve's short-term interest rate hike. (The third increase in two and a half months had been announced earlier in the day.) After discussing it with Lindsey, the President commented on it to the press pool. Then we scrambled back to the vans and aboard Air Force One.

Another Midwestern city provided the President a chance to sample the local food as well. One sunny winter day, the President visited a police academy in London, Ohio. We flew one hour and ten minutes to frozen, windy Columbus and then took helicopters twenty minutes over the flat, barren winter landscape to the Peace Officers Training Academy in London.

In the holding room (a conference room with cold-cut sandwiches, chips, soft drinks and coffee), I dialed in and downloaded coverage of three breaking stories. Saying he had become a "lightning rod" for the Tailhook scandal (in which Naval aviators allegedly fondled women in a hotel hallway), Admiral Kelso held a resignation press conference in Washington. We knew that story was coming. What we didn't know about ahead of time was that North Korea was announcing that it would allow International Atomic Energy Association officials to inspect seven disputed nuclear production sites.

The United States also won another Olympic gold medal in skiing, and since the President had been calling all our gold medalists in Lillehammer, Norway, I printed that story, too. Dee Dee Myers was in the staff hold, so I handed her the stories and verbally briefed her.

The motorcade leaving the police academy didn't get very far before we reached Charlie's House of Meats and Deli. A sign on wheels with removable letters said, "Clinton burgers $1.89/pound." Of course, we stopped. The photographers scrambled out of their van and tromped through the long grass to reach the hungry Commander-in-Chief. A "Clinton Burger," it turned out, was a half-pounder topped with cheese, bacon, mushrooms, onions and special sauce. The press pool, many carrying cameras, long microphones and other equipment, stumbled through the tall, dead roadside weeds and followed the President inside. He later stopped for a second lunch at another deli.

Afterward, six of us on staff were driven in a van forty-five minutes back to the Columbus airport, where the President was to meet and greet local elected officials, contributors, supporters and other distinguished guests. At the airport, I snatched some delicious chocolate dessert before ducking into the holding room down the hall from the reception to check the news.

I found stories saying someone had randomly gunned down a roomful of people at a Wendy's restaurant in Oklahoma, on a day in which we hadn't made much news. Said Myers: "Oh, this is sick, but— we might make the nets now." Sure enough, her news judgment was solid as always: the evening network newscasts ran stories on the Oklahoma shooting and included soundbites from the President's anti-crime remarks in Ohio.

A few of us on staff had a chance to check out the food in yet another Midwestern city one summer evening when the President visited Chicago. He participated in a daylong roundtable discussion on "How Will the New Workplace Benefit Workers, Companies and the Nation's Economy?" and then conducted a news conference with Indiana reporters. I rode to Andrews Air Force Base with Jeff Eller in his car, windows open as he smoked a cigar, country music on the radio on a warm, sunny morning. Since we were flying into Chicago's Midway Airport with its short runway, we couldn't take the 747. So the President flew aboard a twelve-seat jet (called a C-20) and the rest of us boarded a forty-two-seat jet called a C-9 (like a DC-9) for the one-hour, forty-minute flight. Our motorcade was the only traffic on Lake Shore Drive for the twenty-five-minute ride to the Sheraton Chicago Hotel and Towers.

I was kind of lost all day because I hadn't studied the trip book well enough on the flight to Chicago. The trip books were, next to our staff lapel pins, probably the most important items we were issued on trips. They included the President's schedule, aircraft manifests for all flights, diagrams for the sites, background memos and briefing papers, advance team members' names and phone and pager numbers, even the weather of the cities we'd be visiting, in addition to notes about where the staff should go and what we should do during Presidential events. And the books even fit in a suit coat pocket.

During the day, I passed Chief of Staff Mack McLarty backstage, in the Sheraton's kitchen/service area. "Hi, Ken," he said, but he was past me before I could say anything in response. Great, I thought, I didn't realize he even knew my name. Now the Chief of Staff probably thinks I blew him off.

As did just about everybody else around the White House, I really liked McLarty. "How's it going, *Key*-in?" he'd say to me. (I always got a kick out of the way his courtly, Southern accent made my name two syllables.) A former chief executive officer of gas utility Arkla who once ran his family's Ford dealership, McLarty had known the President since kindergarten back in Hope, Arkansas. When McLarty was named Chief of Staff during the transition, a Clinton aide was quoted as saying about the President-elect's decision, "Who can you trust more than a guy you used to eat paste with in Miss Mary's kindergarten class?" A short guy with receding, perfectly-combed hair, smart gray suits, crisply-starched white shirts and striped ties, McLarty's impeccable manners and soft-spoken style got him dubbed "Mack the Nice" by the Washington media in the Administration's early days.

When most of the staff went with the President to a Democratic National Committee fund-raising dinner that evening at the Chicago Historical Society Building, I sat around with our press staff in their office. (I was manifested to fly back on the press plane.) Kathy McKiernan and Jeremy Gaines (press assistants) and Kris Engskov (travel office) and I strolled Michigan Avenue, across the Chicago River, on a pleasant evening. We ate deep-dish pizza at Gino's East and drank Old Style beer. Chicago's a great city, I thought. It was good to be back in the Midwest.

Many of the day trips we took were along the East Coast. New Jersey in particular was a popular site for such trips. We generally liked trips there because they were small, quick and scaled-back in terms of events and aides. One late summer day I was headed to the staff van. I crossed paths near the Old Executive Office Building's west exit with Wendy Smith, who handed me a trip book.

"A thin one—we like those," I said. "The simpler, the better."

"And," Smith said, "we get back at a decent time and can act like we have real lives."

There were only five of us in the staff van about 10:30 A.M. on the way to Andrews Air Force Base. We ate an early lunch of turkey sandwiches and chips on the fifty-minute flight to Newark International Airport.

The motorcade took us fifteen minutes to Jersey City, through a toll booth on the turnpike. It always was fun sailing through those with the traffic arms up, hardly slowing down and not paying the toll. We stopped at a Liberty State Park, where some of us on the staff stood a discreet 100 yards or so away as the President chatted on the boardwalk with some people who had written him letters about health care. The White House received more than one million letters from people concerned about health care, and the President and First Lady tried to meet with letter writers on their trips. It was an overcast, humid day with a breeze blowing off the water.

We then drove just a couple minutes to the nearby event site, where the stage was set up so that the Statue of Liberty was off to the side and the World Trade Center and the rest of the famous Manhattan skyline was behind as a backdrop. The President spoke about the need for universal coverage and employer involvement as Congressional debate on health care reform continued in Washington.

Our staff hold was located inside a former train station. The second-floor, carpeted room was large, well-furnished and air-conditioned, with a table of catered food and drinks and our ubiquitous white plastic phones. Bruce Lindsey and Will Itoh (National Security Council) worked the phones while I dialed in and monitored the wires. After the President's health care speech, Air Force Colonel Ken Campbell (White House Communications Agency deputy commander) walked into the room muttering, "First time *that's* happened. We've had the Presidential seal stolen, but it's never fallen off the podium before."

Sure enough, the President was delivering a literally podium-pounding speech, and the Seal of the President fell off the front of the podium, known as the "Blue Goose." "Gust of wind," the White House Communications Agency guys kept saying. On the "CBS Evening News" that night, Rita Braver reported that the President got so worked up about health care, he knocked the seal off the podium, and CBS aired the video of the President pounding the podium.

When it came time to leave about 3:30 P.M., after the President conducted a meet-and-greet with supporters, I almost missed the motorcade. Nobody gave us a heads-up (which wasn't unusual—it was our responsibility to keep track of where he was), so I ended up dashing to the motorcade, computer and printer bags over both shoulders swinging as I ran. A couple of our guys had to jump into the straggler van and barely made it to the airport. We could hear them on the two-way radios, huffing and puffing as they talked and ran at the same time.

Another time, the First Lady accompanied us to wintry New Jersey for a health care event. Upon arrival, the motorcade drove through clear streets, with enormous snow piles plowed to each side, to Middlesex County College, where the President and First Lady spoke in a gymnasium. The President said parts of his health care reform plan dear to senior citizens were being threatened by political foes. "Fight with us if you want to get something done," he said.

The First Lady gave a harsh assessment of the current system, calling it "the stupidest financial system for health care in the world." Later, New Jersey Governor Christine Todd Whitman, a Republican who had defeated incumbent Jim Florio, went into the on-site press filing center and tore into the Clinton plan. Our press staff was livid.

It was a slow news day. I saw few wire stories of note cross my laptop computer screen while dialed in. (Among the headlines: Michigan Democratic Congressman Bob Carr will run for the Senate seat of the retiring Don Riegle; South Carolina Democratic Congressman Butler Derrick is retiring; Peru's prime minister resigns over a human rights controversy.) But I did e-mail the transcript of the President's remarks back to Washington. "Excellent," Jeff Eller said.

Later, the discussion in the holding room turned to shoes and cars and the toll winter takes on both. Bruce Lindsey told a story, saying he always rode a bus in Washington. One evening in the early days of the administration, he said, a guy came up to him on the bus late at night and said, "Are you Bruce Lindsey?" Lindsey said he thought, "Oh, no." But it turned out the guy just wanted a job in the administration.

One mid-fall day we again took a fifty-minute flight to Newark International Airport, this time followed by a twenty-minute helicopter ride to New Brunswick, where we landed at Johnson Park, surrounded by trees.

We motorcaded five minutes to Robert Wood Johnson University Hospital, and I worked in the staff holding room across the hall from the event site. Just before he entered the atrium to speak to the large crowd, the President stopped in the small restroom across from the staff hold. As usual, a Secret Service agent went in first, checked it out and then stood outside the door when the President went in. And I couldn't help but think to myself, Geez, how badly do you have to want to be President to give up the privacy of your bodily functions? Every time he went to the bathroom, it was a matter of official business discussed on the Secret Service's radio frequency.

The Secret Service, White House Communications Agency and White House staff each had separate frequencies on our otherwise identical WHCA-issued two-way radios. When the advance staffers talked to each other, all the other White House staff could hear them. But sometimes if there was a problem or something semi-private needed to be discussed, one staffer would tell another, "Go to November," which was a backup frequency. Usually that was a clue that something juicy was about to happen—like somebody getting chewed out. And invariably, everybody would switch over to hear.

After the speech, we boarded the motorcade about 5 P.M. When we reached the Johnson Park landing zone, there were hundreds of people—many of them Rutgers University students—cheering and waving yellow HEALTH CARE THAT'S ALWAYS THERE signs in the grassy area surrounded by trees. Governor Jim Florio, running for re-election in less than a month against Republican Christine Todd Whitman, was with the President. And the crowd chanted, "Four more years!"

The President stepped on the ledge of the limo's back seat with the door open and spoke into a microphone through a temporary, portable public address system which staff had hurriedly set up. He mentioned Florio's support for gun control, urged everybody to vote for Florio and headed toward Marine One. The rest of us scrambled to nearby Nighthawks 2, 3 and 4.

In the air, it became obvious that New Jersey was further into fall than we were in Washington. The leaves on the trees were beautiful shades of yellow, brown and orange as we swooped low over them. I looked through the helicopter's small round side windows and saw the other helicopters hovering like giant grasshoppers in formation over the suburban countryside.

Aboard Air Force One for the short flight back to Andrews Air Force Base, I found myself thinking about the crowd cheering Florio. Four more years? You know, I thought, that scene of campaign excitement makes me think...maybe I *could* do one more campaign. The way I feel now, yes, I'd like to be here for four years. But then, I thought, the way I felt last week—or could feel next week—I wonder if I can make it *one* year.

Going to New Jersey got to be almost a routine day trip. (Although not as routine as some other states. In my trips with the President, we visited California eleven times, more than any other state. Other popular destinations were: New York, seven trips; Ohio and Missouri, six trips each; and Illinois, Pennsylvania and Minnesota, five trips each.)

In addition to issues, sometimes day trips were scheduled so the President could attend important ceremonies. Each year, for example, he attended graduation exercises at one of our nation's military academies. Our second year, he went to the U.S. Naval Academy's ceremony in nearby Annapolis, Maryland.

We left a little before 9 A.M., loading the motorcade on the South Lawn driveway outside the Diplomatic Room, under the famous South Portico. We drove to the Pentagon and boarded three helicopters for the twenty-minute flight. With so few staff, the atmosphere was kind of low-key.

We landed on a football practice field and were driven a short distance to Navy/Marine Corps Memorial Stadium. Our holding room was the locker room, where quotations in blue block letters were painted on the white cinder-block walls:

HE WHO WILL NOT RISK SHALL NOT WIN.

HIT HARD. HIT FIRST. HIT FAST.

SHIP. SHIPMATE. SELF.

There was a table of sweet rolls, bananas, apples, soft drinks and bottled water, and I dialed in to check the wires before giving Press Secretary Dee Dee Myers a verbal briefing.

"But due to the time of day…" I said.

"There's not much going on," she finished.

"Not yet," I said.

I walked out of the air-conditioning to watch the graduation ceremony on a bright, sunny, warm day. I stood near the stadium's end zone with Navy Captain Mark Rogers (White House Military Office), who was atypically wearing his white short-sleeved uniform. I told him of former University of Arkansas football coach Lou Holtz's story of when Holtz was coaching at William & Mary and his team played at Navy. One of Holtz's players, pointing out the names on the stadium facade (Iwo Jima, Guadalcanal, Leyte, Midway), said, "Coach, we'll never beat these guys." When Holtz asked why, the player supposedly responded, "Well, look at the schedule they play!"

The Navy Blue Angels stunt air squadron streaked just a few hundred feet overhead in formation. The day turned pretty hot during the ceremony, which seemed to drag. Secretary of the Navy John Dalton's remarks lasted forever, and then the President gave a strong speech on U.S. military responsibilities. He stood and shook hands with all 868 graduates as he handed them their diplomas.

I waited in the air-conditioning before emerging for the traditional toss of Midshipmen's caps into the air. When the caps fell to the ground, our advance staff scrambled to collect as many as they could. (The graduates got new hats upon their commissions.) I took one, and it even fit. I decided I was an honorary ensign, but then one of the guys in the press pool said that I'd have to serve an honorary five years in the Navy. I declined. The motorcade took us through Annapolis, a pretty little town with boats tied to docks, on a beautiful day.

Other ceremonies weren't as uplifting. One early spring day we attended the funeral of long-time Democratic Congressman William Natcher of Kentucky. After a one-hour, thirty-five-minute flight to Bowling Green, Kentucky, I was the only one who rode in the Staff 1 van on a rainy, cold day. (There were only seven political appointee staffers on the trip.) The motorcade took us past cows and a Corvette police car marked "Drug Seized Vehicle" on the front fender in a town that is home to the national Chevrolet Corvette museum.

At Eastward Baptist Church, we held upstairs in a functional room and watched the funeral service live on local TV. There were about 1,250 people there, including 23 Congressmen, 11 former Congressmen, the governor and the mayor. Congressman Natcher the previous month had cast his last vote in a record of 18,401 in a row without missing a vote.

Mark Gearan (communications director) was on the trip in Dee Dee Myers' place, sitting next to me and working on a notepad with a phone to his ear most of the time we were there. I dialed in to the wires to keep him updated, but not much was moving. We sat at long tables, eating a slightly better-than-average staff holding room lunch of cold-cut sandwiches, chips, pasta salad, brownies and soft drinks on ceramic plates with silverware.

On the way back to the airport, the President stopped the motorcade to get out and shake a few hands of people standing by the road.

That sent the press pool spilling out of their vans, hauling cameras, microphones and notepads, and then scurrying back through the mud and tall grass when he headed back to the limo. We got back to the White House by 6 P.M., just in time to check the network TV newscasts.

The President also spoke to organizations. The annual United Negro College Fund brought us to New York for a seventeen-and-a-half-hour day trip. After the regular morning communications meeting in Mark Gearan's office, we rode to Andrews in the staff van and then boarded Air Force One. The plane pulled into its regular spot, with a huge puddle at the foot of the rear steps, at JFK International Airport after a bumpy flight in the rain to begin a busy day trip filled with several stops around New York.

The motorcade took us first to Brooklyn College, where the President spoke at an Americorps Public Safety Forum, a national service event. He urged listeners to "take back our streets, our schools, our lives." An AIDS heckler disrupted the event. After the heckler was removed, a voice from the crowd called to the President during the brief lull: "Welcome to Brooklyn."

I worked upstairs in the carpeted, small staff hold with food, phone lines, electrical outlets, couch, chairs and a TV set with live coverage of the event. I briefed Bruce Lindsey on news coverage of the three White House aides—Mark Gearan, Maggie Williams and Lisa Caputo—who appeared before the Whitewater grand jury back in Washington. Lindsey was one of those subpoenaed as well. (In other stories moving on the wires, former Health, Education and Welfare Secretary Joseph Califano strongly supported the Clinton health care plan before the Senate Finance Committee, and Deval Patrick, the President's nominee for assistant attorney general for civil rights, told Senate Judiciary Committee members he was no extremist and later was praised by the senators.)

Then it was on to the 61st Precinct in Brooklyn, a cramped police station that reminded me of "Barney Miller." We were there only briefly before motorcading twenty-five minutes to the Sheraton in Manhattan. Later we held in a small ballroom while the President addressed a United Negro College Fund dinner. I sat with the medical and military staff as incredibly rude waiters speaking Italian served us beef Wellington. The choir that performed at the UNCF dinner down the hall sat at the other tables. The event seemed to last forever. Finally we headed down the stairs to 53rd Street and the waiting motorcade and back to the airport.

On the flight on the way home, the President slipped into a red, white and blue warmup suit and roamed back to the staff section briefly. Someone on the staff later noted that he looked like "Super Dave" Osborne. ("For my next stunt, I'll ride back to Washington strapped to the nose of Air Force One.")

Other ceremonial event-related day trips included visits to colleges. On a trip one fall day, the President spoke at the 200th anniversary of the founding of the University of North Carolina in Chapel Hill. It seemed half the White House staff was from North Carolina and everybody wanted to go, so I got bumped to the press plane. That always was annoying. It wasn't so much that I didn't like the reporters, but that the press plane always got back later and wasn't as comfortable. Our press staffers said they preferred it because the atmosphere was so much more laid back. But I needed to be near the rest of the staff to do my job. Besides, the press plane included some obnoxious, whining, drunken, egotistical jerks.

We left about 4 p.m. on the fifty-five-minute flight. The plane chartered for the press on that flight belonged to the MGM Grand Hotel. Built in 1957, it was full of first-class seats configured differently in various compartments. Our travel office staff said it had been used by Madonna, Neil Diamond, the Grateful Dead, Guns 'n' Roses and the Boston Celtics. It was interesting, but ultimately kind of tacky—sort of what you'd expect a flying bordello to look like. But the prime rib was pretty good. Everyone was referring to it as "The Madonna Plane" because she used it during her Blonde Ambition tour.

After landing at the Raleigh-Durham airport, the press bus took us to the Field House, where the press office was set up. The President spoke next door at UNC's Kenan Stadium. (The last president to speak there had been President Kennedy.) There was lots of light blue and white (UNC school colors) displayed, which made me think of Somalia's flag. I stood on the low balcony of a building behind the small stadium's end zone, where the President spoke on a comfortable evening with temperatures in the sixties on the wooded, pretty campus.

Another college campus we visited for a ceremony was UCLA. At

Andrews, Air Force One was parked near the hangar, instead of its normal spot in front of the operations building, due to an annual air show. Since there wasn't a land line (a phone line from the plane's nose that plugs into a jack on the tarmac) available at the new location, I couldn't dial in to the wire service computer system before takeoff. Air Force One didn't have the capability for me to dial in while in flight. We did have air-to-ground voice communications for the staff, of course.

I sat in the guest section on the four-hour, fifty-minute flight with California Senators Dianne Feinstein and Barbara Boxer and Representatives Lewis and Miller. The President came back with Californian political staffers John Emerson and Marsha Scott. He sat down and told stories of his Arkansas campaigns, recalling exact voting results, in some cases by county. He then stepped over to Miller, a member of the House Science and Technology Committee: "So, are we gonna pass the space station?"

Then he went back up front to nap, and we were served a breakfast of egg burrito and potatoes. Later, Senator Boxer looked out the window to my right as we flew over the Grand Canyon on a sunny day.

"I don't think I've ever seen this on any other flight," she said, admiring the magnificent view.

"That's the beauty of flying on this aircraft," I said with a smile. "We kind of get to go wherever we want."

We landed about 9:45 A.M. at San Bernardino International Airport, formerly Norton Air Force Base. It looked deserted on a sunny day with palm trees, pretty blue skies and pleasantly dry air, all of it welcome after two weeks of cold, gray weather in Washington. The President gave an outdoor speech, and Bruce Lindsey, Steve Bahar (lead advance), Marsha Scott and Kristie Kenney (National Security Council) and I waited in the hold—the former base commander's office—during the short event beside the building. Outside, the President spoke about defense conversion to a crowd of about 400 people. (Norton had closed less than two months previously.)

Then we boarded helicopters for the forty-five-minute flight to Santa Monica. And it was easily the worst helicopter flight I'd ever been on. Normally I liked flying in the helicopters. But I don't know if it was headwinds or what, but when we loaded into the vans after landing, everybody else said they'd just about thrown up.

The fifteen-minute motorcade took us to the UCLA campus for the school's seventy-fifth anniversary convocation, at which the President spoke. The event was at Pauley Pavilion, and the men's basketball locker room was the President's holding room; the staff's hold (adjoining through a common restroom, oddly) was the women's locker room. It took a while before I recovered enough from the helicopter flight to eat something. After working on my laptop a while (top story: 148 fleeing Haitians repatriated, making 1,024 in the last twelve days), I wandered into the men's locker room, with blue walls and gold lettering listing UCLA's national championship years and All-Americans.

"So this is what it looks like when you win ten NCAA titles," I said.

"Yeah, but when was their last one?" Lindsey said. (It had been in 1975.)

After a long event, the President walked next door to the Acostia Sports Center to tape his weekly radio address a day ahead of its delivery. Afterward, I got the transcript on diskette from the stenographers working in the press office (a nearby tent) and headed toward the motorcade on a perfect Southern California Friday afternoon, past the tennis courts, where Rick James' "Superfreak" was blasting from nearby speakers.

We were driven fifteen minutes to the Sheraton Miramar in Santa Monica, across the street from bluffs that overlooked the Pacific Ocean.

Not many White House staffers got to board Air Force One when it wasn't going anywhere. I got the chance one winter day when the crew and I conducted some testing on the laptop computer dial-in process.

A White House Communications Agency staffer and a civilian Pentagon employee on loan to the White House went with me. We took one of the hourly shuttle vans to WHCA headquarters at Anacostia in southeast D.C. I stood at the fortified Marine guard post waiting for someone to bring the car around and noticed the signs. A MARINE ON DUTY HAS NO FRIENDS, one said.

Based at Andrews Air Force Base, the Military Airlift Command's 89th Military Airlift Wing includes the Presidential Maintenance

Branch. (Trucks called "Eagle One," "Eagle Two" and "Eagle Three" contain tools and equipment.) Andrews is a huge, sprawling complex covering a vast expanse of land in southeast Maryland. When we boarded Air Force One for trips, a staff van would take us onto the tarmac and right to the plane. It stretched virtually as far as the eye could see, and other aircraft usually were parked elsewhere on the tarmac.

At Andrews, we were cleared through security on a bleak, gray day and entered the hangar, an enormous six-sided building created for the new planes' arrival in 1990 and surrounded by fence and barbed wire. The building was large enough for the two planes to be parked wingtip to wingtip, dwarfing the maintenance vehicles. We saw the modern, tidy office space for the Air Force One crew members, then signed the log and were taken aboard by friendly, professional members of the radio crew.

White paper covered the carpeting on the aircraft, and crew members wore plastic bags covering their shoes to prevent dust and dirt from being tracked aboard. No wonder the plane always looked so great.

The crew told me some more about the communications aboard both the 747s. It was amazing what we *didn't* have. It had all sorts of high-technology capabilities, of course, but because of limited funds and the sluggishness of the appropriations process, there were commercial planes with more modern communications technology. Nevertheless, I'd heard that the planes received routine maintenance twice as often as the specifications required. Even the planes which had been in service for years had far fewer miles on them than newer commercial aircraft, because ours were used far less often.

We didn't solve our dial-in problems that day, but it was worth the trip just to visit the hangar and see the operation up-close.

When the plane did leave the hangar, I was almost always on it. There were a couple of exceptions. One was on a zero-degree, icy day. An early-morning earthquake (6.6 on the Richter scale) in Northridge, California, had killed forty-four people. I found out the President was headed out there for a one-day visit the next day. But he took one of the smaller 737s, so I wasn't on the manifest. Neither was Jeff Eller. "If it helps, I got bumped, too," he said. It would've been nice to check out some seventy-two-degree weather, but ten hours on the plane—after having been aboard eleven hours a few days earlier for the flight home from overseas—didn't thrill me.

On other occasions—as on a health care reform-related visit to a Connecticut pharmacy—using a small plane (because of short airport runways) prevented the full traveling staff from accompanying the President. And sometimes, on personal trips (as when the President and First Lady attended their Law School reunion at Yale University or when they attended the funeral in Hope, Arkansas, of White House Deputy Counsel Vince Foster), the traveling staff also was kept to a minimum.

But near the end of my White House "tour of duty," I didn't at all mind being taken off the manifest. The day after we returned from our second trip to Europe in a month, the President flew to Georgia for the day to examine flood damage there. I was exhausted and actually was glad he took a plane too small for all of us. And one Friday, I was asked if it was necessary that I go to Detroit with the President the next night for a political fundraiser. Oh, twist my arm, I thought— *make* me take a Saturday night off.

Other times we had day trips scheduled, only to have them canceled at the last minute. Because of all the logistics and advance work involved, it took a pretty major event to prevent the President from going on a planned trip.

One instance was on a scheduled day trip to Milwaukee. As soon as I got in to the office, Larry Sampas (overnight news analysis) told me the President's mother had died a few hours ago. I had my cell phone on my belt, my staff pin on my lapel and my computer bags draped over my shoulder, but our trip for a foreign policy speech previewing the next week's European trip was off. Instead, I read on the wire, and had confirmed at the 7:30 A.M. communications meeting, the Vice President would go to Milwaukee with his staff.

The President headed to Hot Springs to make funeral preparations. Jeff Eller and I talked briefly and decided he would go to Arkansas without me. That made sense for several reasons: he was going anyway (in Dee Dee Myers' place), the staff for a personal trip should be kept to a minimum, and I had duties in Washington, including getting ready for the Europe trip, which Eller wasn't going on.

I thought of the President's mom all day. Virginia Kelley was a wonderful, special lady. I met her my first couple weeks on the campaign, when she would drive to Little Rock from Hot Springs and help out at headquarters. She always had a smile and a hug for me, even though we barely knew each other. She was, in some ways, much like my mom, who died one year and four days previously: they were both short with black hair, they both had lots of energy and upbeat enthusiasm, and they both died of cancer. It just made me sad all day, one of the most depressing days I had there. I ended up being especially glad I didn't go to Hot Springs.

Other cancellations were less personal and had larger international implications. I walked out the front door and down the Old Executive Buildings steps onto West Executive Drive to board the staff van for Andrews on a sunny, windy, cool fall day. We were supposed to go to New Jersey for a political trip, but after sitting there for maybe half an hour, we found out the trip was canceled.

The President was in the Oval Office, talking to French President François Mitterrand on the phone about the Persian Gulf situation. (On the wires were stories of an Iraqi troop buildup near the Kuwaiti border. The USS *George Washington,* which we had visited a few months before, and other ships had been deployed there, in addition to thousands of U.S. troops.) After we'd sat in the vans for a while, Wendy Smith went inside to see Harold Ickes (Deputy Chief of Staff) for go/no-go decision. It was decided the Vice President and his staff would go in the President's place. That night the President addressed the nation from the Oval Office on the Gulf situation.

Another time, we were supposed to leave for Los Angeles for a weekend trip that was rescheduled into a one-day trip but finally was canceled. (The First Lady went instead.) Trouble in Haiti led the President to threaten and plan for a military invasion, preventing him from taking the planned trip. Former President Jimmy Carter, Georgia Senator Sam Nunn and former Chairman of the Joint Chiefs of Staff Colin Powell went to Haiti to negotiate with the ruling military junta, which refused to allow democratically elected President Jean Bertrand-Aristide to take power. President Clinton called the talks the "last best chance" to avoid an invasion.

I got a call at home one night that there would be a White House meeting about Haiti at 7:30 the next morning and that those attending would need news reports. So early the next morning I clipped, copied and delivered the 103-page sets of clips to several dozen aides in the National Security Council's Situation Room in the West Wing basement. NSC and State Department officials, including Secretary of State Warren Christopher, attended.

That night the U.S. invasion was on its way to Haiti before military junta leader Raoul Cedras acquiesced at the last minute, barely avoiding American military intervention.

Most day trips weren't nearly as dramatic. But there were plenty of them.

5▶One Day at a Time

MINNEAPOLIS: "*HE'S IN A FEISTY MOOD*" · *WELFARE*
REFORM IN KANSAS CITY · *NATIONAL SERVICE/CRIME IN*
ST. LOUIS · "*GONNA RIDE ME A SOUTHBOUND*" *TO*
ATLANTA · *NAFTA 'CAUSE WE HAFTA* · *BACK* "*HOME*" *IN*
THE MONONGAHELA VALLEY

*M*ANY TIMES THE PRESIDENT'S DAY TRIPS are scheduled in
support of specific elements of his agenda. These, of course, change
over time. One week he might focus on welfare reform, another week
on crime, another week on the budget. The great thing about day trips
is, they allow him to bring his message to the people, but still get back
to Washington and deal with other pressing matters.

In late summer 1994, President Clinton's crime bill was being debated on Capitol Hill. The bill called for putting 100,000 additional
police officers on the street and for banning nineteen types of deadly
assault weapons.

I was standing on the South Lawn with fellow Arkansans and
other White House staffers sipping lemonade on an overcast, humid
August afternoon as kind folks from Hope, Arkansas, served their
world-famous watermelon. The Air Force band played country music
as we sat at picnic tables. When I returned to my desk, I found a blue
"urgent" window on my wire services computer screen displaying the
news that a vote on the rule in the House failed 225-210, so members
didn't vote on the bill itself. (In a morning communication meeting,
Rahm Emanuel [deputy communications director] had said the National Rifle Association for whatever reason had decided that a vote
for the rule would count against members, although they could vote
however they wanted on the bill itself.)

Everybody had been saying we'd win a close one. Michigan Democratic Congressman David Bonior, who led the floor fight for us, had said we had the votes. (Of course, he had said that when he was fighting us on the North American Free Trade Agreement, and he was wrong then, too.) The immediate analysis on TV was that it was a "devastating" loss for the President.

Shortly afterward I delivered wire reports to the West Wing for Mark Gearan (communications director) and Dee Dee Myers (press secretary) and passed Kathy McKiernan (press assistant) in the hall. We exchanged disappointed looks. "Sucks, huh?" she said.

When I got to my office at seven the next morning, I started by checking the wire services, as usual. There were references in several stories to the President's trip that day to Minnesota. That was news to me. I read my e-mail, and sure enough, there were manifests and staff van departure notices. There I was, without a staff pin, without my cell phone, and without having given the volunteers in my office a heads-up I'd be gone. (The scheduling and advance office usually sent the manifests via e-mail a day or two before each trip. They showed who would be on Marine One, who would be on Air Force One, when we would take off and where we would land.)

In the morning communications meeting in Mark Gearan's office, David Dreyer (deputy communications director) tried to pump up everybody. "Don't get down," he said, and complimented a not-down-trodden Rahm Emanuel, who had led our crime bill efforts. Don Baer (speechwriter) said he'd met with the President the previous night and said that after the President got over his initial anger, he became combative and ready to go at it. "He's in a feisty mood," Baer said.

As Air Force One began to roll down the runway, I was standing in the conference room talking to Neil Wolin (National Security Council). "Uh-oh, we're moving," I said, and dashed to take my seat in the staff section, sliding on the carpet in my slick-soled dress shoes past the President, who was standing and talking to seated aides. As the plane's nose lifted, I leaned against a nearby bulkhead next to Marcia Hale (intergovernmental affairs), partly pinned by G-forces.

A few feet away, the President went into the "Flying Nun" pose like Dee Dee Myers sometimes did, leaning way forward as the plane sharply angled into the sky. He was in pretty good form. Not as good as Myers' flat-out ski jumper, but not bad at all. Then, glasses perched at the end of his nose, he stood there reading the front page of the *USA Today* Life section in his shirtsleeves. He seemed to be in a good mood as the rest of us laughed and Bob McNeely (staff photographer) took pictures.

I slept part of the two-hour, fifteen-minute flight, awakening long enough to eat a turkey pastrami sandwich and chips. Upon landing at Minneapolis/St. Paul International Airport, the motorcade took us twenty minutes downtown to the Marriott City Center hotel for the National Association of Police Organizations meeting. The group had invited the President some time previously, but was told he couldn't make it. When Congress stalled the crime bill, it was decided he should go on the road to rally support. Was the offer to speak to NAPO still good, its representatives were asked. You bet, they told us.

But the lack of planning meant the advance teams had to scramble. Army Colonel Tom Hawes (White House Communications Agency commander) was standing in the press office when he heard an announcement to the reporters of a "sign-up for tomorrow's trip to Minneapolis." It was the first Hawes had heard of it, and he had to scramble to get a team together and up to Minnesota. As a result, phone lines were still being installed as we arrived. They never did get any in the staff hold, so I used a pay phone and called in on our private 1-800 number reserved for staff use.

During the President's speech, I stood outside the room and listened. Standing in front of rows of about fifty cops standing shoulder-to-shoulder, the President was energized and ready for battle. I thought, This is Bill Clinton at his best: fighting for a cause he believes in, engaged in a political scrap with right on his side, a Washington outsider taking on the entrenched guardians of gridlock in defense of ordinary Americans. And I realized how proud I was to be on his team. It was always true, but I rarely thought about it.

Linda Moore (political affairs) walked over to me as we listened. "It's too bad he's so hoarse, because this is the kind of speech he needs his voice for," she said. She was right. When he spoke of the victims, of the families, of funerals, then his allergy-laden, over-used voice sounded empathetic. But when he got mad at Congress and the NRA and the Republicans, his anger didn't come through as well as it would've if he'd had his full voice.

Afterward, Jose Cerda, our staff liaison to NAPO, mentioned the visuals: "Tonight on the evening news it'll be Newt Gingrich in the House briefing room with those books behind him—and the President with cops behind him."

"I'll take the boys in blue behind us—literally and figuratively—any day," I said.

After we ate nachos with ground turkey and melted cheese on the way to Andrews, the President took Marine One to the South Lawn, where he picked up the First Lady and Chelsea en route to Camp David for the weekend.

Issue-focused day trips weren't always about policy areas with impending Congressional votes. Sometimes when the President wanted to announce an initiative, he would leave Washington.

That was the case when the President unveiled his welfare reform program. On a hot, humid Washington morning, I sat in the plane's staff section, facing the rear of the plane while watching a movie during the two-hour, fifteen-minute flight. Wendy Smith (trip director), Andrew Friendly (personal aide) and I talked about the murders of O.J. Simpson's ex-wife and her friend the previous Sunday night. Friendly and I argued Simpson couldn't have done it because the evidence so obviously pointed to him. Nobody would be that stupid, we said. "Crime of passion," Smith said. Ohhh.

Kansas City was hot but windy. We rode twenty-five minutes downtown to Commerce Bank for the announcement of the President's welfare reform plan. The President met with eleven mothers who were former welfare recipients, four of whom told him their personal stories, in a meeting closed to the press. Then he unveiled his welfare reform plan in a public event.

Afterward, most of the staff went with the President for an "unscheduled" stop (unofficially, but everyone knew about it) at a barbecue place. In the press office, which had a huge, ancient abandoned vault with a tremendously thick door, Bruce Reed (domestic policy) conducted a press briefing that was available via satellite back in the White House press room. I dialed in to check the event coverage on the wires. Top stories, all on health care, included the House Education and Labor Committee voting 25-18 in favor of employer mandates, Senators Patrick Moynihan and Bob Packwood saying employer mandates were dead in the Senate Finance Committee and the First Lady telling the League of Women Voters that abortion coverage could be sacrificed to pass a version of the Clinton plan.

Our van—with Bruce Reed, Dee Dee Myers, Avis LaVelle (a former campaign deputy press secretary who went to Health and Human Services), Mary Jo Bane (an HHS policy aide) and me—was separated from the motorcade. So when we got to an intersection blocked by a policeman, we sent Myers (she being easily the most recognizable among us) in her knee-length blue dress, sunglasses and high heels skittering across the pavement to ask the policeman if we could get through.

Myers left me her cell phone as she dashed out, saying, "It's Tom Ross" of the National Security Council press office. "That's okay," Ross told me after I explained the situation, "I can hold." Just after Myers got back in the van and I handed her the phone, the motorcade—ironically and luckily—pulled in front of us. We got in line behind the last vehicle and followed them to the airport.

Sometimes, however, no matter how well an issue-related day trip was planned, something would happen to overshadow it. That happened one early summer day when we traveled to St. Louis. As we pulled on to Pennsylvania Avenue in the staff van, Jonathan Prince (communications) was working his cell phone. He was telling who was for a particular position ("Oh…me, Rahm, George") and talking about "White House idiots" when Wendy Smith reminded him he was on an easily monitored cell phone. He ignored her. After Prince hung up, there was just a moment of silence before Rick Allen (national service) deadpanned, "You forgot to give 'em the launch codes." Everybody but Prince cracked up.

Democratic Congressman Richard Gephardt of Missouri, his wife and two daughters (all four of them blond) flew on Air Force One with us during the one-hour, fifty-five-minute flight. Lunch—at 10 A.M.—was atypically so awful I just kind of picked at it.

Once we landed at Lambert–St. Louis International Airport, we boarded a bus that took us fifteen minutes to the terminal. I looked at Charles Lindbergh's *Spirit of St. Louis* plane hanging overhead as I headed up the stairs. Andrew Friendly called, "Let's go, you guys. Ken, come on." Sometimes that officious little weasel really bugged me. I think he cited me by name, when others actually were dawdling, because I was just too nice to tell him what a jerk he could be.

We then boarded the MetroLink light rail train. The official unveiling was scheduled for the next day, but our visit marked the first time the whole route was open. The Bi-State Development Agency had just finished the last 3.2 miles of the 17-mile, 17-station route. We rode from Lambert twenty-five minutes to Union Station, enjoying the green scenery on a sunny day. When we exited, a group of (apparently) Arkansans were wearing pig hats and calling the Hogs: "Woo! Pig! Sooey!" Later in the day, we saw a story on a local newscast that included the group. Said the reporter: "Maybe President Clinton understood what it means."

The motorcade took us ten minutes to an inner-city neighborhood where the President walked down a street, chatting with neighbors about crime along the way. As we walked, Dee Dee Myers talked on her cell phone, taking care of business back at the White House since George Stephanopoulos (senior adviser) and Mark Gearan were out for the day.

We then pulled around the corner to Fox Park, a Little League-type field, for the crime bill/Summer of Safety event. STAFF WORK AREA, said the sign in front of folder tables and chairs under the first-base bleachers near the street. The President had conducted a phone interview with KMOX radio in St. Louis aboard Air Force One in which he'd ripped talk shows, cynicism and inaccurate reporting. As I dialed in to check the wires, it become obvious it was the big story of the day.

The Associated Press reported that the President accused Rush Limbaugh and other talk show hosts of fostering a "constant unrelenting drumbeat of cynicism." The President's speech on national service (a good one) got ignored by the media. Poor Eli Segal and Rick Allen. They had worked so hard on their event, only to have it overshadowed by something en route.

After the event, we rode fifteen minutes to the Adams Mark hotel, next to the famous arch and the Mississippi River, for about five hours of Presidential events at the hotel, including a briefing, a meeting with the *St. Louis Post-Dispatch* editorial board and meetings with small groups. Some staffers went shopping. I sat in the staff hold (a regular hotel room upstairs) and dialed in, downloading stories for Bruce Lindsey (senior adviser) and Myers. Live coverage of a World Cup soccer game, being played in the United States, aired on a TV in the background.

Later, as we waited in the motorcade for departure, Rick Allen and I chatted with a uniformed Secret Service officer we knew from the White House. We asked her about the Counter Assault Team (CAT) members in a nearby black Chevrolet Suburban, known as the "war wagon." She said they had to meet extraordinary physical standards, even above those of the other Secret Service agents.

I could believe it. Those were some huge guys, with menacing weapons and "Terminator" sunglasses, wearing black boots, parachute pants and white polo shirts. I remembered Jeff Eller telling me on an early trip, "If those guys ever get out of the back, *get down*." Apparently it had happened in summer 1992 when President Bush went to Panama and a disturbance broke out.

One of the Administration's top priorities its first year was obtaining Senate ratification of the North American Free Trade Agreement. Negotiated during the Bush Administration, the treaty called for creation of a free trade zone among the United States, Mexico and Canada. People around the White House began saying, "NAFTA 'cause we hafta."

We began our campaign with a day trip to New Orleans. The navy blue, fifteen-passenger Dodge Ram staff vans left West Executive Drive on a sunny Washington morning. But after our two-hour, twenty-minute flight to New Orleans, we exited the rear stairs on Air Force One to find a rainy day.

We sat in the motorcade for half an hour on the tarmac as the event site was changed to an indoor location. We rode through the city for thirty minutes ("There's the Superdome"...."Look, a Winn-Dixie—oh, it's good to be back in the South") to reach the Port of New Orleans, one of the many sites we used where President Kennedy had appeared. A huge, dark warehouse was hot and muggy at the Nashville Avenue Wharf, where the President spoke about NAFTA in a short event. I worked in the press office backstage before dashing through the rain to the motorcade.

On the flight home, I finished a wire report with coverage of our event and looked for Dee Dee Myers, who was in the President's office in the aircraft's nose. I thought she might be in there for a while, so I simply stepped in, quickly handed the wire report to her and left. But just as I reached the door, I heard the President's voice. I was out in the hall before I realized I didn't hear exactly what he'd said and didn't know if he was talking to me, or, more likely, to Myers. Do I go back in and look like a geek if he wasn't talking to me? I thought. Or do I keep walking and risk ignoring my boss, the most powerful person in the world? Figuring the odds were in my favor, I kept going. (I asked Myers later, and she confirmed I was right—he'd been talking to her.)

We returned to Washington about 5:30 P.M., but got virtually no news coverage from the event. Debate on health care reform on Capitol Hill was the day's top story. Shortly after we returned, I passed Bruce Lindsey on the Old Executive Office Building's outdoor front steps and asked him what he'd thought of the trip. "Eight hours and no news," he replied. I nodded, unhappily.

We were back out again for NAFTA a couple months later, this time in Kentucky. Staff vans headed to Andrews about 10 A.M., and upon landing at Blue Grass Field in Lexington, we were greeted with gray skies and temperatures in the fifties. The President spoke to the workers at Lexmark International, Inc., and toured the factory. It was a huge plant where the workers made office machines. About 250 workers from five different companies listened as the President downplayed concerns that NAFTA would hurt American workers, especially low-skill and low-wage employees like them. Later he said the Vice President would debate NAFTA opponent Ross Perot. That was news to many of us.

I worked in the press office in another part of the factory as the President spoke and toured an assembly line, where computer laser printers were produced. Afterward, in a conference room elsewhere at the plant, he greeted selected local supporters while I dialed in nearby to check the wires. Dee Dee Myers stood in the hallway, keeping an eye out for departure for me: "He's in the hall…he's stopped to talk to some cops…he's moving. Here we go, Kenny." Out we went to the motorcade just ahead of the President, and the motorcycle cops with lights flashing led us back to the airport. (Waiting around for departure, we could always tell when we were about to leave—even if we weren't carrying two-way radios—by listening for the roar of policemen's firing up their motorcycle engines.)

The action on NAFTA was heating up. The following Sunday, the

President verbally beat up on organized labor on NBC's "Meet the Press," saying unions were engaging in "real roughshod, muscle-bound tactics" by threatening to cut off campaign funds to Congressmen who voted for NAFTA.

A couple days later came the debate between the Vice President and Ross Perot: "Now, just a minute.... If you'd stop interrupting me...." Perot appeared foolish and petulant in the debate, which aired on CNN's "Larry King Live." It wasn't even close. Perot was annoying, sputtering and ridiculous, and the Vice President gave us some momentum on NAFTA. As Michael Waldman (communications) pointed out in the next morning's communications meeting, the coverage in that day's newspapers was good, but stories on that morning's network television newscasts were even better.

Finally, in mid-November, the Senate ratified the North American Free Trade Agreement. It was another huge legislative victory for the President, one that he shoved through with an intense lobbying effort, building momentum after virtually everyone in Washington had thought it was dead.

Like NAFTA, foreign policy was an area receiving Presidential attention during day trips. We headed to Atlanta one spring day for an appearance on CNN. Driving my Plymouth Horizon across the Theodore Roosevelt Bridge to work at 6:15 A.M. that day, I heard the Marshall Tucker Band on the radio: "Gonna ride me a southbound/All the way to Georgia, Lord/'Til the train run out of track...."

After a one-hour, forty-minute flight, rain was falling upon arrival at Dobbins Air Force Base near Atlanta. The press pool stood under the left wing of Air Force One, trying to stay dry until the President emerged. Mary Street (press advance) handed out white baseball caps with the 1996 Olympics/Atlanta logo, and I took one to bring back to co-worker Larry Sampas (news analysis).

The twenty-minute motorcade took us to CNN Center, where our holding room was a dingy, empty area and where white sacks of cold Wendy's burgers and fries awaited us. George Stephanopoulos and Bruce Lindsey reacted with mock excitement: "Oh boy." I was hungry, munching a cold double cheeseburger while downloading wire stories. When the President toured the building and met with Ted Turner, I headed over to the Carter Center ahead of the motorcade in a van with some other staffers.

At the Carter Center, I walked through several spacious reception areas where people in business attire awaited the President's arrival. The staff hold was a large, modern, round, windowless room with tables, chairs, phones, printer, fax, computer and a TV set, with a table loaded with fried chicken, soft drinks, potato salad, cookies and brownies. I cranked out wire reports and went over to the press office (a ten-minute walk there and back) to get Presidential transcripts on diskette so I could e-mail them to the White House staff and others.

The President participated across the hall in the CNN "World Report" Contributors Conference, a live televised town hall meeting with CNN international reporters connected via satellite from four sites around the world. (The word "foreign" is banned on CNN; they only say "international.") A memo in our trip books from National Security Adviser Tony Lake to the President, said, "This is a very good opportunity for you to lay out an overall strategic vision and to explain to the public the pillars of the Administration's foreign policy."

The ninety-minute program was uneventful, except for Christiane Amanpour in Belgrade, who asked pointed questions about Bosnia. A defensive President, momentarily letting his emotions get the better of him, responded, "Madam, I have done everything I know to do on this problem," or words to that effect.

Not only did the President make day trips for specific events, he also did so for specific constituencies. That was true when we spent an early fall day in New Orleans. The weather was cool at 6:45 A.M. when the staff vans drove us to Andrews Air Force Base. The loud, spirited, early-morning discussion was about that week's District of Columbia mayoral Democratic primary election, won by former convict and ex-mayor Marion Barry. Aboard Air Force One before takeoff, I dialed in and tapped away at my laptop's keyboard. Josh King (communications/ advance), who had been the only other white staffer in the van, stuck his head in the tiny office. "That was an interesting cross-cultural experience," he said.

Lovely, tall, friendly Leah, a native Texan—and my favorite steward—worked the guest section, where I sat with Dawn Alexander (assistant press secretary), Lorraine Miller (legislative affairs) and Louisiana Democratic Senator John Breaux during the two-hour, twenty-minute flight. It was good to be back on the plane and to see the crew and our staff again after having been on vacation. Besides the

President's vacation to Martha's Vineyard, we only had taken two trips the previous month.

We found hot and humid weather upon exiting the rear stairs with the press pool at Callendar Field Naval Air Station, stepping onto the same spot on the tarmac where we'd parked during the previous year's trip there. On the thirty-minute trip to the Ernest N. Morial Convention Center, "Fire" by the Ohio Players played on our van's radio. The local volunteer drivers, usually recruited by the state Democratic Party, were told not to play the radios, but we never minded.

Motorcades consisted of about twenty vehicles, plus all the local police cars and motorcycles. There was the lead car, in which the lead advance person rode. Then came the President's limousine and the spare limo (with Secret Service agents, the doctor and the personal aide), in random order. A follow-up vehicle, the Counter Assault Team's Chevrolet Suburban, control (a mini-van), support (another mini-van) and the ID car followed. All those vehicles made up what was called the "secure package" and were driven by Secret Service agents.

Then came the White House Communications Agency car (with a military driver), Staff 1 and Staff 2 vans and about half a dozen vehicles for the press pool, with a straggler mini-van in case anybody got left behind. All those vehicles were driven by local volunteers. Advancing the motorcade could be a nightmare, and it was hardly the most glamorous of advance team duties. But obviously it was important.

After our arrival, the President spoke to the National Baptist Convention in the main hall. The organization was the world's largest body of African American Baptists. The President spoke to a crowd of about 30,000, with more than 120 clergy leaders behind him on the stage.

I spent the afternoon upstairs in the staff hold for five hours, dialing in and occasionally looking out a window at an abandoned warehouse. I downloaded breaking stories covering the President's speech and gave them to Bruce Lindsey and Dee Dee Myers. Lunch was cold-cut sandwiches, bags of chips and cans of soft drinks—typical staff hold fare. The President also attended a Democratic National Committee business leadership forum luncheon, met with the National Conference of Black Mayors' board of directors and talked with the *New Orleans Times-Picayune* editorial board. I never saw him all day.

On the way back to the plane, I rested my throbbing head and closed my eyes as "Superfreak" by Rick James played on the van's radio. We took the same route to the airport as on the previous year's trip to New Orleans, passing a day care center where the kids had waved American flags and the President stopped and shook hands. This time they held up red octagonal paper "Stop" signs, and he shook their hands again. When the staff van passed the kids, they were still waving and jumping up and down.

Back on Air Force One, I sat next to Barb Kinney (staff photographer) and snoozed on the way home. "You can *always* sleep on the plane," she said before takeoff. "As soon as we take off, you're out."

"Out of necessity," I replied.

"I wish I could do that," she said.

Another important constituency for the President was police officers, since battling crime was such a priority for the Administration. One fall day we took a long day trip, this one to Albuquerque: about four hours on the plane, four hours on the ground, four hours back on the plane. On the tarmac at Andrews Air Force Base around 9 A.M., the President addressed the press pool on the historic announcement from the Mideast that Israel and Jordan would sign a peace treaty.

We landed at Kirtland Air Force Base on a cool and sunny day, with scenic mountains in the background. At the Albuquerque Convention Center, the President spoke to a crowd of about 7,000 at the International Association of Chiefs of Police conference. After his speech, the President addressed the pool on the Mideast situation again, largely because part of his remarks at Andrews had been drowned out by the plane's engines and the audio was unusable. He also had some private meetings.

Later I worked in the press office, where Pam Carpenter, one of the White House stenographers, brought me a delicious piece of chocolate cake from the press food table. Arthur Jones (deputy press secretary) wondered aloud how the thousands of chiefs of police at the convention addressed each other:

"Hi, Chief."

"Hey, Chief."

"Hi there, Chief."

"Hiya, Chief."

Unusually, we left a little earlier than scheduled. On the fifteen-minute motorcade back to Kirtland Air Force Base, the President got out of his limousine to shake hands with a bunch of elementary school children lined up on the sidewalk. They were thrilled, as were their teachers.

Sometimes health care would be the focus of the President's day trips. We spent one hot summer day promoting health care reform in Pennsylvania. Due to the short runway in Latrobe, we took a forty-two-seat plane and a twelve-seat plane (instead of the larger 747) on the fifty-minute flight.

A large crowd greeted the President's arrival at the airport, where it was about eighty-five degrees and hazy. He conducted a brief meet-and-greet with health care letter writers. Huge crowds lined the roads leading into town. We saw muffler shops, car dealerships and mom-and-pop diners. We saw dark-rooted blondes with Farrah Fawcett-Majors hairstyles and auto mechanics with their names sewed into oval patches on their shirts. Virtually everyone was smiling and waving to the motorcade.

When we reached the courthouse in Greensburg, I worked in the staff hold (a jury room) and scrolled the wires. In the news, Kansas Senator Bob Dole said Republicans might delay voting on the General Agreement on Trade and Tariffs if the President continued to attack Republicans on health care. Said Dole: "Why should I worry about what President Clinton wants to do on trade when he's beating us up on health care? If this is the kind of hardball they want to play, they need to know there are two teams out there." Afterward, I went outside and briefed Bruce Lindsey, Dee Dee Myers, Ginny Terzano (deputy press secretary) and Tom Ross.

I stood to the left of the speakers' platform as the President spoke on Main Street without his jacket. He talked about the need for universal health care coverage and noted that working, middle-class Americans would suffer the most under a non-universal solution. He shook every hand he could reach on a sweaty day before we boarded the twenty-minute motorcade and headed back to the airport. Rain began to fall en route.

I was bumped to the twelve-seat backup plane for the flight to

Philadelphia. Lorrie McHugh (health care) and I were the only political appointees aboard, and we sat in front chatting and munching pretzels, peanuts and chips and sipping Cokes on the forty-five-minute flight. By the time we landed in Philadelphia, the motorcade already had left, so we took the straggler vehicle, a mini-van. We got caught in the motorcade's backwash, so we slowly crossed a bridge in heavy traffic headed downtown.

Our holding room in the Public Ledger Building was a plain, functional office suite, with sandwiches and soft drinks. I dialed in to the wires in one room while the President talked with the *Philadelphia Inquirer* editorial board and taped his Saturday radio address in another office. (In the news, United Nations Secretary General Boutros Boutros-Ghali said the UN Security Council should authorize 15,000 multinational or inter-American forces to Haiti.)

And in late fall we took a rare trip to an area familiar to me, on another health care day trip to Pennsylvania. The President was headed to southwestern Pennsylvania, where my grandparents and aunts and uncles and cousins lived. My parents grew up along the Monongahela River, and we visited there at least once a year for as long as I can remember.

Air Force One took us to Pittsburgh on a wet, chilly morning. As we neared the runway about 12:30 P.M. after a fifty-minute flight, we looked out the plane's windows.

"What's that white stuff on the ground?" we asked each other.

"Snow?"

"Can't be!"

But it was, white snow on brown grass under gray November skies with dark brown leafless trees on the hills as drove by the dark Ohio River, north to Beaver County. The motorcade took us over hills and two-lane roads, through tiny towns with houses still displaying Halloween decorations, past waving residents standing in their yards by the road on an overcast day with temperatures in the forties.

That area is prettiest when it's ugliest. There's a real character to that part of the country. Old people, young women in jeans, men who drink Iron City beer and cheer the Steelers—all watched the motorcade on our way to Ambridge, which served as the basis for fictional Ampipe in the movie *All the Right Moves*, starring Tom Cruise and Craig T. Nelson.

After a twenty-minute ride, the motorcade stopped at Ambridge's Laughlin Memorial Library. A big crowd stood by the streets outside the library, where the President and First Lady were scheduled to present a copy of the Clinton health plan. On the way inside, the President paused at a window of the house next to the library to wave to a family. A little boy pressed his hand to the glass, and the President did the same from the outside. They stood there silently smiling at each other for a brief moment.

Inside, the library smelled like old wood. We were hardly there long enough for me to dial in and check the wires. (In one story, House Minority Leader Bob Michel of Illinois said the upcoming vote on the North American Free Trade Agreement would be "in many ways the most historic vote since Desert Storm.") Then we drove to Ambridge Area High School, where the President and the First Lady spoke to a literally screaming crowd in the gymnasium as I watched on TV in the press office down the hall.

High school crowds were different than any other crowds. The high-pitched squeal that teenage girls let out is markedly different than the usual roar from any other crowd. Entering an event with the President, listening to that screaming, was what accompanying the Beatles on tour or traveling in Elvis Presley's entourage must have been like.

On the way out of town, we passed the shut-down steel mill, which was deserted with broken windows, as are many mills throughout the Monongahela Valley. It was odd to be back there, to see the familiar scenery from inside the Presidential motorcade.

Health care was only one of many issues that served as the focus of the President's trips. We'd end up traveling in support of virtually every policy area that crossed his desk.

6▶Taking Care of Business

THE PRESIDENT'S TRAVEL SCHEDULE is determined largely by which parts of his agenda he is focusing on. States, cities, constituencies, event sites, types of events...all are chosen based on what issue the White House decides it wants to promote in a given week or day.

Sometimes those trips crisscross the country and last several days. Other times they are shorter. But in all cases they are framed around opportunities for the President to push a specific piece of his agenda.

President Clinton had promised during his 1992 campaign to "focus like a laser beam" on the economy. So the top priority during the first months of the Administration was to pass a budget bill.

One evening in May, Keith Boykin (news analysis) and I joined our volunteers for happy hour at Perry's rooftop restaurant in Washington's Adams Morgan area. All day, CNN and the wire services had been projecting how the House vote on our budget reconciliation bill would go. After leaving Perry's, I took a cab back to the White House, windows down and an oldies radio station playing as neon-lit shops and restaurants and bars flew by while the driver weaved through traffic. Entering the southwest gate, I walked up West Executive Drive and saw Collier Andress, an administrative assistant in the communications office.

"Ken," she called, "we get to keep our jobs for three and a half more years!"

We high-fived, and I asked her what the final vote was.

"I just happen to have it here," she said, rummaging through a stack of papers she was carrying. It was 219-213 with one abstention (and two vacant seats).

Driving home, I was thrilled. 219!

The Senate passed the reconciliation bill as well. Then the process started all over on the actual budget bill itself. After a House-Senate conference committee ironed out differences in the House and Senate versions, the bill went back to each chamber. By August, it was crunch time.

On Monday night, the President presented a televised Oval Office address on the budget bill. He did well, picking up steam as he went, showing charts and using plain language. I stayed late and watched on TV in our office, monitoring Kansas Republican Senator Bob Dole's televised response immediately afterward and distributing a summary to whoever needed it.

Three days later, the House passed the conference committee's report on the budget bill 218-216, thanks to a vote by Pennsylvania Congresswoman Marjorie Margolies-Mezvinsky. Of all Congressional Democrats, she represented the most Republican-leaning district, so it was a tough vote for her politically. Afterward, House Republicans were chanting, "Bye-bye, Marjorie." (In fact, she did lose her re-election bid the following year.)

The next evening, Friday night, the Senate passed the budget bill. It took a one-vote "Clinton landslide," but we did it. Nebraska Democratic Senator Bob Kerrey, saying he couldn't bring down Clinton's presidency with his vote, cast in favor, giving us a 50-50 tie. As Senate President Pro Tempore, the Vice President (who earlier in the day jokingly had sent a scribbled note to Senate Majority Leader George Mitchell that said, "George, I'm wavering") then cast his vote, and the bill passed.

We had figured it would come down to the Vice President's tie-breaker. At the 7:30 A.M. communications staff meeting, I led off as usual with the top news stories, concluding, "And, warming up in the bullpen, from Carthage, Tennessee, wearing No. 2, Al Gore." Later that morning, the wire services moved stories quoting Press Secretary Dee Dee Myers saying that the Vice President was "in the bullpen."

A few hours before the Senate vote, the President and Vice President stopped by the budget "war room" adjoining our News Analysis office. The large room, which had probably at least two dozen aides working there virtually around the clock, was ringed with desks and computers side by side, with stacks of paper everywhere, and trays of bagels and muffins and pitchers of juice delivered each morning.

The atmosphere this evening was that of a big pep rally. Everybody cheered Deputy Treasury Secretary Roger Altman ("Rog-er! Rog-er!"), who headed the war room's effort to get the budget bill passed. The President talked a little about the budget's role in the Administration's "re-inventing government" reduction and reform plan. Then the Vice President told everybody, "It's amazing what you've done working eight hours a day," to much laughter.

The following Monday it was time to take a victory lap. So we loaded the staff vans for Andrews Air Force Base and boarded Air Force One for a day trip to Charleston, West Virginia, where we held an upbeat, campaign-like rally on a sunny, blazing hot day.

The President flew in the twelve-seater, and most of us boarded the forty-two-passenger plane for the fifty-minute flight. We landed at Yeager (as in test pilot Chuck) Airport and held briefly at the West Virginia National Guard Headquarters as the President greeted some local residents. Then it was on to the State Capitol grounds, where 11,000 people (in a city of 57,000) awaited the President. They went nuts, cheering and holding blue and gold signs. "Only in West Virginia could we get cheered for raising taxes," one White House aide said of the heavily Democratic state.

I headed across the Capitol grounds to the press office (where lunch for the press corps was pork barbecue, grilled chicken, baked beans and chocolate cheesecake) to dial in and check the wires while the President spoke to the crowd. An energetic young advance staffer led me through the crowd as we both whined about the heat.

"Hey, it could be worse," I said. "We could be wearing dark suits with ties pulled up to our necks," which, of course, we were. Earlier I'd observed randomly, "You know, I used to watch news footage of politicians campaigning outside in the summer heat, wearing suits and sweating miserably, and think to myself, 'What idiots. There's no way I'd do that.' And here I am."

Advance team members handled a wide variety of duties. Each team included a lead person, who oversaw others. (That person coordinated with the trip director on the traveling staff and the trip scheduler back in Washington.) There was someone in charge of each event site, someone in charge of the press pool, someone in charge of the motorcade and, when we stayed in a city overnight, someone in charge of the hotel. A media affairs staffer usually would be on hand to take care of local reporters. Each of those people often had others working for them.

Advance team members included White House aides, Democratic National Committee staffers, administration political appointees from various agencies, former campaign advance workers working in the private sector and local volunteers. Everyone arrived on site several days early and stayed until everything was wrapped up. Advance work was often a difficult, and usually a thankless, task.

After the event, the President shook some hands along the ropeline while we dashed through the Capitol to the waiting vans. Then it was on to the airport and back to Andrews Air Force Base. When the vans arrived at the White House, a steady rain was falling. David Dreyer (deputy communications director) asked the military driver to pull into a covered driveway, under part of the Old Executive Office building.

"And could you drive up the stairs and drop me off outside my office?" I joked.

After we got out of the van, Dreyer kiddingly chided me.

"What, you think I made you look like a weenie?" I asked.

"In front of those burly military men—yes," he said, and we both laughed.

But as was often the case, it seemed we couldn't win for losing. The President signed the budget bill into law two days later, then he swore in Ruth Bader Ginsburg as a Supreme Court justice. But all that was overshadowed by the Justice Department's release later that day of the report on White House Deputy Counsel Vince Foster's suicide.

The wires that afternoon carried the text of a torn-up note found in Foster's briefcase. "I was not meant for the job or the spotlight of public life in Washington," it said. "Here ruining people is considered sport." Amen to that, I thought.

In addition to the budget battle, that first summer the President also was faced with unexpected concerns. Record flooding in the Midwest affected several states. By mid-July, 40,000 homes and businesses had been damaged or destroyed, and 50,000 people had been left temporarily or permanently homeless. Farm land was flooded, crops were ruined, drinking water was contaminated and bridges were washed away.

So three days after returning from our trip to Japan and Korea, I was back in a suit and at the White House by 7 a.m. on a Saturday to grab my laptop computer and slide into a staff van for the trip to Andrews.

After landing in St. Louis an hour and fifty minutes later, we boarded buses and rode to Fox High School in nearby Arnold, Missouri, while the President got a view of the area's flooding from a helicopter. At the high school, I worked in a non-air-conditioned classroom with cinder block walls and watched the economic summit down the hall on TV. It was too hot to be wearing a suit; the President was in a golf shirt and had shed his blazer.

Afterward, I scrambled around, trying to find the helicopters. I was manifested to be on one but couldn't figure out where they were. How tough could it be? They weren't easy to hide, but it was a big high school. Finally I found and boarded Marine One with the President and several fellow Arkansans (in addition to the ubiquitous Secret Service agents, military aide and doctor) for the fifteen-minute flight back to the airport. The President sat near the front window and put on communications headphones. At the airport, the President boarded a twelve-seat plane, and most of us got on a larger plane built in 1958. It was a museum piece, but it was interesting to compare it to the new 747s normally used as Air Force One.

The temperature in Little Rock was well into the nineties, and the black asphalt tarmac was hot, especially in dark shoes and dark socks. We were driven to the Arkansas Excelsior Hotel downtown, and the President stayed with Chief of Staff Mack McLarty at McLarty's house. I went for a walk downtown, gazing at the vacant *Arkansas Gazette* building where I'd worked twice, most recently in the campaign.

The next morning I produced the clips for the few staff on the trip. The President went to Hot Springs that morning to see his mother. Later a few of us went to the airport to await the President's arrival and ended up sitting around for a couple hours. In fact, the whole short time in Little Rock was a bit of a waste. I was out of touch because my beeper was malfunctioning (probably because I had dropped it on con-

crete when we were in Hawaii earlier that week), there was no schedule and we could leave all of a sudden, whenever the President decided he wanted to go. But at least we were served ribs from Shug's, a
Little Rock restaurant, on the plane back to Andrews.

We returned to St. Louis for another flood-related event in mid-
August. We began a two-day bicoastal trip with aides from Health and
Human Services, Agriculture, Transportation and Federal Emergency
Management Agency with a flight to St. Louis.

Who went with us on trips depended on what issues our events
were intended to address. There always was some combination of a senior adviser, press secretary, National Security Council representative,
trip director, personal aide, staff photographer and non-political appointees like the military and medical staff, White House Communications Agency and of course the Secret Service. Seven of those aides
and two Secret Service agents made up the nine people who accompanied the President on Marine One. For most staffers, traveling was
done on a rotating basis with others in their office. And some offices—
political, public liaison, legislative affairs—only went when we held an
event affecting them. The same was true of Administration agencies.

A twenty-one-vehicle motorcade took us on a ten-minute drive to
the tacky Henry VIII hotel, where the President met with flood victims and signed a flood relief bill. (Flooding by that time covered an
area about twice the size of New Jersey. Seeing it from a helicopter,
the Vice President had said it appeared as if a sixth Great Lake had
been created. The President signed legislation providing federal aid of
$6.2 billion to nine states.) Afterward, I electronically transmitted
transcripts of the events from the press office (down the hall from the
President's events) while Dee Dee Myers sat nearby, talking on a daily
conference call to Washington. She and I missed the motorcade when
the President left early. But we caught a ride in a press van and arrived on time.

Another Administration priority that first summer was the Vice
President's National Performance Review. Commonly called Re-inventing Government (or "Re-Go"), it was a plan that called for reduc-
ing unnecessary bureaucracy, paperwork and personnel in the federal
government. The President devoted several days in September to
traveling with the Vice President in support of the new initiatives.

One late summer day, Air Force One met Air Force Two in Cleveland. During our one-hour, ten-minute flight on the 747, I was woolly-headed and stopped up with a runny nose at the same time. After landing at Cleveland's Hopkins International Airport, we stood around on the tarmac for what seemed forever, waiting for the President to emerge. It turned out he had received official announcement of a peace plan between Israel and the Palestine Liberation Organization and had phoned Israeli Prime Minister Yitzhak Rabin.

A little sick, I muddled through a sunny, pretty day at Church Square Shopping Center, a new-looking strip mall, where the President spoke to the Hough neighborhood group about Re-Go. I worked upstairs in the press office, overlooking the event from an unfurnished would-be store with concrete floors, bare metal rafters and no interior walls. I cranked out a couple of wire reports of breaking news and handed them to key aides.

After the President and Vice President shook hands along a lengthy, enthusiastic ropeline, I rode in the motorcade back to the airport with some of the Veep staff. Back at Andrews, we exited the rear stairs with the press pool as usual. Unlike a typical 747, the planes used as Air Force One have front and rear stairs included, meaning it isn't necessary for airport personnel to wheel a set of stairs up to the plane for passengers to exit. However, exterior stairs are used up front for the President because the plane's stairs are low to the ground. It makes a more dignified arrival—and better media pictures—if he uses a higher staircase.

The next day we headed out to the West Coast for a couple days. We flew five hours and ten minutes to Moffett Naval Air Station in Mountain View, California, north of San Jose.

We landed near Sunnyvale, in Silicon Valley, and visited ILC Technology, where the President and Vice President (having flown separately for security reasons, as always) toured the production line and met with employees who had successfully completed job retraining.

Meanwhile, much of the staff held in a small, crowded, modern conference room and worked the phones. It was easy to tell when we'd been in the air for a while, because whenever we got to a staff hold, everybody would scramble for the phones. Most aides didn't carry cellular phones. There were phones on the plane, but it could be hard to hear and be heard on them. And there were only a limited number of phone lines available, based on seniority.

Then we visited the picturesque Sunnyvale Community Center with pretty trees, a fountain and well-manicured lawns. It was a beautiful, sunny day, so we left open the door to the staff hold. Normally we couldn't do that because of security. The windows often were papered over or curtains were shut. For the National Security Council staff, it was even worse. On overseas trips, their office had the windows sealed shut—even when there was no air-conditioning—for security reasons.

I roamed outside during the event, bottle of orange juice in hand, as the President and Vice President spoke about Re-Go to a small crowd of retrained workers and municipal employees in a grassy area about 150 feet from the staff office. Afterward, I gave the latest wire stories to Bruce Lindsey (senior adviser), Dee Dee Myers, Nancy Soderberg (National Security Adviser) and Marla Romash (Vice President's communications director) as some of the Veep's staff sat near the fountain, basking in the sunshine.

On the way to the airport, the President saw the enormous crowd lining the curbs in an upscale residential area and got out of the limousine. He shook lots of hands and thrilled the masses before getting back in. Unsurprisingly, he would drive the Secret Service nuts when he did that. I got the impression he was even more interested in mingling with crowds than most previous Presidents. But the Secret Service seemed to expect it.

On the three-hour, forty-five-minute flight to Houston (including a standard mid-air interchange with Air Force Two), I sat in the guest area chatting with Jeremy Gaines (press assistant) and Gwen Ifill of *The New York Times*, who was waiting to interview the President in his office. Still bothered by the lingering effects of my cold, I visited the President's doctor, Major Robert Ramsey, in the medical unit in the front of the plane. He gave me some Sudafed, which helped.

A doctor and a nurse, both military, were near the President at all times. The medical compartment aboard Air Force One, next to the President's office in the plane's nose, included virtually every supply imaginable. Closets and cupboards opened to reveal medical equipment, including a fold-down operating table. All but the most major of medical emergencies could be handled aboard the plane.

The next morning was pretty horrendous for me. Nobody was in my Old Executive Office Building office early on Saturday to fax news clips to me, so I had to do it all electronically. Worse, the copy machine jammed every time I touched it and the hotel's front desk staff wouldn't copy the clips for me or let me use their copier.

As I scrambled about the staff office, the President and Vice President stopped by the adjoining room after their jog, sweaty and still in their shorts and T-shirts, sipping juice. They chatted with a few staff and local volunteers. They later delivered a joint live radio address from Room 810 there at the Wyndham Warwick Hotel, and then we boarded a staff bus, where dozens of people on the sidewalk with pro-North American Free Trade Agreement signs awaited us on a hot and humid Houston morning.

We were driven to the Texas Surplus Property Agency, a warehouse, for another Re-Go event. It was a dirty, ugly place without air-conditioning, and the temperature outside hovered around ninety degrees. We stood in the back as the President, Vice President and elected Texas officials discussed Re-Go, and the event seemed to last forever. It wasn't until it was almost over that I found out we had an air-conditioned office for the staff hold. Paul Richard (deputy staff secretary) said later he almost passed out during the event.

Since I was manifested to fly aboard the press plane back to Washington, after the event I boarded the press bus to go to the filing center, which turned out to be the visitors' center of an Anheuser-Busch plant. I couldn't get my computer to connect. On top of being bumped from Air Force One anyway, that really made me mad. Arthur Jones (deputy press secretary) looked on nearby, bemused by my intense frustration. (The press plane, rented by the White House Travel Office and paid for by the news organizations on board, would leave from Andrews before Air Force One and get back later, after the reporters filed their stories.)

In addition to domestic issues, there were matters of foreign policy which demanded the President's attention. One was his annual address to the United Nations General Assembly. During the fifty-minute flight to New York, I sat in the conference room with Bob McNeely (staff photographer) and watched the United States golfers catch up in the Ryder Cup.

McNeely was in charge of the White House Photo Office. He and his staff produced big, beautiful photos of the President's travels, which were displayed throughout the West Wing and updated regularly. McNeely, who also took photos during the campaign, drove a huge, ugly, old car. It was an early 1970s pea-green Oldsmobile 98 or something like that. More than once the Secret Service bomb-detecting dogs sniffed it and, apparently smelling unusual chemicals, sensed a bomb. West Executive Drive, and in fact the facing entrances from the White House and Old Executive Office Building, were shut down, and the bomb squad in protective gear appeared. Barb Kinney (staff photographer) said later of McNeely: "He doesn't understand the difference between a classic car and one that's just plain old."

The motorcade took us from JFK International Airport to Queens, where the President led a discussion about health care with citizens who had written to him, at the crowded Future Diner. Some of the staff watched from the back of the diner, standing on chairs to get a view. Then it was on to our overnight site, the Waldorf-Astoria. (I couldn't help but think about the last time we'd been in New York, when I was working on the campaign staff at the Democratic National Convention and stayed at the YMCA. How things changed in just over a year.)

On the way, our motorcade passed more policemen than I'd ever seen in my life. There was a wall of blue lining the streets everywhere we went, cops standing shoulder to shoulder where there were no other people. We were told later that New York puts 35,000 officers on the streets for every Presidential visit. The cops loved it because they got overtime pay for just standing around. The city loved it because it could bill the State Department due to the existence of the United Nations in New York. One person who didn't love it, I was told, was the President. But apparently there wasn't much we could do about it.

The President spent the afternoon in his Waldorf-Astoria suite preparing his next day's address to the United Nations General Assembly. After he attended a Latin American reception downstairs, the motorcade departed about 7 P.M. for a five-story Upper East Side brownstone owned by Edward Bronfman Jr., the chief executive officer of Seagram's, for a Mayor David Dinkins fund-raiser. Looking around inside the elegant Manhattan home, I couldn't help but think of Tom Wolfe's *The Bonfire of the Vanities.*

The President and Dinkins conducted a meet-and-greet with sup-porters while I climbed the spiral staircase to Bronfman's third-floor study, which was graciously set aside as a staff hold. It had dark panel-ing, bookcases, stereo, bar (Seagram's bottles, of course) and a TV set. I hung out with Bob McNeely, sipping soft drinks and munching sand-wiches, chips and cookies while watching that afternoon's pro football highlights as I dialed in and monitored news moving on the wire ser-vices.

Then it was on to the Sheraton Hotel and Towers for a $1,000-a-plate fund-raiser with the President, Mayor Dinkins, New York Gover-nor Mario Cuomo and New York Senator Daniel Patrick Moynihan. Out in the lobby beforehand, during a reception attended by, among others, Jesse Jackson, I dialed in, and over my shoulder Dee Dee Myers read stories about accusations that Commerce Secretary Ron Brown had dealt improperly with Vietnamese lobbyists. In the large main room, a suntanned blond in a pink dress was sashaying about. David Seldin (press assistant) said she'd told the White House press pool that she was "Mrs. Florida" and was "looking for exposure."

After producing and distributing the news clips the next morning, I had a $7.25 breakfast at the Bunny Deli, the same place I ate virtu-ally every meal during the 1992 convention.

At about 9:30 A.M., the motorcade took us to the United Nations, where a protocol staffer whom someone in the press pool later de-scribed as the most officious jerk they'd ever run into told them, "This is not your country. This is our country."

Inside, the staff didn't fare much better. United Nations officials wouldn't let us go upstairs. Chief of Staff Mack McLarty, at the front of the line, was too classy to do anything but just shake his head and laugh, but he wasn't amused. When that problem was settled, we headed upstairs to the staff hold. We were herded through a huge crowd, but then the UN staff decided to close the doors. Unfortu-nately, Bruce Lindsey and I were still outside. Steve Bahar, lead ad-vance on the trip (and one of our best), said forcefully, "We need these two," and we got in. Once inside, it became obvious that the room was crowded because a bunch of UN secretarial types were standing there with their pocket cameras.

Our holding area was a reception area just outside the door to the

General Assembly, which was a Disney World Tomorrowland-looking place. Dee Dee Myers asked me to fax the speech to the White House press office, and I found the UN equipment was unbelievably antiquated. The place had an early 1960s/futurama feel to it, as if it were left over from the 1964 World's Fair in New York. But it was very cool to be there and to think about the UN's history and its rather utopian goals.

After his address to the General Assembly, the President went to meet the staff at the U.S. Mission, ate lunch with two dozen fellow heads of state and attended several bilateral meetings with fellow world leaders. That night he attended a reception at the Waldorf-Astoria's Starlight Roof Lounge, where he had to shake hands in a huge receiving line. But at his request, the list of 600 or so heads of delegation was trimmed way back, and he got out of there early.

I was sitting with our military and medical aides in a holding room down the hall. At one point Marine Major Leo Mercado (military aide) stepped out to the men's room and asked Army Captain Maureen Donahue (nurse) to watch the "football."

The football is a bulky black briefcase that includes nuclear launch codes for the President. A military aide is always near the President in case of emergency. In a way the football is a Cold War anachronism, but after all, there are still hundreds of thousands of nuclear warheads in the United States and nations of the former Soviet Union. Since the football was around all the time, we didn't think about it much. But when Mercado stepped out, I looked at that briefcase and found myself pondering its significance. Then an advance staffer came in and gave us a heads-up to get ready to move, and we were soon on our way.

Downstairs, I battled my way through the police barricades on the street and ducked into the waiting staff van. The motorcade raced away, in our haste leaving behind David Gergen (counselor) and Alexis Herman (intergovernmental affairs), who would have to get back to Washington on their own. We drove to the Wall Street landing zone, a nearby heliport on the East River, and got a beautiful night view of the lights of Manhattan. I'd forgotten how much fun helicopter rides were...the hot blast of exhaust, the thick smell of fuel, the soft foam earplugs, the minor vibrations, watching the unsure first-timers.

On the flight home aboard Air Force One, the President appeared relaxed but tired. He ambled back to the staff area without his jacket, tie loosened, chomping on an unlit cigar. Talk turned to New York's ongoing mayoral campaign, and a political aide cited a recent poll. "Aw, Harold [Ickes] told me those numbers and I told him he was as full of it as a Christmas goose," the President said.

Sometimes foreign policy-related trips included visits to military sites. It always was interesting to visit aircraft carriers. My first time to do so was when we traveled to the Bay Area in California.

The motorcade that morning drove us from the Parck Oakland Hotel fifteen minutes to the Oakland Naval Supply Center, where the President met with the East Bay Conversion and Reinvestment Commission, a group of local and military officials. He then rode a boat to Alameda Naval Air Station, where he spoke to base military and civilian personnel on a dock at the base on the same topic—defense conversion. It was a gray, cool day, almost cold with the wind whipping in from the bay. Nancy Soderberg (National Security Council) wore a baggy gray Middlebury College sweatshirt over her dress. What's that Mark Twain line, I thought—the coldest winter I ever spent was a summer in San Francisco?

After the speech, we boarded the USS *Carl Vinson* for a lunch of cold-cut sandwiches and baked beans in a large hangar bay. The President ate with the captain and other senior officers in a private mess area nearby. The Navy announced the visiting dignitaries with, literally, bells and whistles. "United States Senate, arriving," said the voice over the speakers, accompanying by clanging bells and a boatswain's whistle. The crew was very courteous and polite. I went downstairs to use the head (as we say in the Navy) and later was disappointed to find out I'd missed a staff tour of the flight deck.

Then we loaded the motorcade, squeezing all our guests in with us for a five-minute ride. California Democratic Senator Dianne Feinstein was in a long black leather coat like Dee Dee Myers', which I mentioned later to Myers. "That's funny," she said. "She used to make fun of mine when I worked for her" (during Feinstein's 1990 gubernatorial campaign).

Then it was back aboard the plane for a two-hour, ten-minute flight back to Denver. On the plane, I was told of a breaking story involving allegations about Commerce Secretary Ron Brown, who was traveling with us, and his dealings with Vietnamese businessmen. I phoned my office from the plane and had some wire stories faxed to the plane, instructing one of my volunteers through the process. As I stood on the tarmac, a military staffer found me ("Mr. Chitester?") and delivered a large envelope. Then I got the information to Brown's aide on site.

The President signed a wilderness preservation bill on the tarmac. On the plane, Paul Richard (deputy staff secretary) had the bill itself, and the official pens the President would use to sign it. I'd never seen an actual bill before. It was about legal-size in a hard, dark blue cover that folded open, kind of like a diploma.

In the staff hold, I was helping myself to a snack at the nearby food table when I noticed Health and Human Services Secretary Donna Shalala standing next to me. I knew she had a dog named after the mascot of the University of Wisconsin, where she had been chancellor before joining the Cabinet.

"Secretary Shalala, how's Bucky?" I asked.

"Oh, he's great," she said. "He won a contest for prettiest eyes."

Later, a fellow staffer asked me, "You asked a Cabinet secretary about her *dog?*"

"You obviously don't own a dog," I said, thinking of Camelot, my then-two-year-old male collie-labrador retriever mixed breed.

After the bill signing, the motorcade took us across the airport to a fund-raiser for Colorado Governor Roy Romer in the United Airlines hangar. Apparently Romer had requested the President's presence but was told the event would have to take place at the airport, and that even an airport hotel was too far or too much trouble. The hangar was decorated festively with red, white and blue balloons, streamers and banners, but it was still an airplane hangar. It also was hot. There was a table provided for White House staff near the stage, where Up With People performed. A bunch of us drank Colorado wine and enjoyed the food, relaxing at the end of another trip.

Afterward, the President and a few aides drove to Aspen for a weekend vacation, where President Clinton was scheduled to play golf with former President Ford. The rest of us boarded the President's 747 (without him aboard, it was no longer Air Force One) for the flight home. There were only about a dozen of us aboard. The last time the 747 took off full of Clinton Administration staff—but without the President—had been after the St. Louis flood event the previous month. Around the White House everybody referred to it as the *Home Alone* flight on which the staff reportedly drank all the alcohol aboard the aircraft and generally had a wild time.

Howie, the head steward, told a few of us sitting on the hallway couch that flight time would be about three hours. "But we could speed it up if Ms. Brophy give us the say-so," he said, gesturing to Susan Brophy (legislative affairs). Brophy gave her assent, and Howie headed upstairs to confer with the flight crew. When he came back down, he said the crew's response was, "Let the big dog eat." Without the President aboard, we had no runway priority for takeoff, but there was virtually no delay.

Howie later told us stories about his career and about the aircraft. "See these ashtrays?" he said, pointing to a beautiful brass set nearby. He said they didn't have the Presidential seal engraved on them because if they did, they would've disappeared a long time ago.

There were other items available to Air Force One visitors, however. An envelope including a photo, fact sheet, cocktail napkin and other trinkets was made available to guests. Among the favorite items were small boxes of M&M's with the Presidential seal. Sometimes the menus, namecards and notepads disappeared as well. The most prized Air Force One souvenir, however, was a plastic-wrapped deck of playing cards with the aircraft's logo. (I'm sure I wasn't the only White House staffer to give away such trinkets as Christmas gifts.)

Howie said when President Clinton boarded Air Force One for the first time and was shown his plush office—with wooden desk, high-backed soft chair, couch and Seal of the President—he was amazed. "This is better than the Oval Office," the President supposedly said. Howie also told us Nancy Reagan was instrumental in selecting the predominantly blue color scheme for the plane's interior.

Our trip a year later to the USS *Eisenhower,* docked at Norfolk, Virginia, was more serious. The *Eisenhower* recently had returned from carrying U.S. occupation forces to Haiti, where they would oversee a peaceful return to democracy with the return of elected President Jean Bertrand-Aristide. We headed out to Andrews on a sunny morning in early fall. I boarded Air Force One for the forty-five-minute flight south, gobbling a bagel, grapes and yogurt for breakfast on the plane.

Upon arrival, we were driven to the nearby U.S. Atlantic Command Headquarters' Joint Operations Command Center so the President could attend a Haiti briefing/video conference. A few of us sat outside a tiny conference room, where the President talked with commanders on the ground in Haiti via satellite.

While he was inside, we sat in high-backed leather chairs at a counter, overlooking a large one-story room below. It included clocks displaying time zones around the world, labeled Honolulu, Zulu and Port-au-Prince. The latter was in a different typeface and probably used to say Mogadishu or Riyadh. There were huge satellite photos of what appeared to be Port-au-Prince, reminding me of photos from the Cuban missile crisis I'd seen in history books. Military intelligence staff sat in cubicles below us. I went elsewhere to find our phones and dialed in to check the wires.

Then it was back into the motorcade for a short ride to Norfolk Naval Base. We boarded the USS *Eisenhower*, which had a crew of 5,500 sailors, 85 aircraft and a 350- by 1,000-yard flight deck. We stopped in a tiny holding room and then walked into a hangar bay for the President's speech. During the introductions, I found Dee Dee Myers and Jonathan Spalter (National Security Council press office).

"It's silly to ask this of somebody who just got out of a Haiti briefing with the President and the U.S. Atlantic Command," I said, "but did y'all know there was a shooting down there this morning?" They didn't, but it didn't involve the military (a warehouse owner trying to prevent looting fired on a crowd, killing one and injuring four), so there was no reason they would've heard. After the President spoke, he shook hands with the sailors, who had returned from leave to meet him, and we returned to the tarmac.

The President spoke to, and shook hands with, base personnel families back at Norfolk Naval Air Station and then conducted a few local interviews inside a building near the plane. We were running late, and the President had to cancel his weekly lunch with the Vice President. I dialed in aboard the plane and ate lunch (turkey sandwich, chips, Coke). We didn't bring many White House staff with us— mainly NSC and Defense personnel—and we got back to the White House about 3:30 P.M.

On other trips the President's foreign policy interests were more economic-oriented than military-focused. Our first year, we traveled to Seattle for the annual Asian Pacific Economic Cooperation summit. For five hours and twenty minutes, sixteen of us flew aboard a 737 backup plane with tail number 27000, which had served as Air Force One until 1990. It was used in 1981 to fly former Presidents Nixon, Ford and Carter to assassinated Egyptian President Anwar Sadat's funeral. It's now one of four used by the Vice President. It always was interesting to fly other aircraft in the fleet. The plane was very nice, but just so small compared to the 747s we usually flew aboard.

We landed mid-afternoon at Seattle's Boeing Field. Advance staffers met us on the tarmac and led us inside a hangar, where a crowd of at least several hundred sat in bleachers while a high school band blared. It looked and sounded like pre-game warmups for a high school basketball game on a Friday night back in the Midwest. Then the band stopped playing, and an enormous door (actually the hangar wall) lifted behind the podium. As it went up, the sparse guitar intro to U-2's "Where the Streets Have No Name" played over the public address system, and Air Force One slowly rolled to a stop on the tarmac. The crowd cheered and literally screamed.

After the President's remarks, we headed to the Westin Hotel. I walked to the press office a few blocks away and returned with the President's speech on diskette. Reporters traveling with us were working on a story about the President saying in a *Rolling Stone* interview just released that he had "not gotten one bit of credit from the knee-jerk liberal press."

The next day I awoke at 5:30 A.M. for another news clips fiasco. I literally blew a fuse, shutting down power in a small part of the hotel by running two copiers at once. I eventually delivered most of the news clips during a staff meeting no one previously had told me about.

That morning we went to the Four Seasons Hotel, where the President gave a speech with colorful "Star Trek"-looking bowls on pillars as backdrops in the Spanish Ballroom. Then it was on to the Rainier Club on a cool, sunny day for the President's afternoon-long bilateral meetings with Japanese and Chinese heads of state as protesters outside chanted "China out of Tibet." In the second-floor staff hold not far from the President's bilateral, we were fed a large lunch, including delicious blackberry pie.

Our carpeted office with windows included the usual assortment of our white plastic phones, tables and chairs, with the added bonus of a fax. The White House Communications Agency dropped phone lines in advance of us wherever we went. They weren't secure lines, but they did allow us five-digit dialing back to the White House complex.

Bruce Lindsey was on the phone, working toward a resolution of the strike between American Airlines and the flight attendants' union. I downloaded hopefully helpful wire stories and printed them for him. (That day 10,000 pilots were to vote on whether to join the strike, and Transportation Secretary Federico Peña was quoted in wire stories as being "very concerned.")

Late in the afternoon, after dark, the motorcade pulled up to the Seattle Art Museum. Enormous lights illuminated the front, and local TV crews with satellite dishes and trucks were parked out front. The President entered the front door, and we were ushered around the back, past the Dumpsters and to the loading dock. (White House aides get used to less-than-scenic entrances.) We went upstairs and saw the local movers and shakers in a classy setting with tables of hors d'oeuvres (seafood, roast beef), bars (with bartenders in uniforms) and a string quartet from the Seattle symphony, with children's artwork displayed on the walls.

Back at the staff office that night at the Westin, I was monitoring the wires when a bulletin popped up on my laptop screen, indicating that the second Senate filibuster of the day trying to sink the Brady Bill had failed. The Senate had remained in session to hammer out the bill, which would require a five-day waiting period to purchase a handgun. So I paged Mark Gearan (communications director), David Gergen (counselor) and Dee Dee Myers, who were at an official dinner with the President.

With everybody leaving at various times to get out to Blake Island for the next morning's leaders' meeting, getting Saturday's clips produced and distributed was a little easier. There was limited room on the island, so few aides were manifested to go. The informally dressed leaders met in a cabin, and even the number of interpreters was limited. So I called a college friend who lived in Seattle, and she and her husband picked me up at the hotel. We went out to lunch and took a driving tour of the city and area. It was fun—and unusual—to actually see something of a city we visited besides airport tarmacs and hotel rooms.

But there would be plenty of airports and hotels to come. And many of those we saw were on trips in which the President promoted his far-reaching health care reform plan.

7►Health Care That's Always There

DURING MY TWO YEARS AT THE WHITE HOUSE, much of the President's traveling time was spent in support of his ill-fated health care reform plan. We probably traveled more to promote the health care plan than we did for all other issues combined, except for political events.

One typical health care trip was a two-day jaunt to Topeka, Kansas City and Minneapolis in early spring. Aboard Air Force One en route to Topeka, we were served tuna salad sandwiches for lunch. Later, Al Maldin (White House Military Office) said it was the first new, healthy menu for the plane that already was being used in the White House Mess, also run by the Military Office. Ugh, I thought…"healthy."

At the Topeka airport, the President gave a health care speech that was well received in Republican Senator Bob Dole's home state. Our holding room in the hangar was a small break room with an old table, some chairs and a beat-up soft drink machine. An Army general walked into the room, and before we could get out, the President strolled in to meet him, blocking the door. So Bob Boorstin (communications), Paul Begala (political consultant) and I tried to look inconspicuous standing a few feet away as the general, prodded by Kansas Congressman Jim Slattery, told the President his compelling life story (born poor in Puerto Rico, educated and empowered by the Army, retiring to care for an ailing daughter).

As we left the hangar, I paused to look for the Staff 1 van in the motorcade parked on the nearby tarmac. "Chit!" Josh King (communications/advance) yelled at me. I looked over, and a whole phalanx of cameras was aimed at me. I suddenly realized the press pool was awaiting the President's departure so they could get some video of him. Even though the President was far behind me, I hustled out of the shot.

Next it was on to the Topeka Foundry and Ironworks Company. Our holding room was a drafting room—small, windowless, old and depressing. Downstairs, the President led a small business/health care roundtable discussion surrounded by large, ancient machinery in the structural fabrication shop. It was almost the most boring event we'd done, second only to a seemingly unending economic roundtable the President had attended in Los Angeles a few months previously. He loved that stuff, though. He was the ultimate policy wonk.

After at least an hour and a half, we headed back out into the afternoon sunlight and boarded the motorcade, which took us back to the Kansas Air National Guard base at the Topeka Airport. There, the President attended a reception of supporters. Then helicopters carried us thirty minutes to Kansas City Downtown Municipal Airport. I was aboard Nighthawk 3, which, as usual, landed first. We watched Nighthawk 2 and then Marine One land nearby. The President briefly addressed the awaiting crowd on a sunny, chilly, windy afternoon before we loaded up the limos, cars and vans for KCTV studios and a town hall meeting.

Upstairs in the holding area, which was a conference room with a TV set, we sampled various types of Kansas City barbecue, tasting both Bates and Rick's. ("Barbecue Wars," we called the taste test.) The town hall meeting itself seemed to go well, even if it didn't make much news outside Kansas City. The President spent a lot of time shaking hands and chatting with people afterward and then headed to the VIP viewing room downstairs for a drop-by.

Trailed by a herd of Secret Service agents, advance staff, White House staff and other hangers-on, he looked around and said, "Where are we going, team?" Lead advance person Kara McGuire said, "This way, sir," and we all followed. After the VIP drop-by, it was back to the airport for a one-hour, five-minute flight to Minneapolis.

Minneapolis was cold and windy when we landed about 1 A.M. Upon arrival on his floor at the Marquette Hotel downtown, the President paused at a hallway sign made by schoolchildren saying, "You're our hero" with their hand prints. He signed it: "Thanks. Bill Clinton." Wendy Smith (trip director) said, "You should've put your hand print there."

In the staff office, I dialed in and found out that Japanese Prime Minister Hosokawa had resigned. I paged Dee Dee Myers (press secretary) and Kristie Kenney (National Security Council) with the news.

Jeff Eller (media affairs) stopped by the staff office as I set up for the next morning. "I think everybody's going to sleep in," he said, encouraging me not to worry about being too early with the morning news clips.

It was painful to get up the next morning, but I got rolling once I did, building some momentum as the adrenaline began to flow from the daily fear of being late with the clips. I was done delivering to staffer's doors by 8:30 A.M., as everyone else was just getting up. The President skipped his usual jog on a rainy, thirty-four-degree morning. Later that morning, the President delivered a health care address downstairs in the Crystal Courtyard, a huge open area of shops in the enormous IDS Tower building, with a cheering crowd of 3,500 and yellow-and-blue pro-health care reform signs all over.

Upstairs in the hotel, he later addressed the traveling press pool with reaction to Hosokawa's resignation before we headed to the motorcade for a short drive to the *Minneapolis Star-Tribune*, where he met with the editorial board. The building had a classy, new, corporate feel. Walking through the reception area, the President stopped to greet a couple of secretaries. He noticed a desk that had an apple, an American flag and photos of two young children.

"That's the most American display I've ever seen," he said.

"Those are my kids," a woman said proudly. The President chatted with her and posed for photos.

The staff holding room upstairs was a conference room a couple of doors from the President's meeting. A Minnesota Twins game was on the TV, but we changed the channel to CNN. I sat at a round table, dialed in to the wires with my laptop and found that rumors of Kurt Cobain's death were true. Soon afterward, CNN showed the Seattle house of the late Nirvana lead singer.

"*Nice* house," Wendy Smith said.

Quipped Dr. Connie Mariano: "It's for sale."

Later, I dove into the food made available for us, loading a plate with glazed teriyaki chicken on a stick, shrimp wrapped in bacon, peanut butter-covered brownies and other artery-clogging food. "Geez, Ken, why not just have a cigarette?" Dr. Mariano said. Then, looking at the brownie, she said, "Oh my gosh. That's not dessert— that's oral sex."

Later I induced her to have a bite and she oohed and ahhed.

"What are you *doing?*" someone asked.

"Oh," Dr. Mariano answered casually, "Ken and I are having oral sex."

Dr. Mariano was one of the funniest people on the White House staff. She would say things other people could never get away with. From San Diego, she was a Navy Major but rarely was in uniform. Unlike previous Presidents, President Clinton didn't have a private physician. Dr. Mariano became his primary physician and was almost always at his side. She once told me that she had to be ready to tend to him 24 hours a day, 365 days a year. She was always on call and couldn't ever, for example, drink.

We went back to the hotel for an hour of down time (the President jogged; I laid down and watched "The Rockford Files") before heading to the KSTP-TV studios for a town hall meeting on health care. Afterward, we stood around backstage and waited for what seemed like an eternity, after a long week of travel, and got home about 3 A.M. On the flight home, I figured out that we'd been on the road fourteen of the previous fifteen days, visiting a total of eight states and traveling 5,077 miles.

Of course, most trips included more than just health care. Such was the case on a three-day excursion to California in early fall. Those of us going on the trip stood on West Executive Drive on a perfect fall day shortly after noon on a Sunday. Why is it, Bob Boorstin wondered aloud, that days we leave Washington invariably are ones with the best weather? It was a sunny afternoon with temperatures in the sixties as we loaded up the vans for the trip to Andrews Air Force Base. The Ellipse was full of people in shorts and sweatshirts playing flag football.

After a five-hour, ten-minute flight, we arrived late afternoon West Coast time at McClellan Air Force Base, near Sacramento. Just before the President was to go on stage, he decided he wanted one of those plastic health care cards that looked like credit cards that he'd held up in a recent speech to Congress announcing his reform plan. I thought of David Dreyer (deputy communications director), who wasn't there. Dreyer kept one in the plastic pouch that held his SecurID card used to dial in to the White House computer system. Like me, he kept that card on the same chain around his neck that held his White House photo ID card. We checked around, but nobody had one. Next time, I thought. Next time I'll have one and I can be a hero: "Oh, *here* you go, Mr. President."

After the rally in a hangar, we were running late. As we piled into the motorcade, an advance staffer ran over yelling for Jeff Eller. The staffer hopped out of the front seat of Staff 1 and raced to the limousine, where he briefed the President en route to the TV studio for a town hall meeting to be televised across the state.

Once there, we were still running late. Our holding room was an upstairs conference room at KCRA-TV, and the President's hold was the adjoining station manager's office, complete with the mounted head of a horned caribou or elk or something. We stood around the receptionist's area sipping bottled water and soft drinks and munching sandwiches as Wendy Smith appeared to be getting nervous.

"Two minutes," she called to the President. "You guys, we need to make some room here."

We backed up, clearing a path for him. He emerged, and with Smith leading him and Secret Service agents surrounding him, they headed through the door, down the stairs and toward the studio. On the TV sets in the conference room, the live town hall meeting came on the air. The hosts, looking perhaps a little nervous at the President's absence, opened the show. They then introduced the President, who thankfully appeared right on cue. Smith came back upstairs. "That was as close as Detroit," she said in reference to another town hall meeting several months ago.

The President stuck around after the ninety-minute show went off the air, shaking hands with members of the audience. Upstairs, we watched CNN's live coverage of a development in the attempted coup in Russia. As I dialed in and scrolled the wires for the latest stories,

CNN showed tanks blasting away in the streets of Moscow. I printed some wire stories and handed them to Bruce Lindsey and Will Itoh (National Security Council), who were seated at the conference table. "I think this is what we're watching," Itoh said, scanning the stories I'd handed him.

Then it was out to the motorcade and aboard the helicopters for the fifty-minute flight to San Francisco. There initially had been some question about the weather, but we got clearance and took off. Nighthawk 3 wasn't the type of helo we usually flew. (Army helicopters are called "choppers"; Navy and Marine helicopters, which we used, are called "helos," pronounced HE-lows.) This one was kind of greasy inside. About halfway through, some type of oil-gas-water mixture leaked on health care coordinator Ira Magaziner's head. He ended up sitting on his briefcase on the floor. We landed at the Presidio, with a cloudy but pretty night view of the nearby Golden Gate Bridge.

The next morning we boarded the motorcade and drove through a colorful, seedy area of town to the Hilton Hotel, site of the AFL-CIO labor convention. I sat in the staff area off to the side during the President's speech in an enormous ballroom. I liked attending labor events. They were real, down-to-earth folks, not like people in Washington, and they were an enthusiastic crowd.

We were at the Hilton much of the day as the President met privately with labor leaders and made an announcement on Housing and Urban Development grants after the speech. I went to the press office, which was part of a small ballroom with temporary walls, down the hall from the President, picking up transcripts on diskette to e-mail. Lunch in the staff hold was good—with real dishes and silverware.

After handing Bruce Lindsey the latest wires in the hallway, I headed downstairs to the motorcade, parked side-by-side on another blocked-off street. It was a cool, windy, typical San Francisco day. The blues played on the van's radio as I settled into a seat in Staff 2 and awaited the President's departure about 2:30 P.M.

It was late afternoon when we reached Los Angeles after a one-hour, ten-minute flight. (Nothing ties up traffic like an afternoon rush-hour presidential motorcade in LA.) We stayed at the Beverly Hilton, owned by Merv Griffin. Upon arrival, the President met Rodney Dangerfield, who lived on the floor where the President stayed that night.

The next morning, as usual, we had rolls and juice in the staff room, one floor below the President's room. A little after 8 A.M., the motorcade took us to Dr. Paul Carlson Memorial Park in nearby Culver City, where the President talked to senior citizens about health care. It was a typical southern California morning—sunny, dry and comfortable. Some of us ate a second breakfast in a white tent with the sides rolled down, and then I strolled to the press tent across the park to collect and transmit transcripts on diskette.

But we left early, by mid-morning, so the President could get back for a national security briefing. (On Sunday in Somalia, fourteen U.S. Army Rangers had been killed, seventy-five had been wounded and one still was being held prisoner. TV coverage since had shown Somalis dragging a U.S. soldier's corpse through the streets of Mogadishu.) By leaving about 10 A.M. PDT, we could get back by 6 P.M. EDT—a five-hour flight plus a three-hour time change.

On the flight, Andrew Friendly (personal aide) was watching *Scent of a Woman,* starring Al Pacino, in the conference room, and I eased into one of the soft tan leather adjustable chairs at the table to check it out. We were maybe halfway through it when an Air Force One crew member handed me some faxed wire stories I'd called back to my office to request. I got up to make copies, leaving Pacino—and Friendly—to mutter "hoo-ah!" without me. When I got back, Washington Democratic Congressman Tom Foley was in my seat, conducting a meeting with other members of Congress flying with us. I wanted to say, "Hey, bud—I don't care if you *are* Speaker of the House. The movie's not over. Now come on, get outta my seat." But of course I didn't.

We also used televised town hall meetings to spread the word on health care reform. Initiated during the campaign, we again used the technique to kick off the President's campaign on health care reform one night in Florida.

The previous evening the President had addressed a joint session of Congress on his plan. About a half dozen aides watched on the television in our office, next door to the health care war room. Afterward, I banged away on my computer, typing in verbatim notes on ABC's wrap-up and then the Republican response, to help the health care war room's efforts.

In the next morning's communications meeting, David Dreyer

told us the story of how the President's TelePrompTer had displayed the wrong speech. The President was ready to go on health care, but appearing was the text of his economic speech he'd delivered to Congress several months previously. He turned to the Vice President behind him and said, "They've got the wrong speech" during the introductory applause, to which the Veep replied, "You're kidding."

Dreyer told us of how he got the correct diskette and then had the White House Communications Agency scroll through the speech so the display matched the cards the President had on the podium. It could have been a real disaster, but the President flawlessly performed in the clutch. Later that day the President told the press that when he saw the economic speech on the TelePrompTer, "I thought to myself, 'That was a good speech, but I don't want to give it twice.'"

After a South Lawn health care rally that afternoon, we left for a two-hour flight to Florida. At the Tampa Bay Performance Arts Center, ABC's "Nightline" was scheduled to televise the President's town hall meeting. I found a spot in the press office backstage to work and ran printouts down the hall to the on-site "war room," which was connected via phone and fax to the Old Executive Office Building's health care war room. David Gergen (counselor), Bruce Lindsey, Dee Dee Myers and Jeff Eller were all there, so I had plenty of staff to get material to.

During one commercial break, the President came backstage after answering a complicated question about some intricacy in the Clinton health plan and asked, "Christine, did I answer that right?" And Christine Heenan, a typical behind-the-scenes young White House aide well-versed in the substance of a specific issue but completely unknown outside the staff, assured the President that he had, running through the topic for him in knowing detail.

After the town hall meeting, I saw Ted Koppel backstage. (Boy, was he short. I was so surprised by his lack of height—especially as he stood next to President Clinton—that I didn't even notice his hair.) The President then ducked into a reception of local supporters down the hall. Before he entered, whoever was in charge addressed the gathered elite: "Now, when he comes in, don't everyone rush toward him. If you do, we'll take him right back out and you won't get to meet him." It was as if second-graders at a birthday party were being told the clown or pony would be taken away if they didn't behave.

I snoozed during the forty-minute motorcade around Tampa Bay to St. Petersburg. I awoke to see the huge, pink, art deco, castle-like Don Ce Sar Beach Hotel and stumbled upstairs to bed about 2:30 A.M.

The next day's first event was a five-minute walk away, down Gulf Boulevard, at the Pinellas Marine Institute. The staff hold was a room above and behind the outdoor podium, and the President spoke to the crowd. As usual, Bruce Lindsey and I were the only ones there. He worked with a phone to his ear, and I used another phone line for my laptop modem, with the windows open on a hot day. After the President worked a street ropeline, the twenty-five-minute motorcade to St. Petersburg International Airport got us aboard Air Force One by noon.

Another health care trip took us to Charlotte, North Carolina. After breakfast in the Hilton at University Place restaurant, Jason Solomon (health care), Christine Heenan, Paul Begala and I boarded a van for a ride on a warm, sunny early spring day as North Carolina awoke on a weekday morning. We headed to rural Troy, about a half hour away in Montgomery County, passing green fields and trees, rolling hills and blooming dogwoods.

We arrived at the landing zone at Troy Elementary School, where I handed aides the morning clips as they stepped off the helicopters. Then it was on to nearby Montgomery County Hospital for a Presidential tour. We returned to the elementary school, where he spoke to area residents in the nearby cafeteria and then conducted satellite interviews with TV stations in Kansas City, Topeka, Omaha and Tulsa.

The President angrily confronted his aides as he entered the school because there wasn't any scheduled opportunity for him to spend time with the townspeople of a tiny area no President ever had visited or probably ever would again. But eventually he cooled off and later left a felt-tip message to the students on a sign in one of the classrooms.

Then after the event, the helicopters took off and headed to the White Homestead in Fort Mill, South Carolina, just across the state line. It was a huge, lovely estate surrounded by trees and including horse stables. Its architecture and grounds reminded me a little bit of the Governor's Mansion in Little Rock. After settling in beside an indoor pool and briefly checking the wires on my laptop, I gave a verbal news report in the kitchen to a few staffers, then went out to the large, well-tended lawn and threw a football with Wendy Smith and Steve Bahar (lead advance). We ran short pass patterns in our suits on the sunny, warm afternoon.

Meanwhile, the President returned from his jog, and the press pool shouted to him, "Mr. President, have you lost confidence in Dave Leavy?" a facetious question about a junior press staffer the reporters knew well. The President looked puzzled and didn't answer as he jogged past. The pool reporters got quite a chuckle out of their impertinence.

We then headed to NBC News Channel for a town hall meeting. We held in a glass-walled conference room, where I dialed in to monitor coverage. No food was provided, so we ordered about a dozen pizzas and then took up a collection. Bob Boorstin, looking around at all the high-ranking senior staff there, set up a donation policy: "Okay, Assistants to the President, twenty dollars; Deputy Assistants, ten; Special Assistants, five; and everybody else, whatever you want."

The President took a couple of nasty Whitewater questions during the town hall meeting. Afterward, we headed out to the motorcade, hustling as usual to get out ahead of the President. That's when I found out the Associated Press was reporting that Supreme Court Justice Harry Blackmun was resigning. But I couldn't go back inside to dial in because we were about to leave.

Standing beside the motorcade in the parking lot, I also found out Army Lieutenant Colonel Rusty Schorsch (military aide) kept me from getting bumped to the press plane, which would've meant getting home later. As it was, we arrived at the White House after midnight.

In addition to North Carolina, rural health care events also took us to New Mexico. The sun was shining on an early winter day as the staff van headed toward Andrews Air Force Base.

A cold and sunny day greeted us in Albuquerque, with picturesque mountains in the background. The motorcade took us north about half an hour to Bernalillo (population: 6,000) where townspeople lined the street to greet us. *"Bienvenido, Señor Presidente,"* one sign said.

The President toured El Pueblo Health Services, Inc. (a rural health clinic), conducted interviews with Denver and Phoenix TV stations and hosted a town hall meeting in a large tent. Some of us worked in the staff hold, which was an antique store across the street. I sat at a countertop and worked on my computer as White House aides and Secret Service agents occasionally came in from the cold to sip coffee.

I'd never been to New Mexico before and was surprised not only at how cold it got at night but by how dry the air was. One of our advance staffers had told me on the phone a couple of days before the trip that he had been getting nosebleeds from the dry air and had been drinking virtually gallons of water.

After Bernalillo, we headed back to the Albuquerque Convention Center for a couple of fund-raisers. The President attended a reception and dinner for New Mexico Governor Bruce King, Senator Jeff Bingaman and Congressman Bill Richardson.

Not only did we focus on rural health care, but also on how health care reform would affect the elderly. That was the purpose of an early spring trip to Miami. It was an unusual trip in that it was thirty hours long, including an overnight, just for two events. Usually we crammed a lot more activity into a lot less time. After a two-hour, fifteen-minute flight, we landed to find palm trees, mostly sunny skies and humidity. Our motorcade was momentarily halted by a raised drawbridge en route to the Sheraton Bal Harbour. Usually, not even toll booths stopped us.

Since the President had no events on his public schedule that Sunday night, the press and a few White House aides went to South Beach for dinner at Mulberry Street Cafe, sponsored by a local magazine publisher. We took a bus to SoBe, as it's called locally, a hip area dominated by art deco architecture. After dinner, the host magazine's associate publisher called a nearby nightclub, and about sixteen of us—local magazine staff, White House aides, models, national reporters—ambled down the street to see Screamin' Jay Hawkins perform.

The next morning, a staff van took us forty-five minutes north to Century Village East, a senior citizens community center (population: 15,000), for a health care event on a sunny, hot day. The temperature reached a record 91 degrees by mid-day. The crowd was all elderly people—most of them loud, obnoxious, former New Yorkers. They were like little children, saying anything that came into their heads. One of our advance staffers said some seated themselves on the stage. When told those seats were for distinguished visitors—members of

Congress, local elected officials—one of the senior citizens refused to get up, saying, "I voted for him. I'm entitled." Others were passing out, getting lightheaded in the heat and being brought to a tent and given water.

Afterward, we headed back to the hotel for a Democratic National Committee fund-raiser downstairs. A DNC videotape featuring highlights of the President's first year in office was shown in a huge ballroom. Wow, I thought, we really *did* get a lot done. We eventually got underway for the flight back to Andrews Air Force Base.

We motorcaded back to the White House about midnight, driving around the South Lawn to enter through the Diplomatic Room under the South Portico. A few minutes later, I exited the West Wing ground floor doors, following Jeff Eller by a decent distance, and walked out onto West Executive Drive just after he did.

"Geez! Did you see that?" he asked, gesturing to a large trash bin in the dark about ten feet away.

"No, what?"

"A rat! Thing was as big as a cat!"

Sometimes the schedule called for combining day events with town hall meetings at night. That was the case when we visited New York and Rhode Island. Breakfast was juice and a bagel during the fifty-five-minute hop up the coast to JFK International, where, as usual, we flew in helicopters to the Wall Street landing zone right next to the East River.

We held a health care event at a Pathmark grocery store, located under an expressway bridge, ten minutes by motorcade from the helicopter landing zone. The President gave a quick speech near the checkout counters as we stood a few aisles away and strained for a look over the press pool. Pathmark hadn't endorsed the Clinton health plan, but they did support the five principles our plan was based on. The store was distributing bag inserts that said, "Pathmark and the UFCS support Health Benefits at Work and Quality Health Care Coverage including Prescription Medicines for All Americans."

Then we stopped at a fire station where one of the firefighters recently had died in the line of duty. The addition to the schedule was the idea of New York Mayor Rudolph Giuliani, who had greeted the President at the airport and was escorting him around town. When they were inside, health care staffers and I stood on the blocked-off street beside the motorcade on a sunny day. Next it was on to the Hilton, where I ate a stale ham sandwich and scrambled around a little bit in the staff office, a regular hotel room without the furniture. The President spoke about health care to the Association for a Better New York downstairs in the Trianon Ballroom, greeted health care letter writers, was briefed and then conducted a health care reporters' roundtable discussion before departure about 4 P.M.

The motorcade then took us fifteen minutes back to the helicopters, and then we boarded Air Force One for a forty-five-minute flight to Rhode Island.

At the Green State Airport in Warwick, Rhode Island, the President addressed an enthusiastic crowd and then shook hands along a ropeline. He stopped in the midst of it to take a call on the limousine phone from the First Lady, who was in South Africa for President Nelson Mandela's inauguration. The motorcade then took us twenty minutes to the studios of WJAR-TV in Cranston for a televised town hall meeting.

Backstage, chefs in white hats from a nearby culinary school prepared a delicious dinner for us. During the town hall meeting, I hustled back and forth between the staff hold and the press office in another part of the TV station, five minutes away. Afterward, the President seemed to take forever hanging out with the studio audience and then shaking hands backstage. We didn't get home until 1:30 A.M.

Another time, we were in Boston so the President could present a health care address to the National Governors Association summer meeting. After producing the morning clips, I headed down the Park Plaza Hotel stairs (one elevator always was held for the President, and Secret Service didn't allow the others to stop on the floor where he was staying) and into the motorcade and on to the Hynes Convention Center.

Upstairs, our staff hold was a large room with dark blue carpeting, tables, chairs, a couch, a computer, printer and phones. I scrolled the wires on my laptop, monitoring his speech on C-SPAN. Catered lunch consisted of luncheon meat, pasta salad, cookies and soft drinks. In his speech, the President appeared to change his definition of "universal coverage" for health care, indicating he might accept coverage for 95 percent of Americans instead of 100 percent. The early wire stories showed the trouble we knew we'd have as soon as he said it. As soon as stories crossed my computer screen, I hustled to get them to Mack McLarty (counselor), Mark Gearan (communications director), Dee Dee Myers and Lorrie McHugh (health care).

"How's it look?" one of them asked upon entering the holding room immediately after the speech.

I shook my head. "Not good," I said, handing over the first paragraphs of an Associated Press story.

The senior aides then hurried downstairs to the filing center to anxiously interpret the President's remarks for the press.

We were at the convention center until almost 3 P.M. as the President met with the *Boston Globe* editorial board. Then we stopped briefly back at the Park Plaza for a reception with supporters in the Plaza Ballroom. Upstairs in the staff office, I created one last wire report before dashing to the motorcade. In our crowded staff van, Boston native Arthur Jones (deputy press secretary) pointed out sites through the window.

Aboard the plane, I ate nachos and refried beans during the one-hour, fifteen-minute flight before wondering where everyone had gone. I strolled to the conference room, where the President and the rest of the staff were sitting around chatting. The conversation turned to jogging, and then to Indiana Democratic Governor Evan Bayh. Said the President: "He's got the best physique of any governor."

One of the rallying points President Clinton sometimes called upon in fighting for health care reform was the image of President Harry Truman, who also had fought for health care reform. One summer Saturday, we took a day trip to Missouri for health care and then to Ohio for a political fund-raiser.

The First Lady joined the President on the two-hour, twenty-minute flight to Kansas City. We ate chicken sandwiches for lunch as I sat next to Barb Kinney (staff photographer). She clarified a story from a few months ago for me. The President, appearing at a Washington news correspondents' black-tie dinner one night, mentioned President Truman's quote: "If you want a friend in Washington, get a dog." Clinton then told the crowd, "I wish somebody had told me that before I showed up with a neutered cat."

A few days later, Kinney took a photo of Socks getting, uh, intimate with a stray cat near the Rose Garden. (Stray cats used to crawl through the outside fence all the time.) Kinney printed the photo and on the border wrote, "Dear Mr. President: I can run with the big dogs, too. Your new best friend, Socks." She gave it to the President, and apparently he got a big laugh out of it.

Kinney was funny. She was probably in her early thirties, with short dark hair. She was from Evansville, Indiana, and she and her roommate had a whole houseful of dogs and cats. Like the other White House photographers, she hadn't worked on the campaign (although chief photographer Bob McNeely had.) She was very down-to-earth, and I always enjoyed talking with her.

Upon arrival at Kansas City International Airport, Air Force Two was waiting for us. It was great to see the Vice President's and Mrs. Gore's aides on the tarmac. We rarely traveled with the Veep. In fact, that Saturday was the first time the four of them had appeared together outside Washington since the 1992 campaign. We boarded the motorcade, and I rode in the staff van with Ira Magaziner (health care), Lorrie McHugh, Paul Begala and Steve Richetti (legislative affairs) during the forty-minute motorcade to Independence. "Anybody know any songs?" Magaziner asked facetiously on the long ride.

A large crowd jamming the streets around Independence Square and the Truman Courthouse awaited the President on a sunny, eighty-degree day, but so did protesters. One held up a sign with a photo of controversial Surgeon General Joycelyn Elders that said, "Clinton picked this doctor. Do you want him to pick yours?"

The President, First Lady, Vice President and Mrs. Gore all spoke about health care in front of a statue of Harry Truman, who as President fought for universal coverage. (When President Johnson signed Medicare into law, he went to Independence and gave the first Medicare cards to former President and Mrs. Truman.)

After the event, Willie Nelson played "On the Road Again" on a nearby stage in honor of the health care bus caravan that was traveling across the country and which had stopped that day there in Jackson County. Dee Dee Myers, ever wary of something the press would jump on, asked me, "Did he ever pay his taxes?" referring to Nelson's difficulties with the Internal Revenue Service.

The motorcade then took us five minutes to the Harry S. Truman Library. I dialed in to check the wires and then ate Gates barbecue with the rest of the staff in our holding room as the President and

First Lady toured the library and museum. After they passed our door, I ducked out to see what I could in the few minutes before departure. I only had time to check out the Oval Office display, set up as it was during Truman's presidency, complete with the THE BUCK STOPS HERE sign on his desk.

After the long drive back to the airport, we took off on a one-hour, forty-minute flight to Cleveland. I ambled up to the plane's senior staff section and told Bruce Lindsey that based on the coverage I'd seen so far, our event appeared to be not a home run, but certainly a solid line drive up the middle.

"So far, so good," I said.

"Let's see if we can hold it," he replied.

Upon arrival at Cleveland-Hopkins International Airport, about 400 people greeted the President. He tried to speak to the crowd through a portable public address system, with a White House Communications Agency staffer holding a speaker, but the sound cut out in the middle of virtually every sentence. After we'd motorcaded thirty-five minutes to Landerhaven Country Club for the next event, Wendy Smith told Navy Captain Mark Rogers of the military office, which is in charge of WHCA: "I guess I don't have to tell you how pissed he is."

Upstairs at Landerhaven, our holding room had catered food (salad, pasta, chicken, rolls, cookies, soft drinks), a TV, phones, tables and comfortable chairs. I dialed in, finding news on U.S.-Japan trade talks and possible United Nations action on Haiti. Sitting to eat dinner with Neil Wolin (National Security Council) and Bruce Lindsey, I said, "Well, as you know, Bruce, our hearts and souls were with you this week" when he and other staffers appeared before the House Banking Committee's Whitewater investigation.

"Well, I appreciate that," Lindsey said. He said that while it was never fun, it got much better after the first break. But as he pointed out, that was the easy half. The Senate appearance next week won't be as easy, he said.

After the President spoke at a fund-raiser next door for Senate candidate Joel Hyatt, the motorcade took us five minutes away to another fund-raiser. The house in nearby Hunting Valley where the fund-raising dinner for Hyatt was held was more like a complex. It included tennis courts, a pool and several buildings (garages and guest houses, probably). The staff hold was the basement, where Lindsey, Wolin, Kinney, Dr. Connie Mariano and Army Captain Maureen Donahue (nurse), sporting a huge new engagement ring, and I sat down to watch Arnold Schwarzenegger's awful *Last Action Hero* on a big-screen TV.

Afterward, I stood next to the motorcade and awaited departure. I chatted in the dark with Coast Guard Lieutenant Commander Bob Walters (military aide), who said he would have to get up at 6 A.M. the next day to get to New Jersey for an upcoming Presidential visit. It was already almost midnight when he said, "But I keep telling myself that I could be on a ship off Haiti about now, so I have no complaints."

We finally rode thirty-five minutes back to the airport and flew one hour, five minutes back to Washington. En route, I asked Captain Mark Rogers something I'd always been curious about: What exactly are the rules about shutting down airports when Air Force One arrives? Quoting Air Force Colonel Danny Barr (Presidential aircraft commander and Air Force One pilot), Rogers said his understanding was that Federal Aviation Administration regulations say ten to fifteen minutes before and after landing, runway freezes go into effect. That's triggered by Air Force One notifying the tower it is approaching. Then the Secret Service performs its security sweep of the area. But ramp freezes only affect adjacent runways. Airlines always blamed us for making them late, but that was a myth. They just used it as an excuse.

That Saturday night fund-raiser in Ohio was far from the only political event the President attended. With the mid-term Congressional elections coming up, we'd be on the road for a seemingly endless series of fund-raising receptions, dinners and campaign rallies.

8▶On the Campaign Trail

"*LOOK AT THE VOTES WE'RE LOSING!*" · *KENNEDY-STYLE
CAMPAIGNING IN MASSACHUSETTS* · "*WHAT DO THEY
WANT ME TO SAY?*" · *ACCENTS IN RHODE ISLAND* · *STUMP
SPEECH IN ALBANY AND DES MOINES* · *EIGHT-DAY DASH
TO ELECTION DAY*

*I*N ADDITION TO ALL HIS OTHER DUTIES, the President serves as de facto head of his political party. Whether it's working toward his own re-election or campaigning for members of Congress, the President spends a tremendous amount of time speaking, shaking hands and meeting supporters across the country. Whether it's a fund-raising reception or dinner or a campaign rally, the President spends a large percentage of his travel time on politics.

The mid-term or so-called "off-year" Congressional elections take place halfway through a President's four years. President Clinton's trips in 1994 were typical of how a President campaigns on behalf of Congressional members of his own party.

One summer day we were in Philadelphia. In the staff hold, a small office suite in the Public Ledger Building, political consultant Paul Begala told a presidential campaign story that included his partner, James Carville. The President, Carville, Begala and others in 1992 were meeting with Hollywood celebrities, including Warren Beatty and his wife, Annette Bening. And Begala said Carville kept muttering to him, "Look at her, man—she's staring at my crotch."

Begala also said it was interesting to see Hollywood and Washington people interact. "Hollywood people would love to do what you guys do," he told Lorrie McHugh (health care) and me. "You talk to Barbra Streisand, and she wants to be [health care adviser]

Ira Magaziner."

Shortly afterward, the President came through on his way upstairs, discussing Pennsylvania politics with Begala. "Would you tell that to [gubernatorial candidate Mark] Singel's people?" the President said in reference to their discussion. "I'll tell Mark when I see him later, but would you tell them that?"

I'd liked Paul Begala since I first met him the night after the 1992 California primary. A Texan who always wore cowboy boots, even with suits, Begala had receding reddish hair and a well-trimmed beard. A warm and friendly veteran of gubernatorial and senatorial campaigns, he traveled everywhere with then-Governor Clinton during the general election. He was one of the best writers I'd met and had an amazing ability to understand complex issues and boil them down to memorable sound bites.

Then we went upstairs, where the President attended a reception and fund-raiser for Singel, Senator Harris Wofford and the Pennsylvania Democratic Party. In the staff hold across the hall, Bruce Lindsey (senior adviser) was sipping a glass of wine and looking out the window, appearing atypically relaxed. He talked about how Chelsea Clinton was growing up and about one of his daughters working as a Congressional page.

Then he asked, "Ken, where do you say you're from?"

"Depends on who's asking," I replied. "I was born in Indiana, but I usually say I'm from Arkansas. Why?"

"Because I think of you as being from Arkansas, but I read my e-mail and saw you were nominated as 'Hoosier of the Month' for a reporter's profile piece."

"Yeah, I saw that," I said. "I don't know who they ended up getting."

Meanwhile, Press Secretary Dee Dee Myers, a huge Los Angeles Dodgers fan, had gone to see part of the first game of a Phillies-Dodgers doubleheader. Soon afterward, we headed back to the airport about 8:30 P.M., and we passed brightly lit Veterans Stadium.

I rode in a staff van with Begala and Democratic National Committee Chairman David Wilhelm, whom I knew from the campaign's early days. Begala and Wilhelm were talking politics: policy, strategy and tactics. It was fascinating to hear those pros talk shop. Begala and James Carville got Harris Wofford elected to the Senate from Pennsylvania in 1991, and Begala was advising Wofford's re-election campaign. He said that listing the President's accomplishments wasn't enough.

The Republicans' message is simple, he said. "I can give Rick Santorum's stump speech right now," he said of Wofford's opponent. "'I'll get government off your backs.' What do *we* stand for? Government that's on your side.... Ultimately, I think they want government on their side and not off their backs."

He continued riffing, working out the sound bites aloud, saying we had to tie the message to our accomplishments. Then, sitting next to me and turned backward to face Wilhelm, he began pounding the back of the seat. "That's it! That's right!" I couldn't help but think that people would pay big bucks to hear these guys expound on politics, and here I was getting it for free.

I met David Wilhelm, a Chicago resident and Ohio native, during my first weeks at the campaign. A veteran of campaigns for Illinois Senator Paul Simon and Chicago Mayor Richard Daley, he hired Matt Smith, whom I worked with in those early days. A youngish-looking guy with brown hair and dark eyes, Wilhelm was down-to-earth and friendly to me ("Hey, Chief") when I was but a lowly volunteer. He'd been called a Boy Scout who was too nice to be Democratic National Committee chairman, but he was very effective in the campaign and remained extremely loyal to the President. Wilhelm and his wife, DeeGee, were expecting their first child that fall.

During the forty-five-minute drive to the airport, we passed a long, long line of headlights where traffic had been stopped on interstate entrance ramps. "David, look at the votes!" Begala whined. "Look at the votes we're losing!"

People don't like it when the motorcade keeps them stuck in traffic. Sometimes local politicians traveling with us would duck in their seats so their constituents couldn't see them holding up traffic. But I never figured out if getting stopped by the motorcade ultimately affected the way people voted.

Later that summer we were staying overnight in Miami. The day's first events were downstairs in the Sheraton Bal Harbour hotel, where the President met with the *Miami Herald* editorial board, a group of local business leaders and then the host committee for the upcoming Summit of the Americas, to be held in Miami.

Around noon we rode fifteen minutes to the Miami Beach Convention Center (site of the 1972 Democratic and Republican national conventions), where the President addressed the annual convention of La Raza, a national Hispanic organization. We then boarded the motorcade for the twenty-five-minute ride to Miami International Airport.

After a two-hour, forty-five-minute flight (pasta salad for lunch), we touched down in Brunswick, Maine, about 6 P.M. After sunny, ninety-two-degree weather in Miami, we found clouds and a cool breeze upon arriving. "You can tell we're in Maine," said one of the guys in the press pool, who had traveled there with then-President Bush to Bush's Kennebunkport home, as we exited the plane's rear steps.

We then boarded the helicopters for a fifteen-minute flight to Portland, where crowds lined the streets. I liked going to new places, especially smaller cities and towns, because the President's reception always was so enthusiastic. After viewing the oceanside art deco of Miami earlier that day, we saw old brick and clapboard houses in the green countryside of Maine.

The President attended receptions and fund-raisers for Senate candidate Tom Andrews and Maine gubernatorial candidate Joe Brennan at a couple of hotels. On the way into one hotel, advance staff led the President to a non-working elevator, so he had to turn around and walk past a bunch of hotel staff and local people in a service area. I was standing next to Ralph Alswang (staff photographer) when the President came up to us.

"How's it goin', man?" he said, patting me on the arm.

"Good to see you," I replied, not having seen him earlier in the day.

Upstairs in the staff holding room, I told Bruce Lindsey about a Whitewater story moving on the wires, and he asked me to print it for him. A little later, Air Force Major Darren McDew said fog was closing in and we couldn't take the helicopters directly to Boston as we'd planned. Instead, we'd have to helicopter back to Brunswick and then take Air Force One to Boston, meaning an even longer day. Everybody groaned in unison.

While the President attended a fund-raiser downstairs, a small group of us headed into a room down the hall where a reception he'd attended had just ended. There were JOSEPH BRENNAN FOR GOVERNOR signs on the door, and inside was a buffet table with shrimp, mushroom caps stuffed with crab, salmon, roast beef and sliced turkey. We shamelessly attacked the leftover food.

Afterward, we headed to the motorcade, to the helicopters and then to the plane for a one-hour flight and—finally—to Boston's Logan Airport. I was dead on my feet after a nineteen-hour day. By the time we reached the familiar Park Plaza Hotel and our usual fifteenth floor, I was sagging. I walked past the staff office (as usual, in the Towers Club), where the early clips from Washington already were coming through the fax. Army Lieutenant Colonel Rusty Schorsch (military aide) was waiting at the end of the hallway: "I think you're down here, Kenny." Good ol' Rusty, I thought...always looking out for us.

The first time I met Schorsch, I remembered thinking that he was the type of officer the Army wants. He was a tall, broad-shouldered, redheaded guy, polite, softspoken, charming and professional. He was part of the elite Rangers and once was injured paratrooping, spending some time recovering at Washington's Walter Reed Army Hospital. I liked all the military aides, but Schorsch may have been my favorite because he was the first military aide I met on my first trip. And like the others, he went out of his way to help us.

On another trip, we left about 4 P.M. on a Friday for a weekend trip to Chicago, Minneapolis, Kansas City and New York. We landed at Chicago's O'Hare International Airport after an uneventful one-hour, forty-five-minute flight. In the van on the way to the hotel, Martha Phipps of the Democratic National Committee and I talked about how burned out we were. We both had started in the early days of the campaign. How nice it would be, we said, to be home about now, free to do whatever we wanted for the weekend, including just nothing.

The President took Marine One to Meigs Field and attended a Democratic Senatorial Campaign Committee fund-raiser and dinner at the Ritz-Carlton Hotel. Those of us riding in the vans arrived at the hotel a little later, and I worked in the staff office. If you've seen one fund-raiser, I thought, you've seen 'em all.

The next day was "just" another twenty-one-hour, four-state day. We found rainy, cool weather throughout the middle of the country. After delivering clips to staffers' doors, I waited while the President finished his regular live Saturday morning radio address at 9:06 A.M. Central time. In the lobby, I briefly chatted with my old campaign buddy Matt Smith, who was back home in Chicago working for the city's transportation department after leaving Washington. Coming home seemed to agree with him.

Air Force One took off about 10:30 A.M. for the one-hour, five-minute flight to Minneapolis. The motorcade took us thirty minutes to the Minneapolis Club, where the President attended a "Minnesota Campaign '94" luncheon with David Wilhelm, Minnesota Senator Paul Wellstone, Florida Senator Bob Graham (who was chairman of the Democratic Senatorial Campaign Committee) and Ann Wynia, Minnesota's Democratic Senate nominee. I tapped away on my laptop in a nearby room, scrolling the wires, while Deputy Chief of Staff Harold Ickes sat beside me, working the phones in an effort to smooth out problems in New York with the President's schedule for the next morning.

After a thirty-minute ride back to Minneapolis/St. Paul International Airport, we boarded the plane again for a one-hour, ten-minute flight to Kansas City, followed by a thirty-minute motorcade from Kansas City International Airport to the Ritz-Carlton Hotel. The President attended a fundraising reception and dinner for Senate candidate Alan Wheat of Missouri. What some folks wear to meet the President! At the reception I saw an aging, leather-skinned, tanned and sagging blond in a leopardskin dress that didn't cover nearly enough.

Back in the staff hold next door, I watched college football on TV, seeing Colorado pull out a come-from-behind victory over Michigan with a Hail Mary pass on the game's final play. "Did you see that?" I said, stunned, turning to Navy Captain Mark Rogers (military office).

After the fund-raiser, which seemed to last forever, we flew two hours and twenty-five minutes to New York, my least favorite U.S. city we ever visited. As usual, we took four helicopters from JFK International Airport to the Wall Street landing zone and from there took the motorcade to the Waldorf-Astoria Hotel, finally getting to bed about 2:30 A.M.

The President got involved in the mid-term campaign in earnest on a Monday in mid-October 1994, when he traveled to Michigan. We visited the Ford assembly plant in Dearborn, where Mustangs are produced, and got to see the shiny new models on the assembly line. It was a sunny, pleasant day as the President spoke outside to the auto workers. He bashed the Republicans' "Contract with America," saying what they promised couldn't be paid for, and deploring a return to the trickle-down economics of the '80s. There was a current model and a classic Mustang on each side of the stage behind him, and a trailer behind him full of cars fresh off the assembly line.

That afternoon we traveled downtown to Detroit's Westin Hotel, where the President met separately with auto company executives and United Auto Workers leaders. We also visited the *Detroit Free Press*, where he talked with the editorial board. They were one of the few editorial pages that had remained friendly to us.

On the thirty-minute ride back to Willow Run Airport, the motorcade stopped at a strip mall so the President could buy an anniversary present for the First Lady at Borders. The press pool was kept outside, but I went inside and looked around at the books. Customers already inside weren't allowed in the back section, where the President, Wendy Smith (trip director) and some other staff perused the CDs. I poked around the blues section. (Later, I realized that I'd gone CD shopping with both the President and with John F. Kennedy, Jr.)

The President, meanwhile, was of course surrounded by staff and Secret Service agents while he shopped, and afterward the press asked what he bought. I realize he's the President, I thought, but that particular lack of privacy has to get old for him.

Campaigning was a family affair on a long Saturday in October, when the President visited Connecticut and then Florida, where his brother-in-law was running for the Senate. We spent nineteen hours traveling up and down the East Coast, beginning with a one-hour flight to Hartford, Connecticut, and then a thirty-five-minute helicopter ride on a pretty fall day, the leaves near peak color as we flew over them. It was cool, windy and sunny—perfect college football weather on an autumn Saturday.

We attended a political rally at Stratford's Sikorsky Airport for gubernatorial candidate Bill Curry. When Marine One landed, Secret Service agent Dave Carpenter appeared as the rear door opened first. The crowd saw a tall guy in his forties with gray hair in a dark suit and cheered wildly. Those of us on staff standing nearby laughed. Then the President himself appeared and gave an upbeat speech. He and the First Lady, who was along for the day, then both worked the ropeline in the slightly chilly wind. Afterward, the motorcade took us to the nearby Bridgeport Holiday Inn, where the President attended a reception and then spoke to about 300 people at a luncheon in the ballroom. Both events were Curry fund-raisers.

I worked in the staff hold across the hall, munching a cold-cut sandwich with a brownie and a Coke while scrolling the wires on my laptop. My pager went off, and I called Julia Payne of the Vice President's press office at her home in Washington. She said the Veep, who was in Milwaukee, wanted to see the wires. So I called Washington to track down the Milwaukee fax number and then compiled a wire report. But I knew it would take forever to print and fax it. So— quite cleverly, I thought—I dialed into the White House main computer system and used the communications software there to fax it to the Veep's advance staff. I was able to take a document on my diskette in Connecticut and electronically transmit it through Washington to Milwaukee, where it appeared on paper.

We took the helicopters back to Hartford and flew Air Force One two hours and forty minutes south to Miami, where it was hot and humid upon arrival. We drove past the Orange Bowl on the way to a rally for Senate candidate Hugh Rodham, the First Lady's brother. We heard radio traffic from the advance staff just before we got there that the candidate hadn't shown up yet for his own rally. When the twenty-minute motorcade arrived at the Port of Miami, however, he stood waiting to welcome the President and First Lady.

In the tiny, sparse staff hold downstairs, I took a quick look at the wires, mainly college football scores. When we traveled on autumn Saturdays, I always tried to get an Arkansas score in case the President asked, or in case the Razorbacks won so we could have some good news for him. That day, the Hogs beat Ole Miss 31-7. National Security Adviser Tony Lake looked over my shoulder. "Got a Harvard score?" he asked.

Upstairs, the President and First Lady posed for photos with various VIPs before walking to the other side of the curtain for the main rally. The sparse crowd couldn't even fill the small site. They cheered at the wrong times and were politically ignorant. I thought it was embarrassing for the President, but Wendy Smith was closer. "Humiliating," she muttered.

Then it was on to a huge, ocean-side estate for a Democratic Senatorial Campaign Committee fund-raiser expected to raise $700,000. There were tennis courts, a guest house and a huge air-conditioned tent set up on the lawn. The press had a tent next door to the guest house, where the staff ate dinner and sat around talking. The event lasted an hour and fifteen minutes longer than scheduled, and, unable to dial in for some technical reason, I sat on the couch in the guest house and fell asleep. A fellow staffer awoke me shortly before we moved out, and we headed back to the plane.

Aboard Air Force One on the two-hour, ten-minute flight home, Lieutenant Colonel Rusty Schorsch said there was room for all of us on the helicopters at Andrews. I was pleasantly surprised not only because we'd get home sooner, but because I'd only been on Nighthawk 2 once before. The white-top helicopter with ten of us aboard swooped over the nation's capital, swinging around the Washington Monument on a quiet, starry night, streetlights glittering below. The helicopter set down just a few feet from 17th Street, about halfway between the Washington Monument and the Lincoln Memorial. After a very short ride back to the White House, I got home about 2 A.M. on a chilly morning.

One Thursday morning in late October, I was finishing the clips in our staff office, Room 1591 of Boston's Park Plaza Hotel. I called my office and asked if there was anything else I should know. Larry Sampas (news analysis) said there was a late-arriving story in that day's *Arkansas Democrat-Gazette* in which an Arkansas state trooper denied statements about the President attributed to him in that morning's *Washington Post.* Sampas faxed it to me and I handed it to Dee Dee Myers a few minutes later, and she was interested and excited. She then showed it to the President, who happened to be walking down the hall after his morning jog. He, too, appeared interested and pleased.

Then it was on to nearby Framingham (population: 65,000), the motorcade taking us onto the Massachusetts Turnpike for a beautiful, thirty-five-minute autumn drive on a cloudy day. At Framingham High School, the President spoke to 1,700 students and faculty in the hot John F. Kennedy Gymnasium. He also signed the Elementary and Secondary Education Act, which over the next five years would provide approximately $60 billion in aid for schools across the country. I stayed in the staff hold, which was a physics classroom, to dial in to the wires. Top news stories included North Korea telling the International Atomic Energy Association that the IAEA would get access to nuclear sites but no guarantees, and U.S. personal income and housing starts both rising.

Bruce Lindsey asked if I could track down a story from the previous day's *Boston Globe,* so I called the Old Executive Office Building library and Lindsey's assistant and had them fax it to us. Outside afterward, several dozen elementary school students lined up to meet the President as he headed to the limo.

But the best part of the day was yet to come. The motorcade headed toward downtown Framingham for a Senator Ted Kennedy rally. As we got closer, townspeople lined the streets. They stood in yards with campaign signs, waving American flags, kids and parents together, on sidewalks in front of big old houses. Nearby, a school bus stopped under big trees full of colorful fall leaves. It was absolutely pure Norman Rockwell. As we got to the town square, the crowds were spilling over the sidewalks onto the street. They were waving Kennedy signs (and admittedly a few Republican challenger Mitt Romney signs) behind ropes.

In the staff hold downstairs in the old Nevins Hall building, I dialed in and ate meatballs, manicotti and chicken dumplings with rolls during the rally. (Don't think getting a chance to eat wasn't a big deal on the road. As much energy as it took to keep up with the President, missing lunch could ruin a traveling White House aide's whole day.)

Then outside, we experienced what it must've been like to campaign with Jack Kennedy in 1960. It was October, we were in Massachusetts, the crowds were screaming and there were Kennedy signs everywhere. And President Clinton looks a little like President Kennedy, especially from the back or when he does that hand-in-the-suit-jacket-pocket-while-speaking gesture.

After President Clinton and Senator Kennedy worked the crowd, we headed back to the airport and a one-hour, ten-minute flight back to Andrews, arriving back to the office late in the afternoon.

Also late in October, we spent a weekend in San Francisco, Seattle and Cleveland/Akron for a variety of events. By Sunday evening, we were in Ohio to campaign.

I was up at 6:30 A.M. the next day to produce and distribute the clips in our hotel staff office, overlooking Lake Erie with Municipal Stadium across the street, where the hometown Browns had beaten the Cincinnati Bengals Sunday. The under-construction Rock and Roll Hall of Fame was visible a little further away. The big news was a memo by Office of Management and Budget Director Alice Rivlin which had leaked. But the budget deficit figures came out that morning, and they were the best in two years. The President promoted that fact during some local morning radio interviews he conducted at the hotel.

The motorcade then took us five minutes to the Statler Tower Building, where the President spoke to the Cleveland City Club. After his speech, as was traditional, members chosen by blind draw asked questions. The first question just happened to come from Ohio Republican Congressman Martin Hoke, who verbally attacked the President. Clinton gave a strong rebuttal and closed by chiding Hoke for his vote against the crime bill. The crowd gave the President a standing ovation. Gene Sperling (economic aide) and Harold Ickes stood next to me, their heads together, and chortled with glee.

The President attended a fund-raising reception for Ohio Attorney General candidate Lee Fisher, then flew via helicopter to Akron, where we took a brief hard-hat tour of Inventure Place, a construction site that the following spring would become the National Inventors Hall of Fame and the National Invention Center.

We then headed to the Akron Civic Theater, an old, ornately detailed former vaudeville performance hall, for a fund-raiser. Backstage, Ohio Democratic Senators John Glenn and Howard Metzenbaum hung out with us. I was saddened to find how old and apparently hard of hearing Metzenbaum was. It's probably a good thing he's retiring, I thought, but what a great loss to liberal causes. Then I thought and realized that Glenn took *Friendship 7* around the Earth exactly 355 days before I was born. As a long-time space exploration aficionado, I wanted to introduce myself and chat with him, but he was busy eating and I didn't want to bother him.

Then we got word that Republican Mayor Rudolph Giuliani of New York had endorsed Democratic Governor Mario Cuomo. It was huge news, and Marsha Scott (political affairs) and I told the senators, neither of whom had heard. Metzenbaum read the wires over my shoulder as I worked on my laptop computer. I found a story that the

Senate Ethics Committee had announced that several months ago it had cleared Senator Ted Kennedy of allegations made in a book by one of his former staffers. The senators (neither of whom were on the Ethics Committee) didn't know about it. Metzenbaum showed interest in my computer and in what I was receiving on my screen.

Then he and Glenn began to discuss who was the worst Senator, the most harmful. Metzenbaum said it was New York Republican Al D'Amato, but Glenn said D'Amato was a joke who undermined his own credibility. He said the worst was Texas Republican Phil Gramm: "He's a bastard, but he's not stupid." I was fascinated to hear such frank talk from guys who on C-SPAN refer to "the gentleman from Ohio" or "my distinguished colleague."

Glenn had flown on Air Force One a couple of times with us, and we sometimes joked that, unlike most guests, he could fly the plane if necessary. After all, in addition to being a former astronaut, he also was once a record-setting Marine pilot.

After the event, we headed five minutes to another fund-raising dinner at the John Knight Convention Center, where a huge room was divided by pipe and blue drape for our and the President's holding areas. The President called Giuliani to thank him for endorsing Cuomo.

In our hold on the other side of the drape, we talked about a photo on the front page of that day's Akron newspaper that identified a former Japanese prime minister as "Clinton." But nobody could remember the guy's real name. Even Tom Ross (National Security Council) couldn't recall when the President asked him. "Talk about embarrassed," Ross said.

The motorcade then took us fifteen minutes through a cold rain back to the plane. The 747 (tail number 28000) earlier in the day had been sent back to Andrews to be prepared for the next day's Middle East trip. So we boarded 27000, one of the old 737s that used to be flown primarily as Air Force One. Only three of us who made it all the way through that grueling coast-to-coast, five-day political trip (personal aide Andrew Friendly, staff photographer Sharon Farmer and I) were going to the Mideast the next day.

It was crowded aboard the 737, and I was standing behind my seat, facing the rear of the plane. There were two tables and maybe a dozen seats in the staff section. Then I heard someone behind me enthusiastically say, "*Yesss!*" I looked, and it was the President, in his shirtsleeves, pumping his fist. "This was a day to live for," he said, excited over the budget deficit numbers, Giuliani's endorsement, the enthusiastic crowds and the building momentum toward Election Day.

He talked about what the endorsement would mean for Giuliani's political future. Arthur Jones (deputy press secretary) and Harold Ickes talked with him about whether he should comment to the press pool about it, as the press wanted him to. Standing less than five feet in front of me, the President thought about it aloud.

"Why do I want to be in that story?" he asked rhetorically. "What do they want me to say? 'I'm happy as a pig in....' *Oops*," he said, clapping a hand over his mouth.

"That's what they want you to say," Jones said, laughing.

After we returned from the five-day, six-country trip to the Middle East in late October, we embarked on an eight-day sprint to Election Day. There was a nip in the air in late fall, and it was campaign season—a great time of year.

After a forty-minute flight to Philadelphia International Airport, the President spoke at the City Hall courtyard during a cloudy noon rally before a small crowd, apparently shy of the 2,000 we'd expected. I worked on my laptop in the staff hold, seeing and hearing the event below through the windows. The President warned that Republicans favored cuts that would "devastate Social Security and senior citizens.... Say no to this radical attack on Social Security." Sounding "weary and hoarse," according to a wire story, he told the crowd, "Don't turn back" to Reaganomics.

Moving on the wires was coverage of a *Pittsburgh Post-Gazette* poll showing Republican Congressman Tom Ridge leading Democratic Lieutenant Governor Mark Singel 46 percent to 30 percent in the Pennsylvania governor's race, with 13 percent for independent Peg Lukzig. Congressman Rick Santorum, a Republican, led Senator Harris Wofford, a Democrat, in the Senate race 46-35. Philadelphia was only a quick stop, and soon after the event, the motorcade took us twenty minutes back to the airport. Then we flew fifty minutes to Pittsburgh.

The President spent the afternoon conducting satellite TV and phone radio interviews with Detroit, Cleveland and Pennsylvania media outlets and attending a fund-raising reception, all at the David Lawrence Convention Center. I worked in the staff hold for about three hours (the main story on the wires was about proposed Social Security cuts by the Republicans) before we all went downstairs to a big, loud rally with about 3,500 raucous loyal Democrats.

As the President was shaking hands along the ropeline while departing, I found out an American Eagle airplane with about fifty passengers aboard had crashed near Chicago. I called the White House on my cell phone to get details from someone who could check the wires and then paged Dee Dee Myers, who was somewhere in the convention center, with the information so she would at least be aware if the reporters traveling with us brought it up.

After a thirty-minute motorcade in a cold rain, we reached the plane and flew home, getting back to the White House about 9 P.M.

The President still had another event, though. Shortly after he returned to the White House, he headed to McLean, Virginia, for a Senator Chuck Robb fund-raiser. In fact, I was about to drive onto the Theodore Roosevelt Bridge on my way home when a police officer blocked the road for no apparent reason. But within a few minutes, the familiar motorcade came whizzing past. So this is what it feels like to get stopped by the motorcade, I thought.

The next day we headed to Michigan and Ohio, both key states where Democrats were resigning, leaving behind open Senate seats.

Air Force One flew one hour and twenty minutes to Willow Run Airport near Detroit. After a thirty-minute motorcade to the University of Michigan at Dearborn, the President attended a roundtable discussion at the student union. We held in a nearby conference room, and I dialed in to check the wires (U.S. consumer spending up 1.6 percent in September, the biggest leap in six months; National Traffic Safety Board Chairman Jim Hall says weather alone didn't cause Monday's American Eagle plane crash near Chicago).

Then it was back to the motorcade for a twenty-minute ride on a chilly, windy, gray day to Detroit's Cobo Convention Center. The President spoke to about 5,000 people at a loud Democratic rally with a bad sound system. (The White House Communications Agency couldn't provide equipment for purely political events, and the local folks didn't get the sound right.) There were about 100 people seated behind the President on the enormous stage.

Then it was on to the Westin Hotel and Renaissance Center downtown, where upstairs in a holding room, I dialed in as pollster

Stanley Greenberg worked the phone beside me and watched as I printed out wire coverage of the rally. Meanwhile, the President attended a fund-raising luncheon for Democratic Senate candidate Bob Carr from Michigan.

Then we moved down the hall, into a large room where the President was scheduled to conduct live radio and TV satellite interviews with New York, Providence, Detroit and Philadelphia stations. But there weren't any walls in the small carpeted ballroom with acoustic ceiling tiles—only pipe and drape separated the live interview area from the staff section, where we busily filled our plates with lunch (cold-cut sandwiches, pasta salad, cookies and cans of soft drinks from a large, plastic ice-filled bowl). Any noise would carry into the interview area.

"This is outrageous," Bruce Lindsey said to Andrew Friendly, as Lindsey made a sandwich.

"I *know* this is outrageous!" Friendly said about the setup. "Did I advance this?" Then, muttering, Friendly added, "This is outrageous," and Lindsey laughed.

During the President's interviews, Ralph Alswang (staff photographer), Marsha Scott and I crashed out on couches and snoozed. We were told that if we were going to stay in the room, we had to remain absolutely silent during the President's live interviews. Fortunately, nobody snored.

Afterward we made our way through the underground garage, where the motorcade whisked us past a view across Lake St. Clair of Windsor, Ontario, and back to the airport thirty-five minutes later. We flew forty minutes to Cleveland, where the weather was raw: rainy, windy and cold. The President spoke at a GOTV (Get Out the Vote) rally at Antioch Baptist Church. I worked in the staff hold (a small carpeted room with a couch, soft chairs and food) and read headlines off the wires to Dee Dee Myers, who phoned her office to find out what was on the evening TV network newscasts.

The following day, we flew one hour from Andrews Air Force Base to Rhode Island for our third straight political day trip.

Our first stop in Providence was the Portuguese Social Club, where the President spoke to a group of about 650 senior citizens. (Rhode Island has the country's fourth-largest population of residents sixty-five and older.) Most of us waited or worked downstairs in the staff hold, which was the club's bar. Then it was a ten-minute motorcade to the Rhode Island Convention Center, where we stayed for several hours while the President conducted live radio and satellite TV interviews, getting into the Des Moines and Minneapolis/St. Paul media markets, where we'd be heading that weekend. His holding room adjoined ours, so when he took a nap later, the lights in both rooms dimmed.

That evening, we all headed downstairs to a coordinated campaign fund-raising rally with Rhode Island Democratic candidates. I had to laugh when gubernatorial candidate Myrth York spoke. She had the classic nasal Rhode Island accent. (Granted, anybody like me who speaks with an Arkansas accent—"y'all," "fixin' to"—has little room to talk.) I had a friend who lived in Rhode Island for two years. She used to imitate that Northeastern accent, and it was so annoying I'd make her stop. But Myrth York really talked like that. The sound system went out for ten minutes during the event, putting a damper on an otherwise upbeat rally with about 2,000 in attendance.

On the way out, a local golf club craftsman presented a handmade driver to the President, complete with the Seal of the President and "Bill Clinton" on it. It was an impressive piece of work, and the President was very appreciative. As a long line of volunteer motorcade drivers (and aides wanting to go home) stood nearby, the President talked earnestly with the man and posed for photos with him.

We left the next morning, Thursday, and wouldn't be back until Monday night. It was my last domestic trip, and I was glad. I was so burned out by that point that I was just going through the motions.

We flew one hour and five minutes to Albany, New York, to start our magical misery tour at the State University of New York-Albany campus. The President attended an interactive technology event as he and New York Governor Mario Cuomo talked with students at three other sites, promoting education and the information superhighway. Backstage, the Cuomo campaign staff instructed a TV crew, which was videotaping Cuomo with the President for use in a campaign commercial.

Afterward, we headed to the SUNY-Albany gymnasium in the Physical Education Building, which was filled with red, white and blue balloons and signs and a noisy, excited crowd of about 1,500. The tiny gym was jammed for the Get Out the Vote rally. Afterward, the staff ate lunch (sandwiches, chips, brownies, soft drinks) in the wrestling room upstairs. In the coaches' office, I dialed in on my laptop to check the wires, gobbling a little lunch before dashing to the motorcade about 1:30 P.M. on a sunny day. (On the wires: Susan Smith arrested in Union City, South Carolina, for the murder of her two toddler sons, whose bodies were found in a submerged car she had been driving.)

Then it was back aboard Air Force One for a two-hour, thirty-minute flight to Des Moines, Iowa, where we held a rally in an airport hangar on a cloudy, windy, chilly day. (Like a doofus, I'd forgotten my overcoat back in my Old Executive Office Building office.) The President spoke to about 1,000 people, with the limo and Air Force One behind him in the distance.

Then the motorcade took us fifteen minutes downtown to the Savery Hotel, where the President worked a fund-raiser reception crowd and conducted more radio and TV interviews for Seattle, Minneapolis, Detroit and Los Angeles. Then we headed downstairs for a rally for Iowa Attorney General and gubernatorial candidate Bonnie Campbell. The President's speech became a little longer and less focused as the day wore on and as he got more tired. But it was still basically the same stump speech, extolling Democratic achievements of the previous two years and warning of the effects of returning Congressional control to the Republicans.

Finally we flew one hour and ten minutes north to Duluth, Minnesota. At the airport, we landed in the dark to find sub-forty-degree temperatures on the Iron Range. A huge crowd waited at the airport to shake hands with the President, and our motorcade passed what must have been half the town lining the streets on our way to the Holiday Inn.

Friday morning our hotel advance staff pretty much took care of the clips, so I monitored NBC's "Today" show and enjoyed a continental breakfast and a view of Duluth out the staff office window. Located next to Lake Superior, Duluth is very hilly, with Victorian houses, looking sort of like a little San Francisco.

After the President conducted satellite TV and phone radio interviews with some San Francisco and Los Angeles stations, we left on a cloudy but dry day for a ten-minute motorcade to the University of Minnesota-Duluth gymnasium. The President spoke at a rally for Democratic Senate candidate Ann Wynia of Minnesota. The liberal

Democratic Farm Labor crowd of the 8th District cheered the President, and we headed back to the airport about noon local time.

We then flew three hours and forty-five minutes to Los Alamitos Naval Air Station in Orange County, California. The President announced the creation of aircraft-related jobs in an event on the tarmac with California Democratic Senators Dianne Feinstein and Barbara Boxer. The President took a helicopter to his next event. Some of the staff boarded vans for a rush-hour drive on the southern California freeways, past the famous Hollywood sign in the distance, on our way to City Hall. By the time the rally started, night had fallen. Huge temporary outdoor lights illuminated the cheering, sign-waving crowd.

Saturday morning I had to get the clips produced and delivered before a 7:45 A.M. departure to the Anaheim Convention Center, where the President addressed perhaps a couple thousand people at the National Association of Realtors conference.

The staff hold was a tiny, cold, sterile dressing room in a corner of the convention center. I stood in the back of the large arena during the President's address, which was less campaign-related and less partisan than others on the trip and which focused on the economy. At one point he listed the Administration's actions on the economy and then mentioned a series of positive economic indicators. "Now, where I come from, we say if you see a turtle settin' on a fence post, chances are it didn't get there by itself," he said. The crowd was silent for just a moment, and then broke into laughter and applause as he said, "Now, you think about it."

I noted the scoreboard overhead and got the impression that the arena was normally used for roller derby. Afterward, the President attended a meet-and-greet with local supporters and then conducted radio interviews with Los Angeles and New York stations in a dressing room next door to the staff hold. I listened on a phone in our hold (we had an open line back to Media Affairs aides in Washington) shortly after lunch for the staff finally arrived. On the way to the freeway, we drove past Disneyland and could see the Matterhorn rising above Anaheim on a perfect sunny Saturday afternoon.

From Los Alamitos Naval Air Station, we flew one hour and five minutes to Alameda Naval Air Station near the San Francisco Bay, where the weather was cold and wet. Without an umbrella, I tried to dodge raindrops, dashing down the sidewalk from the motorcade to the entrance to Oakland's Henry J. Kaiser Convention Center. As sometimes happened upon arrival, the President stopped to shake hands with some greeters. We caught up to him too quickly and had to hold momentarily until he went inside.

I quickly found the holding room, which was a dressing room with food, bottled water, soft drinks, phones and a printer. My laptop's internal modem squealed, connecting to the White House wire service computer system. In the blue "Urgent" window was a story that former President Reagan had released a letter saying he had been diagnosed with Alzheimer's disease. I checked, and Dee Dee Myers already knew about it; the President later mentioned it at the beginning of his remarks. The crowd, which hadn't heard about Reagan's illness, reacted with shock.

The President addressed a large, lively crowd at a campaign rally. Senator Boxer and state treasurer and gubernatorial candidate Kathleen Brown flew from southern California with us and were on stage, but Senator Feinstein stayed in Los Angeles to woo swing voters in her re-election campaign against multimillionaire Michael Huffington. The President delivered another strong stump speech, and rap star/actress Queen Latifah arrived at the end after being delayed by her commercial flight connections. Then the motorcade hauled us twenty-five minutes across the Bay Bridge in a downpour to the familiar Fairmont Hotel.

In the twenty-third-floor staff office, I thought it fitting that since the Fairmont was my first overnight site, there I was on my last domestic trip. But due to the last-minute scheduling of the trip, there weren't enough rooms at the Fairmont for everyone. So I got bumped to the Holiday Inn several blocks away, on Kearney Street. Shuttles between the two allegedly set up for us didn't exist. I was angry, but there wasn't any point in complaining to anyone on the advance team because it wouldn't change anything, and I figured it was my last domestic trip anyway. So I trudged without an umbrella down the hilly sidewalks in a downpour, arriving at the Holiday Inn soaked.

The Holiday Inn's alarm clock didn't go off Sunday morning, and I was awakened by the ringing phone. Larry Sampas in my Washington office called to say the staff office's fax machine wasn't answering and he couldn't send me the clips until I fixed it. So I showered, dressed and packed, only to find that the roof had leaked overnight and that my wet suit from the previous night, which I'd hung over a chair, was even soggier than before. I muttered under my breath and packed it anyway.

I quickly trudged up the steep San Francisco hills as a light, steady rain fell. I had to stop twice in the early-morning darkness and catch my breath. After cranking out the clips, I perused the Sunday papers, ate bagels and muffins and drank some orange juice. Other staffers, some in fluffy white Fairmont bathrobes, sat around the staff office doing the same thing. The President went to a church too small for us to accompany him.

Then it was on to the airport and a one-hour, forty-minute flight to Seattle around noon. We found cool and windy but sunny weather upon arrival, the rain there having halted shortly before we arrived, we were told. We were driven fifteen minutes downtown to an outdoor Get Out the Vote rally near Pike Place Market, the same scene as a huge 1992 rally late in the campaign. I stood on the street, behind the stage, overlooking lovely Puget Sound and its surrounding mountains.

Afterward, the President walked to the nearby Market Place North office building and taped an appearance on "Larry King Live." We sat in an adjacent office, quietly watching on a monitor. After checking the wires on my laptop in the press office, it was on to the motorcade, noting how cold the weather had turned after dark.

"Chit, don't you have a coat?" asked Jeremy Gaines (press assistant), who stood awaiting departure with the press pool.

"Back in my office," I answered with a shrug.

The motorcade then took us back to King County Airport. After a two-hour, fifty-five-minute flight to Minneapolis, we arrived at the Minneapolis Hilton and Towers after midnight.

In the staff office the next morning, some of the First Lady's staff, who had arrived with her the previous night, joined us for the usual juice-and-muffins breakfast with the morning news shows on TV in the background. DNC Chairman David Wilhelm was there as well.

"Well, David," I told him, "I know there's at least one state you don't have to worry about today. Just like the President and the First Lady, I voted absentee in the governor's race back in Arkansas."

"Good," Wilhelm replied. "Put a stake in Sheffield's heart," he said in reference to Republican gubernatorial challenger Sheffield Nelson, who also had lost the 1990 race to then-Governor Clinton.

The first event was an early-morning rally for Senate candidate Ann Wynia at North Hennepin Community College in nearby Brooklyn Park. Afterward we headed to the motorcade and rode thirty-five minutes to the plane.

We arrived in Flint, Michigan, on a sunny, windy day and headed to the University of Michigan-Flint gymnasium for a mid-day rally for Senate candidate Bob Carr. An enormous American flag adorned the wall behind the stage. I worked in the staff hold, which was a carpeted women's dressing room with orange lockers. I ate a delicious catered lunch while working on my laptop.

After another fifteen-minute motorcade back to the plane, we flew one hour and forty minutes to Wilmington, Delaware, for one final rally. Aside from the gubernatorial race there, the Philadelphia TV market included Wilmington, and we had a Senate campaign in Pennsylvania, where incumbent Harris Wofford needed all the help he could get. The outdoor event was held at downtown Rodney Square, and the weather was cold.

The traveling staff hung out in a recreational vehicle parked on the street behind the stage. Bruce Lindsey laid down on his back on the bed during the President's speech and looked at his watch. "This is the twenty-five-minute version," he said. "He must be tired."

On Air Force One back to Andrews, the crew brought out a cake and champagne, and we gathered in the conference room to say goodbye to Wendy Smith, who was ending her last trip as trip director. The President and First Lady were there, and the President stood in the doorway talking about the next day's elections with David Wilhelm and Harold Ickes. The mood at the end of the five-day, seven-state campaign swing was tired but upbeat. We knew we'd take some losses since the party in power always does during off-year elections. But we expected to be able to hang on to slim majorities in at least one chamber of Congress.

We were wrong, of course. The mood in Washington would change drastically, and I would be getting out of town just in time.

What's the "Western White House"?
My first visit to the White House, with my cousin Ron Smith (left), was during a family vacation in August 1971. President Nixon was vacationing in San Clemente, California—much to the annoyance of a certain eight year old.

Cheering for "The Comeback Kid"
Early returns from the 1992 New Hampshire primary showed Bill Clinton narrowly trailing Paul Tsongas. I was among the Clinton supporters at the Arkansas Democratic Party headquarters watching CNN's coverage. (Arkansas Democrat-Gazette, Stanton Briedenthal)

"*Don't Stop Thinking About Tomorrow*"
Fleetwood Mac's song served as a backdrop for key 1992 campaign moments. Here confetti falls after Governor Clinton secured the nomination at the Democratic convention at Madison Square Garden.

The Ears Have It
Catherine Cornelius and Jeff Eller (wearing Mickey Mouse ears, for some reason) at the 1992 Democratic convention. Eller would become White House Director of Media Affairs. He envisioned a real-time wire service computer system that would allow the traveling staff to have access to all breaking news, and I ended up being in charge of it.

Trying to Change the Country

That's me with Press Secretary Dee Dee Myers in her campaign office. Myers was the first person I met on the campaign staff. I went to work for her in January 1992, and stayed until we left the White House within a month of each other at the end of 1994. I was always impressed with her energy, enthusiasm and sense of humor.

"And They Have Earned This"

President-Elect Clinton and Vice President-Elect Gore celebrate their 1992 victory at the Old State House in Little Rock. A few of us campaign staffers stood fifteen feet away as Clinton thanked his "brilliant, aggressive, unconventional but always winning campaign staff" on live national television.

WELCOME TO WASHINGTON
Keith Boykin (far right) and I were roaming the halls of the Old Executive Office Building the week after the inauguration when who should we run into but President Clinton and Vice President Gore. (Director of Administration and Management David Watkins is behind the . President.) Boykin and I were discussing staffing for our Offfice of News Analysis when we crossed paths with our bosses, who were visiting with their new staffs. (White House Photo Office, Bob McNeely)

"MY FELLOW AMERICANS..."
On Inauguration Day, we roamed all over the White House to check it out. Everything seemed so much smaller in person that it appears on television. Here I'm posing behind the podium in the briefing room normally used by the Press Secretary.

MEETING THE PRESIDENT
President Clinton shakes hands with my dad, Ray Chitester, at the
Indiana Convention Center. I'm answering my cellular phone, which
happened to ring just as I was about to achieve a personal highlight
by introducing the President of the United States to my father. (White
House Photo Office, Barb Kinney)

ABOARD THE USS GEORGE WASHINGTON

White House aides Pat Griffin (legislative affairs), Will Itoh (National Security Council), Christine Varney (cabinet secretary), Mike Lufrano (scheduling and advance), myself and John Podesta (staff secretary) cross the English Channel. Those are F-18 fighter jets on the carrier's flight deck behind us. We were on the way to Normandy to commemorate the 50th anniversary of D-Day. (White House Photo Office, Bob McNeely)

"WHAT DO THEY WANT ME TO SAY?"
President Clinton confers with Deputy Press Secretary Arthur Jones aboard Air Force One somewhere over Ohio as I look on. Deputy Chief of Staff Harold Ickes is behind the President. Republican New York Mayor Rudolph Giuliani had endorsed Democratic Governor Mario Cuomo, and the White House press pool wanted the President's reaction. (White House Photo Office, Sharon Farmer)

ANOTHER CITY, ANOTHER EVENT
White House Trip Director Wendy Smith talks with an unidentified advance staffer during a 1994 Congressional campaign rally in Seattle. Smith had a particularly difficult job, but handled the pressure well.

"Mr. President!"
The traveling White House press pool watches from the tarmac in Michigan as the President and First Lady descend the front stairs of Air Force One. About a dozen members of the pool, selected on a rotating basis, traveled aboard Air Force One.

Briefing the Press
Press Secretary Dee Dee Myers answers questions from the traveling press pool on the tarmac in Michigan. We were campaigning for Congressional Democrats in the 1994 mid-term elections.

KEEPING IN TOUCH
*Senior adviser Bruce Lindsey, one of the President's
closest aides, calls his office from the staff hold during
a 1994 campaign rally on the campus of the University of Michigan at Flint. Lindsey and I were often the
only aides in the staff holding rooms. He'd talk on one
phone, and I'd use another to dial in to the White
House wire service computer system on my laptop
computer.*

9▸A Ticket to Ride

ONE DAY, A FEW WEEKS BEFORE CHRISTMAS, I found out the President and First Lady had decided to visit Arkansas for a couple days of vacation, followed by a long holiday weekend at Hilton Head Island, South Carolina, where they would go to the annual Renaissance Weekend they had attended for years.

Director of Media Affairs Jeff Eller and I discussed how we'd keep the President and traveling aides informed of news stories. "I'd better go," I said, even if it was over the holidays.

"Do you *want* to go?" he asked.

Does a dog have fleas? I thought. I *always* want to go. "Sure," I said.

In later months, that wouldn't always be the case. But having been in Washington less than a year at that point, overwhelming exhaustion, frustration and general burnout hadn't yet set in.

Presidential vacations were a chance for the staff to get a break as well. Of course, some aides always were needed on site. I usually took off a week or two during August, when the President went to Martha's Vineyard and all of Washington virtually shut down. But other vacations, such as the one to Arkansas and South Carolina, I performed my usual duties on site.

Vacations, unlike the normal trips, were fun. So was attending sporting events, which we did on vacations with the President.

Two days after Christmas, Jeff Eller, Dave Seldin (press assistant),

Ralph Alswang (staff photographer) and I—virtually the only White House aides on the trip—left mid-afternoon in a van for Andrews Air Force Base. The Old Executive Office Building was empty that holiday week.

Partly because so few aides were on the President's and First Lady's personal trip to Arkansas, we took a forty-two-seat C-9 instead of one of the 747s. I was reading one of the weekly news magazines on board while we awaited the President's arrival. As I flipped through a story about Arkansas state troopers' allegations that they arranged for and then covered up then-Governor Clinton's supposed romantic liaisons, Dave Seldin said, "Chit, you won't want to be reading that when they come on board." I knew that, of course, but it made me think. I read literally thousands of stories a week about the President. But sometimes, even though I worked for him, it was easy to forget that there was a real person being written and talked about.

Unusually, there were no name cards on our seats, so we sat in the small front section. But then, when the President arrived, he had more family and friends with him than we'd expected. Even though there was room, he understandably wanted the front cabin solely for himself and his guests.

So after takeoff, I moved to the large rear section of the plane, behind the press pool. Howie, the chief steward, later told me he got chewed out because of that. "I'm not blaming *you, sir…*" Howie said, and I thought, Well, then why tell me? I mean, why didn't somebody *tell* us where to sit? Now I'll have to stay out of the President's sight for a while, I thought.

In the President's boyhood hometown of Hot Springs, an enthusiastic crowd with signs greeted him at the airport soon after dark. He shook plenty of hands, and then we went to dinner at Rocky's Corner, across the street from Oaklawn horse racing track. Staff and press sat in a separate room from the President and his family, watching "Monday Night Football" on an unseasonably warm sixty-five-degree evening.

Afterward, we tagged along as he went bowling at the local lanes of his youth, slipping into rented shoes and still wearing a tie. The staff stayed overnight on Bathhouse Row in the Arlington Hotel, an old place without soundproofing. The President stayed at his mother's house beside Lake Hamilton. Hot Springs is a neat little tourist town that includes a national park.

After I produced and distributed the clips the next morning, the motorcade drove the hour northeast to Little Rock on a wet, windy, raw day with temperatures in the mid-thirties. (A cold front had moved through overnight.) In Little Rock, the motorcade drove not far from my house, and I thought, Wouldn't that be something—to take the Presidential motorcade through your own neighborhood?

The President, First Lady and Chelsea went to their dentist in west Little Rock, and a few of us on the staff ate lunch with some of the press pool at a Chinese restaurant across the street. Then the President attended a reception downtown at the Old State House. I stood in the press office next door at the Excelsior Hotel and tried to figure out how I was going to get to Fayetteville. I was manifested for a car that, it turned out, didn't exist. (There were no trip books, few advance staff and of course everything was at the President's whim because the trip was his personal time.) I got on the two-way radio and also worked the phones, and some of our staff came to my aid and got me on the press plane.

Low-lying fog in northwest Arkansas caused us to land at nearby Rogers instead of Fayetteville. The reporters, photographers and technicians whined all the way about the weather and safety. I'd never seen such a group of wimpy fliers in my life. After a short drive to Bud Walton Arena on the University of Arkansas campus, we were issued press credentials and ushered into the press entrance. We entered during the first half and sat in the front row, across from the team's benches.

The Razorbacks decimated poor Texas Southern. Afterward, we all headed to the Hogs' locker room. The President and First Lady chatted with the coaches and players and posed for photos. Everybody seemed to have fun.

The President and First Lady stayed at their friends' house in Fayetteville, while the staff stayed at the Hilton downtown.

The next morning I headed to where the President was staying. The Secret Service, as was typical, rented the house next to the President for its operations. I went there and dialed in briefly (very little news that early in the day, especially during the holidays) and then sat around with the agents in the living room, watching trashy TV talk shows, awaiting news of the First Family's impending departure.

The motorcade stopped briefly at the Ozark Mountain Smoke-house en route to the airport, and then we flew to Hilton Head Island, South Carolina, on a sunny day. The President and First Lady were taken to the multimillion dollar house where they were staying, and the rest of us then went to the hotel on the beach.

I was up at 5:30 A.M. the next morning to produce the clips and get them over to the President and First Lady with the advance team. After that, I wasn't really needed much. So I just hung out in the staff office and dialed in, monitoring the wires and watching CNN to see what was going on. But with Washington deserted, there wasn't much news.

That afternoon I went for a walk around the resort. There was a lot to do in summer, but the weather was too cold, and the only folks I knew were all working. It was a good thing I was there to do the clips, because if I weren't, they wouldn't get done. But I couldn't help but feel a little guilty for being there. I kept my two-way radio turned on in case I was needed. Every once in a while I'd hear somebody else on the radio: "Chitester, Chitester—Eller."

"Go, Eller."

"Will you meet me in the staff room?"

"Roger, copy."

On New Year's Eve, I spent a routine morning producing the clips and sending them to the President's rented house with an advance staffer. Even though I had a beige nametag admitting me to the Renaissance Weekend workshop sessions, I had no interest in all that baby-boomer, New Age, touchy-feely stuff. The President attended at least one session.

That afternoon the President played some touch football on the hard sand of the beach. The field was less than half a regulation field, with about twice as many players as regulation, many of them little kids. I looked around the crowd and didn't see any metal-detecting magnetometers. "The President and two hundred of his closest unmagged friends," White House Communications Agency Commander Colonel Tom Hawes said, as we stood watching.

Two Secret Service agents in shorts and T-shirts were on the "field" at all times with the President, looking especially concerned when he took a tumble. The President played quarterback, of course, and didn't do too badly, all things considered. On defense, he leaped and intercepted a pass. There was such a jumble of bodies out there it was kind of ridiculous. But he seemed to be having a good time.

The advance staff, Jeff Eller, Ralph Alswang and I went out to dinner that night. It was a fun time. We'd been talking in the morning communications meetings recently about how approachable the President is, how huggy he is. (The previous Sunday night a five-year-old boy at the Kennedy Center had broken free of his parents and ran all the way down the aisle to the President and gave him a big hug.) So we decided he was President Barney, after the popular children's purple dinosaur. At dinner, we sang "Ruffles and Flourishes," the traditional horn segment that precedes "Hail to the Chief." And then we sang the Barney song: "I love you, you love me/We're a hap-py fam-i-ly...."

There was a New Year's Eve party back at the hotel, with the President in attendance. I saw him across the room and barely made it to midnight before going to bed.

New Year's Day fell on a weekend, but in the insular world of traveling with the President, it was hard to tell. Once inside the bubble, White House travel was almost like going into a sensory deprivation experiment. All that affected us was what happened in that little world.

That night I went out to dinner again with the traveling and advance staffs, probably about fifteen of us. Jeff Eller got started on his barnyard animal imitations and had everyone cracking up: "Do the donkey noise, Jeff."

After several windy days with temperatures in the forties, Sunday morning was warmer and sunny. I cranked out the clips and then ordered breakfast from room service and sat at a glass table with the sliding patio door open, waves crashing below my third-floor balcony and sea birds squawking as they flew nearby. I read the local papers and *The New York Times* and monitored news on television before departure.

A few months later, I was walking down the outdoor Old Executive Office Building steps to West Executive Drive when I passed Mike Lufrano (scheduling and advance), who put together all the aircraft manifests on Presidential trips.

"Are you going to Dallas this weekend?" he asked.

"Yeah, I was planning on it."

"What about next week?" (on the President's vacation to California), he asked.

"Well, yeah. Why? Is that a problem?"

"It might raise a few eyebrows," he said, noting that staff was being kept to a minimum.

But it was decided I should go, as usual, to provide morning news clippings and to monitor breaking news to keep the President and top aides on site informed.

Later that week, the President went to Pope Air Force Base in Fort Bragg, North Carolina, but I didn't find out until he'd already left. It was a last-minute addition to the schedule (in the wake of an airplane crash that killed some crew members), and nobody had told me. When I boarded Air Force One later, a few of the military and medical aides and Air Force One crew said they'd looked for me and that I'd been missed.

The plane came back to Washington, and the rest of us left at 3:00 P.M. for Andrews. The plane was full, including a lot of Arkansans getting rides to the Hogs' NCAA Tournament game against Tulsa in Dallas. Some aides went to the game; others went to the wedding rehearsal dinner for Roger Clinton, the President's brother.

The rest of us rode to the Mansion on Turtle Creek, which turned out to be arguably the nicest place we ever stayed. It was a five-star hotel, and there were tea and snacks awaiting us in our rooms, along with bottles of Evian water and ice in the ice bucket, with handwritten notes welcoming guests by name. I went to the staff office briefly and then returned to my room to order room service and watch the Hogs beat overmatched, outsized Tulsa.

The next morning I managed to get news clips delivered while most aides were having breakfast there in the staff office.

We then rode five minutes in a moderate, constant drizzle to Scottish Rite Hospital for Children, where the President toured and then delivered his weekly radio address. I dialed in from a staff hold overlooking a grassy area with trees and the interstate in the background, everything wet, as I drank a small glass of orange juice and ate a muffin and a danish. Upon departure in the staff van, I could hear radio traffic: "Chitester, Chitester—Eller."

Jeremy Gaines (press assistant) answered, "Eller, I don't think Chitester is on radio."

I picked up the radio in the van and said, "That's okay, Jeremy, I've got it. Go ahead, Jeff."

"When we get back, come straight to the staff office. We've got something that needs attention."

"Roger, copy."

We returned to the hotel about 11:00 A.M. and I began to track down a *Time* magazine story in the upcoming issue that claimed George Stephanopoulos (senior adviser) and Treasury Chief of Staff Josh Steiner had a possibly improper conversation about who was heading the Resolution Trust Corporation's investigation of Madison Guaranty Savings and Loan. It was another potentially damaging Whitewater story, and the staff and press were focusing on it.

That afternoon I didn't go to Roger Clinton's wedding. It turned out that about everybody else on the traveling staff did, but I didn't think I should. It was a private ceremony, and I didn't foresee much I could do to help there. So I decided to take a stroll through the residential area surrounding the hotel on a humid, warm, overcast late spring afternoon in Texas.

Later I headed back to the hotel and upstairs to the staff office, where Bruce Lindsey asked for the latest news, so I downloaded a few relevant stories for him and Jeff Eller. The President stopped by in his tuxedo (his suite was across the hall), looked around and said to no one in particular, "I'm gonna go put on some jeans." I went to bed soon afterward, but the President stayed up late and played cards.

The next morning the President stopped by the staff office and read *The Dallas Morning News* sports section, glasses down at the tip of his nose: "Look at this—Arizona shot forty-one free throws…and Missouri shot fifteen. That's not right. The referees shouldn't be in the game that much."

He talked briefly with Jeff Eller about what was in the news, and Eller asked if he wanted to see the clips. "Not unless there's something I need to see," the President said.

"No," Eller said. That little exchange reminded me how important it was that I do my job, to support Eller and the other senior staffers.

The motorcade left the hotel loading dock about 2:30 P.M. for Reunion Arena. What a way to beat game-day traffic! We pulled up to the entrance near the media's work area and found our seats. The President and about two dozen others sat at mid-court, and he was interviewed at halftime by Jim Nance of CBS, which was carrying the game live. In my khakis and red shirt, I sat with fellow Arkansans Ashley Bell (advance) and Kris Engskov (travel office), just past the Hogs' bench. We chanted "H-O-G-S" and clapped and cheered and had a great time. I was wearing my two-way radio with earpiece, but the crowd noise was so great, I couldn't hear any chatter. The Hogs went ahead early and held on to win, 76-68.

Elated, we dashed to the staff van (in the motorcade, the President called Alabama Governor Jim Folsom regarding tornadoes which earlier in the day had killed nineteen in Alabama) and headed back to Love Field. Air Force One took us to North Island Naval Air Station, located on the Coronado peninsula across the bay from San Diego. We had very few aides aboard. Two advance staffers were in the guest section, Jeff Eller, Jeremy Gaines, Kelly Craighead (First Lady's trip director), Helen Dickey (Chelsea advance) and I were in the staff section, Colonel Jim Reed (National Security Council) was in the senior staff room and Andrew Friendly (personal aide) was in the conference room. Normally, we traveled with a lot more staff.

We ate salad, teriyaki chicken over rice, roll and apple pie while watching a movie during the two-hour, forty-five-minute flight. Night had fallen when we landed. The motorcade took the President and First Lady to the vacated mansion of U.S. Ambassador (to Switzerland) Larry Lawrence, while the rest of us went to the Hotel del Coronado, which Lawrence owned.

I delivered clips the next morning to fellow aides' doors, strolling around the Hotel Del, a National Historic Landmark with red-shingled spires, ornate woodwork, a well-manicured courtyard and Victorian gazebos. Since it opened February 19, 1888, fourteen U.S. Presidents had stayed there, in addition to such early guests as Joseph Pulitzer, L. Frank Baum, Mae West, Greta Garbo, Jack Dempsey and Babe Ruth.

After delivering the clips, I ate breakfast in the Crown Room, where on September 3, 1970, President Nixon hosted the largest state dinner ever held outside of Washington for Mexican President Gustavo Diaz Ordaz. A half-dozen aides enjoyed muffins, ham, bacon, sausage, hash browns, fresh fruit and made-to-order omelets, with a white-hatted chef flipping four at a time in skillets over blue flames.

That afternoon I sat around the pool in seventy-degree weather, military planes overhead flying to the nearby naval base. That evening a bunch of us headed to San Diego's Gaslight District to Dick's Last Resort, part of a restaurant chain owned by Debi Schiff (VIP lobby receptionist) and her husband. It was a huge place, with brick and wood, very low-scale and unpretentious with long tables, and very loud. Bras hung behind the bar, and there were thirteen condom machines in the men's room. The band played 1970s classic rock. We ordered buckets of crab legs, buckets of ribs, buckets of fries and ice-filled buckets of quart beer bottles, running up a $400-plus tab.

Lawrence ("not Larry"), our approximately six-foot-six, 300-pound waiter in T-shirt and shorts, was hilarious. At one point he loudly blew a referee's whistle, pointed at a guy at the end of our table and yelled, "Ladies and gentlemen, I'm sorry to do that, but this man just ordered a *Zima!*" The waiters and customers tossed rolled-up napkins at each other.

Later, Lawrence danced on a chair, hip-pumping and gyrating. We goaded Kathy McKiernan (press assistant) to join him before she quickly sat down, giggling and embarrassed. I sat next to Josh Silverman (media affairs), a former high school football player and former campaign co-worker. Everybody kept saying things like, "That Josh can *eat.*"

Later we (Kris Engskov, actually) decided it was Ashley Adams' (travel office) birthday. So Lawrence brought her a birthday drink. "Tap it," he told her. When she did, he lifted the inverted plastic cup atop it, and an inflated condom sprung up. She squealed and everybody laughed as Lawrence sprayed whipped cream over it. It was that kind of place, and that kind of night.

Tuesday I was up early again for the clips, and then a breakfast buffet and made-to-order omelets (ham, cheese and mushrooms). About a dozen or more of us went to dinner that night at Brewski's across the San Diego Harbor in the Gaslight District. It was a clean, light, yuppified microbrewery. Kim Hopper, a former media affairs staffer living in California, joined us. She wanted a regular American beer, and Jeff Eller yelled, "No! You can *not* have a Bud Light."

We then walked a few doors down the street to Fat's, a pool hall with chrome and purple neon, and shot some pool.

The next day I rented a bike and went for a ride around the 4,100-acre Coronado peninsula. It only took about forty-five minutes to pedal that old Schwinn-like bike with balloon tires and no gear shift around the peninsula. I saw residential areas with nice little California-style houses on tiny, neat lawns.

Later, I passed through the staff office and found a few young aides were going to Tijuana, about twelve miles south. So Jeremy Gaines, Chad Griffin, Kathy McKiernan (press assistants), Kris Engskov and I loaded a minivan and parked on the U.S. side, walking over a bridge and making jokes about what would happen if we got into trouble. We had the pager number of the lead Secret Service agent and phone numbers of some staffers, just in case. "Do you think the President would send in a helicopter for us? I mean, you know, if we were like, taken hostage or something?" It was a pretty silly but amusing conversation.

We strolled past sidewalk vendors and shops with questionable food and souvenir junk and onto Avenida de Revolución, several blocks of bars, restaurants, fast food joints and strip bars. All evening we were "amigos" to the guys who tried to hand us advertising fliers: "Amigos! No cover charge! Free tequila!"

We finally went into a place with booming disco music, sitting outside on a balcony overlooking the street to munch nachos and sip Coronas. The place was much like all of Tijuana: tacky, dirty, hot, loud, crass, cheap and disgusting. That, of course, is its charm. It was full of high-schoolers and young military recruits who drank shots and danced to booming disco songs.

We finally left after midnight, passing through U.S. Customs at San Ysidro, where President Clinton's photo hung on the wall.

The President went across the San Diego-Coronado Bay Bridge to San Diego the next day to sign the Goals 2000 education bill. After breakfast, I walked down the street to the beachfront residence where he and the First Lady and Chelsea were staying. I didn't bring my laptop computer because I didn't figure there'd be much need for it. But when I got there, Jeff Eller said the stock market was going up and down like a yo-yo (I'd compiled the clips but hadn't yet dialed in) and said he needed to see some coverage. So I traipsed back to the hotel and picked up my computer, getting back to the street just as the motorcade passed. If it had stopped at the light, I could've hopped in the Staff 1 van, but of course we didn't stop at traffic lights. So I went back inside and tried to reach Eller via pager and fax. I watched the event live on local TV, and the President returned after lunch on a cool, cloudy afternoon.

The weather was cool and cloudy again the next day. After a routine morning of producing and distributing the news clippings to the White House staff, at lunch I strolled Orange Boulevard in jeans and a light jacket, picking up the local paper. I ambled into Danny's Palm Bar & Grill, a small, narrow dark place with a couple of booths in back. HOME OF THE SLAM BURGER, the sign said. A waitress wearing shorts and a sweatshirt brought me a greasy half-pound cheeseburger with fries and a Coke as I read baseball season previews in the *San Diego Union-Tribune.*

Not long after I returned, our press office declared a full lid (meaning we didn't expect to make any more news for the day), so we were free to take off. Since the President was in Coronado on vacation, no one expected there to be much news that week. In fact, he had signed the education bill earlier in the week because the ten-day period following Congressional passage was almost up, meaning the bill would've automatically become law without the President's signature. But since we wanted to make a big deal out of it (because it was our initiative), we scheduled an event.

I found Arthur Jones (deputy press secretary) in our temporary press office at the Hotel del Coronado and suggested we head to the veranda overlooking the ocean for screwdrivers or bloody marys.

"Something fresh and fruity, perhaps?" I suggested.

"I think you've already *had* something fresh and fruity," he said, laughing.

Jones was press secretary to Boston Mayor Raymond Flynn (later the U.S. Ambassador to the Vatican) and didn't work in the campaign. So I didn't know him until we both got to the White House. An African American and a Catholic, Jones was a tall guy with a mustache who had gotten married the previous fall. He was one of the few laid-back people on the staff, and always was really nice to me. I found myself laughing around him, and the way things went around the White House, that was a rare thing.

We sat outside sipping beers on the veranda, waves rolling onto the beach below, until the evening turned dark and cold. So we walked down the street for dinner at McP's, a casual pseudo-Irish place with a lit fireplace and Boston Bruins hockey on TV. We stopped in briefly at Danny's, listening to oldies on the jukebox, before getting back to the Hotel Del by 10:30 P.M.

The next morning I walked the clip packages a couple blocks down the street to the residence where the President was staying, past all the local gawkers and local TV crews held behind yellow police tape. Needing to dial in one last time and check the wires, I ducked into the mansion, where Colonel Tom Hawes led me into the Secret Service office (actually a small kitchen). I used one of their phone lines and dialed in to our wire service computer system back in Washington.

Then we stood on the street by the motorcade, awaiting the President's arrival after his morning round of golf. Josh King (communications/advance) had a basketball for the President to hold up as he boarded Air Force One for a photo opportunity. It was for his departure for the Final Four. We tossed the ball around and soon afterward drove only a mile or two down the street to North Island Naval Air Station to head for Charlotte, North Carolina, to watch Arkansas play Arizona.

We took off about 9:00 A.M. There were very few of us aboard. At one point, Will Itoh (National Security Council) had some papers in his hand and asked the President, as they walked past me in the staff section, "Do you want this basketball stuff?"

"No," said the President, not unpleasantly. Itoh was referring to the talking points I'd prepared on both games. But the President was such a fan apparently he figured he already knew all about them.

We landed in North Carolina to find sunny weather, warmer than San Diego had been. We were handed passes to the game and hung them around our necks as we boarded the motorcade for Charlotte Coliseum. The President and a few others headed to a luxury box, while I roamed, eventually standing next to the Hogwild Band. Arkansas finally pulled away from Arizona with eight minutes remaining and won to advance to the title game.

On the plane on the way back, I sat in the staff section with fellow Arkansans Marsha Scott (correspondence) and Helen Dickey. We waved our red pompons, sang the school song, cheered, called the Hogs ("Woo! Pig! Sooey!") and had a great time. Later, the President, still in his dark suit, and Secretary of the Interior Bruce Babbitt (former governor of Arizona) and his wife Hattie came back to the staff section. The President stood behind me, hand on my headrest, and spoke lavishly of Arizona's team. "We were lucky to win," he said. We munched baskets of peanuts, cheese nips and pretzels on the hour-long flight.

The President's vacation officially ended that Saturday night upon arriving in Washington. But we took the next day off for Easter. And the day after that, we attended Opening Day in baseball and the NCAA championship in basketball. In addition to going on Presidential vacations, going to major sporting events also was a highlight of traveling aboard Air Force One.

The President and First Lady attended the annual Easter Egg Roll on the South Lawn that morning. Bruce Lindsey kiddingly suggested that, with Whitewater allegations looming, we cancel the Easter egg hunt. Why, someone asked. "Because," he explained, "we have nothing to hide."

Our motorcade included the First Lady and her staff, who were on the way to Chicago so she could throw out the first ball at Wrigley Field. After our 9:30 A.M. departure aboard the staff bus, James Carville (the famous political consultant taking a rare trip with us) told stories about attending the recent Academy Awards ceremony. He had met actress and former *Playboy* model Anna Nicole Smith, and he told us she was fat. "Why, her ass was so wide she couldn't get through that door," he said in his loud, familiar Louisiana accent.

We loaded up the forty-two- and twelve-seat aircraft, with the President on the larger, primary plane. We landed at the downtown Burke Lakefront Airport, which has a shorter runway than Cleveland's main airport, necessitating that we forego the 747 and instead take two smaller planes. We landed within sight of Lake Erie, and the motorcade took us to nearby Jacobs Field, the brand-new home of the Indians.

We received credential stickers on the way into the stadium, and I stuck mine to my overcoat, computer bags slung over my shoulders. The President and a few aides and Secret Service agents headed to the clubhouse and dugout en route to the field. The rest of us walked to a luxury box, smelling sizzling meat and hearing the vendor's call of "cold beer" as we walked above a concessions area. Our skybox was in the right-field corner. Everybody was as excited as kids as we put on Indians' caps left for us on the table. We ate hot dogs and chicken, chips and popcorn and watched the pre-game ceremonies, including opening pitches by Hall of Famer Bob Feller and the President, whose throw from the pitcher's mound was a floater down the middle.

We sat outside briefly in the cold, admiring the great view of the city skyline, the huge scoreboard in left field and the bright green grass and unmarked infield dirt. But unbelievably, we couldn't see home plate from our seats. A section of the stands jutted out, blocking our view. How can you build a brand-new stadium and not know that? So we watched the game on TV, turning to the field when the ball was put into play.

We left in the eighth inning with Seattle's Randy Johnson pitching a no-hitter. But after most of us got to the motorcade (parked in the stadium's concrete garage area), we waited around as the President stayed to watch the Indians rally to tie. The motorcade took us to the Sheraton City Centre hotel, where the President conducted satellite interviews with half a dozen various media outlets and attended a meet-and-greet reception.

Upstairs, the staff hold was two ordinary adjoining hotel rooms, where we watched on TV as the Indians came back to win in eleven innings. Then it was back downstairs to the motorcade for a five-minute ride back to the airport. We were actually running ahead of schedule, which was unheard of. The President must have been excited about getting to Charlotte to see Arkansas play for the national championship.

After a one-hour, ten-minute flight, the backup plane landed across the tarmac from Air Force One. A few of us scampered past the Secret Service Counter Assault Team's black Chevrolet Suburban that always escorted the President, even aboard Air Force One on the tarmac, to board the motorcade and head to Charlotte Coliseum. Once there, I ducked in the same side entrance as on our previous visit, calling to Dee Dee Myers and Paul Begala (political consultant), who had never been there before: "The staff entrance is over here."

Inside, I wandered through the press row and found a couple college friends covering the Final Four for different newspapers. I took a seat at the end of the court, next to the Hogwild Band. Duke went up ten points with seventeen minutes to go, but as always the Hogs fought back. We cheered mightily when Scotty Thurman hit an incredible rainbow, a twenty-two-foot three-pointer with less than a minute remaining, the shot clock expiring and Duke's Antonio Lang all over him. The victory gave Arkansas its first national basketball championship.

As exciting as vacations and sporting events were, traveling with the President also provided other thrills, such as seeing famous faces. Other times White House aides would become inventive trying to stave off boredom brought on by the sheer monotony of the seemingly endless travel routine.

10▶A Sea of Faces

"JOLLY GLAD" TO DINE WITH THE PRIME MINISTER · BEVERLY HILLS: "WE DIDN'T HAVE A LOT OF THIS IN INDIANA" · NEW YORK: "GUESS WHO I JUST SAW" · TEXAS: "WE'RE REALLY HEADING INTO NUT COUNTRY TODAY" · "CAPTAIN HOOK" IN SHREVEPORT · "THE MOTHER OF ALL FARTS" IN NEW HAMPSHIRE

TRAVELING ABOARD AIR FORCE ONE provides an opportunity to view a seemingly endless variety of fresh faces, a cornucopia of American diversity. Everybody wants to meet the President. And celebrities are no exception.

But whether it was a celebrity-filled fund-raising cocktail party or a trip to a blue-collar factory assembly line, traveling with the President provided me with a chance to encounter people I otherwise might never have met.

Certainly that was the case when it came to meeting world leaders. One example came on a weekday in late summer. After concluding an event in St. Louis, we boarded two planes for a two-hour flight to Denver's Stapleton International Airport, where Pope John Paul II was to arrive. When His Holiness emerged from his red, white and green customized Alitalia 747 and descended the steps, it admittedly was impressive. John Hart (political affairs) was so excited he'd met the Pope that he called his mother from his cellular phone on the tarmac to tell her. "I know," his mother told him. "You're wearing a white shirt and a red tie. I just saw you on CNN."

And Susan Brophy (legislative affairs) was literally speechless when she met the Pope. When the President introduced her to the Pontiff, he hinted at her Boston accent, telling her to say something so the Pope (who speaks several languages) could guess where she was from. Said an awestruck Brophy: "Uhhh...." And immediately the Pope, in his Polish-accented English, said, "Boston."

Rain fell throughout the Pope's and President's speeches, and I went inside to check the wire services on my laptop computer. After I distributed the latest news to a couple of key staffers, the President boarded Marine One for nearby Regis University, where he and the Pope made statements to the media.

Another meeting with a world leader was more social. After a morning of Presidential events in Chicago, British Prime Minister John Major was scheduled to meet the President in Pittsburgh. We were running even later than usual, but Colonel Danny Barr, Presidential aircraft commander and Air Force One pilot, made up the time in the air, as he always seemed to.

When we got to Pittsburgh International Airport, we stood on the tarmac awaiting the Prime Minister's plane. Soon enough, a white Viscount 10 with the familiar British symbol (a red dot surrounded by white and blue circles) rolled down the runway. Clinton and Major walked a couple hundred yards together to the nearby hangar, eschewing the approximately forty-five-car motorcade.

A high school band was blasting away in the hangar. I walked into the staff hold, which was a maintenance workers' break room with a table, refrigerator and TV, all of them old and beat-up, and a Snap-On Tools calendar.

Just outside our door, in the hangar, Major told the crowd about his meeting with Clinton the previous summer at the Tokyo Group of Seven summit and mentioned "that second whisky." Said Major: "I'm jolly glad we had it, because I'm delighted to be here."

Major's grandfather worked in the steel mills near Pittsburgh and his father was in the circus. I mentioned that my grandfathers both worked in the steel mills near there, too. "Was your dad in the circus?" Bruce Lindsey (senior adviser) joked.

We then went to the Tin Angel restaurant atop Mount Washington, overlooking Pittsburgh and the Monongahela, Allegheny and Ohio rivers. Most of us waited there as Clinton and Major rode the Duquesne Incline up the side of the mountain. As they did, fireworks exploded, eye-level with where we stood. A ground display of U.S. and U.K. flags also went off in red, white and blue.

The White House and 10 Downing Street staffs sat together at long eight-seat tables. Our British counterparts were civil service secretaries who said some of the staff at 10 Downing Street had been there twenty-five years. As we sat talking, Clinton and Major walked in.

"Hey, y'all had a better view of the fireworks than we did," the President said, examining the beautiful view of the city, lights in buildings twinkling below. He and Major met each other's staffs. Major's secretaries introduced us to him, and he said something about "how hard these girls are on me." (For the record, the President is two inches taller than Major, who is six feet, one half inch.) As we sat dining, looking out at the view, I told Major's jet-lagged staff, "You know, this is *fun*. We don't do many things that are actually *fun*."

As we talked with our British counterparts, we tried to avoid topics like the campaign-related British search of Clinton's passport file, Major's support of Bush during the 1992 campaign and England's failure to qualify for the World Cup, which was to be played in the United States in a few months. We enjoyed the New York strip steak, gulping it down because Clinton and Major, dining downstairs, were served first and were ready to leave soon afterward.

Then the waitresses brought around the bills. The *what?* Granted, we were spoiled. When we traveled, people took very good care of us. So we got used to never having to reach for our wallets. But fifty bucks? It was no big deal because we got per diem money, of course. So we just handed our credit cards or cash to the waitress.

After we scrambled into the vans, some aides whined on the way to the airport. "Fifty bucks!" said Ralph Alswang (staff photographer), adding at least half-facetiously, "That's my food budget for a week. I can't eat for the rest of the week now."

Major and a couple of his security staff flew with us aboard Air Force One, followed by Major's plane. We got back to the White House about 12:30 A.M., the end of another eighteen-hour day on the road.

Sometimes the famous names and faces came from within the United States and were from the entertainment industry rather than the political realm. That was the case when we traveled to California, waking one early winter Saturday in a Los Angeles hotel.

The President delivered his weekly radio address live at 7:06 A.M.

local time. Afterward, nearly everybody who was in the room said it was a mistake for him to deliver it live when we were on the West Coast. President Clinton is *not* a morning person.

Around 9:00 A.M. the motorcade left the hotel for a twenty-five-minute drive to Rockwell International's Canoga Park Facility in the west San Fernando Valley, which was much like other plants we'd visited. The President's economic roundtable in the final assembly area went on for three and a half hours and was the most boring Presidential event I ever attended. I sat in the adjacent staff area behind some pipe-and-drape and dialed in to the wires, but there was no news of note. Some of us went outside to a small fenced parking lot beside railroad tracks and sat in the sun on a beautiful southern California day.

That night we attended a fund-raiser at Creative Arts Agency, a star-studded Beverly Hills cocktail party where the President spoke about Hollywood's responsibilities in portraying violence. We saw Chevy Chase, Teri Garr, Whoopi Goldberg, Quincy Jones, Nastassia Kinski and Donna Mills mingling among the guests. Shortly after we arrived, I noticed Will Itoh (National Security Council) chatting with Chevy Chase, whose talk show recently had been canceled for low ratings. Later I asked Itoh about it.

"Well," he said, "I started talking to the first attractive blonde I saw, and it turned out to be his wife." Noting recent improvement in the President's approval rating, Itoh also said, "I was going to say, 'Our guy's numbers look great. How about yours?' But I didn't."

Looking around at the glittering Hollywood celebrities sipping wine and chatting, I turned to fellow native Hoosier Jeff Eller (media affairs director). "We didn't have a lot of this in Indiana, did we?" I said. It was fascinating to see the mix of East Coast and West Coast, of Washington and Hollywood, of entertainment and politics. I stood there soaking in the scene and thought, This truly is, as John Kilzer sings, "a memory in the making."

Afterward the President attended a private fund-raising dinner at Marvin and Barbara Davis' house. About a half dozen of us had a staff van take us back to the plane, which was nearly full. I sat in the crew section for the four-hour, thirty-minute flight, putting on headphones and turning to the "Selection of the Month" channel on the Air Force One audio system. I listened to John Cougar Mellencamp's *Human Wheels* and fell asleep.

The audio system on board featured about a half-dozen channels—oldies rock, country, jazz, classical and others. Some of the traveling staff used to tell the story about President Clinton's first trip aboard Air Force One. One of his aides boarded the aircraft and heard Elvis Presley, a Clinton favorite, playing on the overhead speakers.

"Could you turn it...up?" the staffer asked.

"Oh, we've been *waiting* for you," a steward supposedly replied.

Whether we visited the West Coast or the East, celebrities flocked to the President. On a fall day, we left the White House for a two-day trip to New York and Boston. Air Force One rolled to a stop at TWA's familiar Gate 12 at New York's JFK International after a fifty-five-minute flight. We took helicopters to the Wall Street landing zone (also as usual) and motorcaded to the Sheraton (at least the second time we'd been there).

The President addressed the plenary session of a state-federal partnership at the Governor's Leadership Conference on the Future of the Economy in the Imperial Ballroom. Meanwhile, I worked upstairs in the staff hold, a normal hotel room with the furniture removed, with some other staff. Stories moving on the wires included bombings in Tel Aviv and Baghdad, flooding in Texas and a health study on eating seafood. But most of the aides I briefed were most interested in fifty-four-year-old actor Raul Julia's stroke.

Then Susan Brophy walked into the room and said she'd just seen Madonna downstairs. Press Secretary Dee Dee Myers, a southern California native and our resident expert purveyor of the entertainment scene, told her, "No way. She's in Europe with her boyfriend." I'd just seen Madonna on CNN that afternoon, attending a fashion show in Paris, and the wires said Madonna had just been in London to tape an interview with the BBC last weekend. So Brophy decided she was mistaken.

But when we went downstairs for the $2 million New York Governor Mario Cuomo fund-raising reception and dinner, there was Madonna, sitting at a corner table with some friends, her blond hair short and slicked back, smoking a cigarette and wearing lots of eye makeup and a black (presumably fake) fur coat with a short skirt. Brophy saw her and said, "Where's that Dee Dee? 'Oh, no, you didn't see Madonna.'" (In fact, Myers later had her photo taken with Madonna.)

Meanwhile, looking around the pre-dinner reception, I saw Alec Baldwin, Marissa Tomei and Dr. Ruth Westheimer making cocktail chatter. I called a friend back in Washington on my cell phone: "Guess who I just saw."

Inside at the dinner, I saw Robin Williams, Lee Iacocca and George Steinbrenner looking for their tables. Charles Grodin, Rita Moreno and Marvin Hamlisch performed, but virtually everyone in the huge ballroom kept talking and paid them no attention. Cuomo gave his typical excellent speech (although it wasn't particularly political and was probably better suited for another time and place). The President then spoke, and afterward, because I mistakenly thought I had time to go to the men's room, I dashed—literally—to the motorcade.

The helicopters lifted us over the East River, kicking up a spray of water we could faintly feel through the open windows, and providing a spectacular view of the glistening lights of Manhattan below.

Other up-close encounters were more personal. One gray spring day we headed to my hometown of Indianapolis. Jeff Eller (taking Dee Dee Myers' place, as was common on weekend trips) was sitting in the front seat of the staff van to Andrews Air Force Base. "Eller, put on Ralph's station," I said, referring to an oldies station Ralph Alswang (staff photographer) had selected on a previous trip. "I did," Eller said.

It was hard not to like Alswang. A former New Yorker, he'd lived the last few years in Washington taking photos for *Newsweek*. He was probably in his early thirties, with thinning black hair and brown eyes. He was energetic and talkative. Any room with Alswang in it was not a quiet one.

As we descended on our one-hour, thirty-minute flight on a cloudy, cool morning, the phone at my seat rang. "Mr. Chitester, I have Mr. Chitester on the line for you. Go ahead, sir," the Air Force One crew member on the line said. My dad said he and my cousins were having a little trouble finding the arrival site, which had changed without my knowledge, at Indianapolis International Airport.

On board, I chatted briefly in the guest section with Indiana Republican Senator Dick Lugar, who was interested to know I was an Indianapolis native and Pike High School graduate. He talked a little about the night in 1968 when he was mayor of Indianapolis, where

Robert Kennedy spoke downtown hours after Martin Luther King had been killed in Memphis. He said he didn't want Kennedy to speak that night, fearing for his safety. I disagree with Lugar on just about everything politically, but you can't help but respect him. (Although up close, he looks like comedian Gilbert Gottfreid, without the annoying voice and eye squint.)

I also talked with Indiana Democratic Congressmen Lee Hamilton and Frank McCloskey on the plane. I lived in Hamilton's district while at Indiana University, and McCloskey was mayor of Bloomington part of the time I was there. I asked McCloskey about his controversial first congressional race, which he barely won and which was finally settled by the House itself. Gesturing to Hamilton sitting across the table, McCloskey joked, "If Lee hadn't voted for me six times, I wouldn't have won."

Upon landing, I exited via the rear stairs and walked across the windy tarmac to the roped VIP area, where my dad, my cousin Ron and his wife Anita stood. "That's quite an entrance," Anita said. Dad said Marine Major Leo Mercado (military aide) already had greeted them. On the plane, I'd talked to Navy Lieutenant Commander Rich Fitzpatrick to tell him I had family there. The military aides were great. I knew they'd take care of my family.

While the President took a fifteen-minute helicopter flight, two police-escorted vans took the rest of us to Mt. Helm Missionary Baptist Church downtown. Riding with us were two of Martin Luther King's sons, Senator Ted Kennedy and his wife, Victoria, and Ethel Kennedy, Bobby's widow. (Late-night talk show jokes aside, Ted Kennedy really *is* a big guy.)

At the church, the President delivered his weekly radio address. Even though I'd eaten eggs, potatoes and ham on the plane, I tasted the biscuits and gravy, eggs with potatoes, and orange juice in the holding room a couple doors away, which was usually used as a nursery. I dialed in to the White House wire service computer system, but there was little news moving on a Saturday morning.

Then we walked next door to a park where Robert Kennedy spoke on April 4, 1968, the night Martin Luther King was assassinated. The President spoke at the dedication of a statue to nonviolence created in the memories of Kennedy and King, and rain fell throughout the event. Fortunately, I was needed inside to download a *Los Angeles*

Times story, which the reporters were asking our staff about. Irish Prime Minister Albert Reynolds was in the holding room, as was Indiana Governor Evan Bayh and his perky Tipper Gore-look-alike wife, Susan.

Next it was back into the motorcade for a five-minute ride to the Indiana Convention Center, where I found my dad and cousins. They said they'd enjoyed their tour of Air Force One, even getting to sit in the President's office chair and in the pilot's seat. (Even I never did that.) Dad said there were crumbs in the President's office chair where apparently he'd been eating cookies.

We sat around a large, bland, carpeted Convention Center holding room with temporary walls, where about fifty other people watched the President's televised speech down the hall at the annual Jefferson-Jackson Day luncheon. Virtually everyone in the room was a family member of a White House aide from Indiana. Eller had at least three dozen relatives there, standing on risers. Jamie Lindsay, the site advance person, instructed them to hold up red-and-blue plastic health care cards, in reference to Eller's work as health care spokesperson, and cigars, because Eller was a cigar aficionado.

Soon afterward, the President entered with his usual entourage of Bruce Lindsey, Wendy Smith (trip director), Dave Carpenter (Secret Service agent), Dr. Connie Mariano, the nurse and military aide. When the President saw that huge group of Ellers displaying health care cards and chomping plastic-wrapped cigars, he just cracked up—leaning back, knees bent, eyes crinkled with his high-pitched laugh. That was the hardest I ever saw him laugh, maybe except for when the Vice President would crack him up.

Then he made his way to us in the corner. Just as he was about to shake my dad's hand and I was about to reach perhaps the personal pinnacle of my political career by introducing my father to the President of the United States…my cellular phone rang. I'd put it on the rear of my belt so it wouldn't stick out in the photos, and it took me a couple rings to grab it. By that time it was as easy to answer it as it was to shut it off. (A friend from college, a reporter for *The Indianapolis News*, was calling from the press filing center down the hall.) I flipped it shut just as the President stepped in front of me.

"Thank you, man," he said, smiling.

"Thank *you*, Mr. President," I said with a grin.

Later I showed my dad and cousins the press office, filing center and speech site, meeting a couple of fellow staffers en route. The President went to Crooked Stick Country Club in nearby Carmel, Indiana, via helicopter, to play golf.

Before takeoff for Washington, several of us were in the Air Force One conference room when Dr. Mariano beckoned everybody to the staff section. The President told Leo Mercado that he was disappointed, and that we had a serious problem. But his tone and demeanor belied his words, and Mercado was laughing.

Then the President showed him a photo that Barb Kinney (staff photographer) had taken during a Presidential golf outing. It was of Mercado with his back to the camera, apparently urinating in the woods. Dr. Mariano had it framed and had written clever quips and double entendres around the matting.

The President was going to sign it for Mercado and add a quote of his own, but he looked at Wendy Smith and said, "I can't even touch this." Then, looking at the photo and Dr. Mariano's quotes, he said, "She knows so much about anatomy, I'm gonna have her be my expert witness."

After a stunned second of silence, we all howled with laughter. He was referring to a lawsuit filed the previous week by former Arkansas state employee Paula Jones, who alleged then-Governor Clinton had propositioned her and exposed himself in a hotel room. Jones claimed she could identify "distinguishing marks" on the President.

Mercado, meanwhile, was laughing and sweating heavily in embarrassment. Everybody on the trip stood crowded around him.

Several of us watched a movie in the conference room on the way home while eating pork roast, broccoli, salad, baked potato and apple pie with whipped cream during the flight.

Unlike his loyal staff, not all the people we met were enamored of President Clinton. Nowhere was that more obvious than during one trip to Texas. After a week of ice and snow, sunny, forty-five-degree weather prevailed as we loaded the vans about 2:00 P.M. on a Sunday to head out to Andrews for a two-day trip to Texas and Louisiana. Washingtonians were out and about town for the first time in weeks. It never failed—good weather on departure days.

After the three-hour flight to Houston, the President and most of the staff stopped at an American Cancer Society children's party. The Staff 2 van went straight to the fund-raiser at the Wortham Theater. Lorraine Miller (legislative affairs) was aboard Staff 2 with us. She told a story about Tupperware parties she used to host at which she'd serve Mad Dog 20/20 punch. Mad Dog is a cheap, powerful wine ("Serve *very* cold," says the label), and Miller said women would drink glasses of it and then start buying like crazy. "Do you think that would work with members of Congress?" I asked.

We also talked about the recent decision to list prices on menus in the White House mess. Miller said she was glad because she'd gotten monthly bills of $200. Two hundred dollars? Yes, she said, because her guests from Capitol Hill would order virtually everything on the menu, figuring that since there were no prices, everything was free.

At the Wortham Theater, protesters with pickets were jammed against the barricades on either side of the sidewalk as we arrived. I had heard and seen plenty of protesters in my job, but I'd never experienced the venom those people spewed. I made a point to block out their exact words, but there were Vietnam veterans in fatigues who were upset about the President's recent lifting of the Vietnam trade embargo, and of course the ever-present abortion protesters with their familiar signs. They all were screaming horrible things about the President, mere feet from us. We stared straight ahead, ignoring them on our way inside. But I couldn't help but think of what President Kennedy said to his wife after seeing a negative newspaper ad in another Texas city in November 1963: "We're really heading into nut country today."

Inside, I dialed in and downloaded stories on United Nations and North Atlantic Treaty Organization responses to the previous day's shelling of a Sarajevo market that had killed sixty-eight people. Dee Dee Myers tried to piece together what everyone was saying and where the process stood through phone calls back to Washington and the stories I was handing her. Bosnia, of course, was a messy situation. Poor Dee Dee had to figure out what the UN, NATO, North Atlantic Council and each of our allies were doing, not to mention making sure the White House, National Security Council, State Department and UN Ambassador were all on the same page in explaining our policy.

On that same trip, I saw a side of the President all too familiar to some of his closest aides. We stayed overnight in Shreveport, Louisiana. I left the Holiday Inn the next morning, carrying an armload of heavy news clip packages to take to the other staff hotel a half dozen blocks away, when I saw Josh King (communications/advance). Since it was a pleasant morning, I hauled the clips over there on foot, but I was sweating and nearly panting by the time I arrived. Soon afterward, I saw King there.

"How'd you get here so fast?" I asked.

"I had one of the motorcade vans bring me over," he said.

I just shook my head. I'll never have the attitude that it takes to fit in around here, I thought.

"Captain Hook" made an appearance that morning. Jeff Eller was summoned to the President's limousine as we prepared to leave. An unhappy, gesturing President went over the speech with him in the limo. "Remember," Eller said later, "*this* (imitating Clinton's gesturing fist with pointing thumb) is better than *this*" (imitating an angry Clinton hooking his index finger in a tight circular motion). The latter was what some of us sometimes referred to as "Captain Hook." When the President was really mad, he'd make that hooking gesture with his finger. Whenever I saw that, I gave him even more room than usual. Believe me, nobody wanted to see Captain Hook.

The day's event was at a General Motors assembly plant, where GM built trucks. All right, I thought: here were real people, living in the middle of the country, working with their hands, who actually *made stuff.* We saw the assembly line, with transmissions and engines hanging from chains and moving down the line. It was a huge factory, covering several acres. The President spoke to the workers in the chassis dock about health care reform and joked about the AstroTurf he had in the back of his El Camino in his youth. "You don't want to know what it was for," he told a puzzled press corps.

Afterward, he conducted satellite interviews with Detroit media and met the publisher and editors from *The Times* of Shreveport while I worked in the staff hold in another part of the plant.

When I walked outside to the motorcade, the day was sunny, windy and eighty degrees. The area around the GM plant was green and spacious, with grass and trees. Back in Washington, we later heard on the staff van's radio, a plane had slid off the runway at National Airport. When we landed at Andrews at about 5:30 P.M., freezing rain was falling.

The weather prevented the President from flying in Marine One back to the South Lawn, however. So we rode in a long, slow motorcade north on Suitland Parkway and got back to the White House about 6:00 P.M. Our van stopped on the South Lawn driveway, right in front of the ground-floor entrance to the Diplomatic Room.

"Watch your step, sir," one of the military drivers said as I started to exit the van. Right, I thought—what am I, a little old lady? Whereupon I promptly slipped in my slick-soled dress shoes, and the guy caught me and my two computer shoulder bags. Sometimes those military guys must have thought we were pathetic. We strolled into the Diplomatic Room, and I thought, This is just like the opening of the movie *Dave*.

But as exciting as traveling with the President could be, sometimes we'd get bored from the sheer repetition and occasional monotony. So aides would come up with little changes of pace to amuse themselves.

One summer Sunday evening we flew to Miami. All of us fit in one staff van and were dressed casually. I had on sneakers, khakis, a madras shirt and a navy blazer.

Before we loaded up, Wendy Smith asked our military driver, "Is it against your orders to stop at the Tastee Freeze?"

The driver replied, "I'm following your orders."

"Oh...okay," Smith said, and then told us, "I've always wanted to stop there."

Actually, so had I. We passed it every time we went to Andrews Air Force Base. So as we approached the Tastee Freeze, our driver said, "I, uh, think I hear a rattle in the rear end. I'd better pull over and check it out." He pulled into the Tastee Freeze parking lot, and, well ahead of the President's arrival and feeling like school kids on a field trip, we went inside and got ice cream. I had the hot fudge sundae in a white Styrofoam cup ($1.74) and thought of John Mellencamp's "Jack and Diane": "Suckin' on a chili dog, outside the Tastee Freeze...."

On board Air Force One, I downloaded, printed and delivered wire stories to Dee Dee Myers in the conference room. About a half dozen aides were watching *Tombstone* on the TV sets at each end of the room, and the President was standing near the end of the table. Val Kilmer appeared on the screen, and Wendy Smith said he'd once kissed her ("On the lips, no tongue") because she was with Nelson Mandela. "In fact," she said, "it was a two-fer" because Kilmer was then filming *The Doors* and looked like Jim Morrison.

Other times we'd come up with other ways to amuse ourselves when the President was running late. One late night in Minneapolis, Jeff Eller started an arrival pool, something we sometimes did when we were hopelessly off schedule. Everybody would toss in a dollar and give an exact time they expected Air Force One to land. (Half the fun was defining what time it was we were trying to predict. "Now, is that wheels down, or is it in the blocks, or what?")

One time, in Los Angeles, I almost won a pool. The arrival time was defined as when the President's foot hit the ground when he stepped out of the limousine upon arrival at the hotel. (Once the time you'd chosen passed, you were eliminated.) I was closing in on it, but Bob McNeely (staff photographer) had an earlier time in the pool than me. He and I were the only remaining contenders.

So when the motorcade pulled into the hotel parking garage, McNeely hopped out of a van and yelled to Navy Lieutenant Commander Rich Fitzpatrick (military aide), who was standing beside the limo, "Rich! Rich! Open the door!" Fitzpatrick, not knowing why but sensing the urgency in McNeely's voice, opened the door. The President, who had been sitting there reading, saw the open door and put his foot down. And McNeely won the pot.

Another time, Bruce Lindsey was in on the pool. He told the President what time he'd predicted and told him he'd split the pot if the President would meet it. It was only about $30, but that wasn't the point. It isn't that they're cheap; they're painfully competitive. So the President met the time, and he and Lindsey split the money. But after that incident, Lindsey was banned from arrival pools.

So in Minneapolis we included the press pool, and the pot got up to about $80. I picked 1:22 A.M. for arrival at Andrews (in the blocks, as we say, meaning a full stop, with the wheels blocked in by the ground crew) but was about half an hour too early.

Other times the press would be part of the amusement themselves. That was the case one late winter day while we were visiting New Hampshire.

We had a late morning departure from the Sheraton Tara Hotel in Nashua. After producing and distributing clips, I had time to sit around the staff room and munch on rolls and sip some juice, reading the local paper and keeping an eye on the morning network news shows.

Our first event was a town hall meeting at Elm Street Junior High's gymnasium, where a supporter told the President, "Whitewater is for rafting and canoeing," to cheers. I worked in the press office down the hall while the President headed to nearby Keene, New Hampshire, for another event.

As I sat with press staffers, Pool Report No. 2 came in. The pool reports were produced by the reporters who followed the President, representing the dozens or hundreds who weren't allowed to accompany him everywhere. Reporters sent pool reports throughout the day to the on-site White House press office, which distributed them. That day, Pool Report No. 2 said the President, shaking hands along a ropeline, turned to the pool and "emitted what sounded like flatulence." We were shocked, then we laughed, then we were disbelieving, then disgusted, then angry at the reporters who would file something like that. (It was occurrences like that which fed the distrust between the White House and the Washington media, feeding the abrasive nature of the relationship and helping to make the staff feel a little paranoid at times.)

Later a rickety old press plane took us about an hour to Fort Drum in upstate New York. From the air, it looked like Siberia, a vast frozen tundra. Upon landing, we could see snow plows had cut through several feet of snow, banked to each side, to clear the runways. A bus took us to the event, where a 21-gun salute was fired, and the President welcomed the 10th Mountain Division home from Somalia. We motorcaded a couple minutes to a hot, noisy gymnasium, where a raucous crowd of enthusiastic soldiers ("*Hoo*-ah!") welcomed the President. Staff holding areas were nearby racquetball courts with tables of hors d'oeuvres, a little unusual but practical.

I told Paul Richard (deputy staff secretary) and Susan Brophy of the pool report. Brophy tried to seriously analyze the likelihood: "Wait a minute—they could hear it over the crowd noise, several feet away, through his overcoat, which would muffle it?" Then, in her Boston accent, amazed: "That had to be the mother of all farts." She later added, "Not to fuel the fire, but he's capable of it," saying she'd heard for herself. Later we asked Wendy Smith, who said the President hadn't been wearing his overcoat. We looked at each other and some-one said, "It's possible." We were all laughing and aghast at the same time.

After the event, we boarded the motorcade and headed back to the planes for the flight home. We flew a C-9 and a C-20. I was on the twelve-seat backup, which actually was fine with me, because I'd never flown on a C-20 before. Navy Captain Mark Rogers (military office) said it was like a sports car, compared to the luxury car equiva-lent of the 747. As we raced down the runway, Army Colonel Tom Hawes (White House Communications Agency commander) shifted gears on an imaginary gearshift. The plane held twelve and a crew of four, but we weren't full. Dinner on the quick trip was grilled chicken, cucumber salad and cheesecake, just as good as on the big plane.

In addition to the press, sometimes the Secret Service interacted with the President's aides and kept us amused. That was true during the President's vacation to Hilton Head Island, South Carolina, where several aides and off-duty agents sat around the upstairs staff room at the hotel, watching college football bowl games and eating some of the seemingly tons of donated food. We watched *In The Line Of Fire*, starring Clint Eastwood as a Secret Service agent, on Spectravision. One of the agents hadn't seen it before. As John Malkovich's would-be assassin character loaded bullets into a key ring and created a wooden gun to get past the metal detectors, he was aghast. "They shouldn't show that! That could give people ideas!" He was also amazed at some of the accuracies ("Those are our [lapel] pins!") and inaccuracies ("I've never seen a [female] agent who looks like *that*.")

On a trip to California, another agent provided entertainment for us. It was a late spring morning, and we were staying at the Sheraton Miramar in Santa Monica. I delivered the news clips as everyone else was emerging from their rooms. Wendy Smith, Dee Dee Myers and Andrew Friendly (personal aide) were relaxing around a poolside table, while others were lounging on the patios outside their rooms reading or suntanning as I scurried about. The President played golf all morning, and our vans left the hotel at noon for a twenty-minute drive to the airport, where we met him.

We flew Air Force One to Sacramento's McClellan Air Force Base on Armed Forces Day. The motorcade then took us to a fund-raiser at a private home on Rockwood Drive. It was strange to ride in the motorcade through a neighborhood. People stood in their front yards and waved on a pleasant evening. There were lovely homes, but not huge, with white sidewalks and pretty lawns.

The President spoke briefly and then greeted the crowd along a ropeline. As the President shook hands, a man down the line kept yelling, "Bill! Bill! Bill!" The President shook his hand and moved on. Whereupon Wendy Smith turned and told the guy, "You know, some people call him 'Mr. President.'" (Later, aboard the plane, Smith told the President what she'd done. "Really?" he replied. "You said that?")

On the flight back to Andrews Air Force Base, a bunch of us sat around the Air Force One conference room table. Smith prodded Secret Service Agent Dave Carpenter into telling one of his "booger stories." He told one about when he was in college (where he was a big basketball star) and, after chatting with a flirtatious girl sitting next to him, sneezed and blew an enormous booger on her notebook. She screamed and, leaving her books behind, got up and ran out of the class. Carpenter, who is a terrific storyteller, said he never saw her in class again. We all laughed loudly. Carpenter was the tall, gray-haired agent many people recognized because he was always at the President's side and who looked a little like Clinton. He was married to Pam Gray, one of the White House stenographers, and everybody at the White House just loved him.

Bob Walters, whose real name is Barney, then told of a romantic evening on the couch with his then-girlfriend that ended when he accidentally blew a snot bubble. I'd heard a couple staffers call him "Barney Bubble" and suddenly knew why.

Other Secret Service encounters were more serious, like the time agent Lew Merletti conducted a briefing in Jeff Eller's office for Media Affairs staffers. He told several long stories of recent incidents in which people who shouldn't have gotten access to the President and the First Lady did so. He said agents went to one suspect's home and found a wall display of clippings and photos, just like in the movie *In the Line of Fire*. There had been a lot of incidents recently, and he wanted us to be aware, to keep our eyes open, and to provide information to the agents if we saw anything.

It was serious stuff. It wasn't anything that any of us liked to think about, but it was fascinating. In Atlanta, a man had been arrested for carrying weapons during the President's visit to CNN Center. Afterward, in the limousine, Bruce Lindsey was talking with the President and then said, "I think Lew has something he wants to talk to you about." And Merletti then read us some of his notes from the conversation. The President said there were more incidents because of passage of the assault weapons ban and the Brady Bill. And he told Merletti a story of a friend who was an Arkansas sheriff and who had been gunned down in a setup.

Merletti, who would later become director of the Secret Service, told us President Clinton was the fourth President he'd protected, and previously he'd never even *heard* of such of a rash of incidents. The Secret Service obviously was embarrassed and concerned (an understatement, I'm sure).

Then Merletti, who would later become director of the Secret Service, talked about weapons and metal detectors and bomb-sniffing dogs and how there was only so much agents could do. He told us how the Secret Service takes advantage of the armor in the limousine, the podium (the "Blue Goose") and the newly-redesigned toast lectern. Bulletproof vests are heavy and difficult to breathe in, but have been used by both agents and the President. He said the key is to keep armor near him, so that if anything happened they could pull him down and protect him.

Then he said, matter-of-factly, "We can use our bodies, but a bullet will go through a body." And finally, he said, "Not to be too melodramatic about it, but I would give my life for the President. I don't *want* to, but I would do it."

Even though we all knew it was the Secret Service's job, it still was rather extraordinary to hear. I'd always had great respect for the agents, but after that briefing, I had even more.

11▶Inside the Bubble

NOT ONLY DID TRAVELING aboard Air Force One provide an opportunity to encounter a wide variety of people and places, but sometimes it was like experiencing a mobile American history lesson. Partly because of the time in which President Clinton grew up and partly because of other circumstances, we ended up visiting several events and sites with connections to the 1960s.

Certainly President Richard Nixon was a major figure of the '60s. And when Nixon died in April 1994, President Clinton attended the funeral late that month.

Air Force One was full of current and former White House staff. That must've been weird, the mix of Clinton and Nixon administration officials. Among those on board were Nixon aides Caspar Weinberger, Alexander Haig, Brent Scowcroft and Elliot Richardson. Director of Communications Mark Gearan said later, "It was like Madame Tussaud's Wax Museum."

Upon landing at El Toro Marine Base, we motorcaded to the Richard Nixon Library and Birthplace in nearby Yorba Linda. I ducked into the staff hold so I could check the wires after being out of touch all afternoon. But the only stories of note were on Nixon's funeral and Nelson Mandela's election as South Africa's president.

During the televised ceremony, held in what was normally the parking lot, howitzers fired a 21-gun salute and jet fighters flew overhead in the "missing man" formation. As a member of the honor guard presented Nixon's daughters Julie and Tricia the folded U.S. flag from their father's coffin, Coast Guard Lieutenant Commander Bob Walters (military aide) stood next to me quietly reciting the standard speech: "On behalf of a grateful nation...."

It was very sad. Oh, Nixon was a criminal who defaced the Presidency, an evil, twisted villain who betrayed his office and his country. But he did leave behind a family who was in pain, something with which I could empathize. I just had a hard time being as magnanimous and gracious as President Clinton was in his eulogy. It was hard enough just wearing a black suit and keeping my mouth shut all day.

After the ceremony, I waited outside a room where President and Mrs. Clinton greeted the former Presidents and First Ladies. I stood next to a narrow floor-to-ceiling window, watching them like a little kid with his nose pressed to the candy store window. There in one room was American history in my lifetime. The first President I could remember in my life was Nixon, and I could recall what was going on in my life when each—Ford, Carter, Reagan, Bush—was President. Just seeing them in person brought back a flood of personal memories.

Then it was upstairs to a reception for VIPs attending the funeral. I put on my purple admittance lapel button with the circled "RN," a reproduction of the way Nixon signed memos. Oh, well, I thought—at least they didn't make us wear those "Nixon's the One" campaign buttons. Inside the large room, it was like a Republican National Convention in Salt Lake City. There were old, white, rich, male Republicans as far as the eye could see. And not just garden-variety, long-time party loyalists, either. These were the big, bad, heavy hitters: Dole, Gingrich, Kemp, Helms, Hatch. When I saw Henry Kissinger, I had to stop myself from saying, "So, Hank...talk to me about the Christmas bombing of Hanoi. What were you *thinking?*"

I was standing with fellow White House aides, huddled together for strength, when we saw Virginia Democratic Senator Chuck Robb walk by. "You know," I said, "I live in Virginia," and started to say something about being registered to vote back in Arkansas, but Lisa Caputo (First Lady's press secretary) beat me to it. "So do I," she said, "and *that's* one reason I'm registered to vote in Pennsylvania," motioning toward Robb.

Later I saw Bob Hope. The man looked like wax. For a minute I thought they'd buried the wrong guy.

Our group of aides talked about what the current and former Presidents must have been thinking during the service. We figured each could be excused for wondering what their own send-off would be like and for wondering how they would be remembered. Then we debated who would be next. "We'll be going to another one of these in our eight years," someone said after looking at the former Presidents. Most bets were on Reagan being the next to go. He did not look at all like the Gipper of the '80s. (A little over five months later, Reagan's office announced he had been diagnosed with Alzheimer's disease.)

Soon afterward, we got word that we had "imminent departure." So I headed for the parking lot, where I saw former Senator George McGovern get on the VIP bus. McGovern was one of the reasons I got into politics, and his 1972 Presidential campaign was the first one I studied. I thought about it and then decided, Oh, why not? So I followed him onto the bus and introduced myself and briefly told him of the influence he'd had on me. "And you're on the White House staff now?" he asked. We chatted very briefly and I prepared to leave.

"Ken, do you know the Senator?" McGovern said, gesturing to New York Democratic Senator Daniel Patrick Moynihan, the only other person on the bus. I hadn't met him, but I'd seen him at the White House. Later, I thought of the story everybody at the White House used to tell about Moynihan's flight home aboard Air Force One from a Presidential visit to Hyde Park, New York, the previous spring. Upon boarding, he reached the staff section and allegedly began bellowing, "Whiskey! *Whiskey! WHISKEY!* Somebody get me some whiskey!"

During our departure, unbeknownst to us, former President Bush's two or three cars pulled out into our motorcade. In the confusion, the staff bus, two VIP buses and Roadrunner (the White House Communications Agency communications van) all followed, getting in the wrong motorcade. We pulled up to a major intersection and saw the instantly recognizable two limousines going in the opposite direction.

"Hey," we said, "isn't that…?"

"That's *our* President!"

So Mort Engelberg, the lead advance person, got out and frantically waved us through the intersection—with traffic stopped by local police officers—so we could swing a U-turn and get back in the motorcade. Whereupon we all burst out laughing. I'd been in probably 150 motorcades at that point, and I'd never seen anything like that. And it couldn't have been Carter or Ford or even Reagan. No, it had to be Bush. "That guy's *still* trying to lead people in the wrong direction," somebody said.

Another major figure of the '60s was Martin Luther King, Jr. A visit to Memphis one wet fall Saturday turned into a bit of a tribute to the late civil rights leader. Sometimes I realized while something was happening just how lucky I was to be a part of it. Usually I was too busy working, but that day was an exception.

We left the White House about 7:45 A.M. and after a two-hour flight arrived in Memphis, where rain fell off and on all day, for the President's late-morning address on crime and values. Upon arrival, he gave a brief speech outdoors at the airport and picked up some Congressional endorsements for the North American Free Trade Agreement. The wind on the tarmac was so strong it even messed up Chief of Staff Mack McLarty's normally perfectly combed hair.

The motorcade then took us to Mason Temple, headquarters of the Church of God in Christ, where Martin Luther King gave his last speech, the night before he was assassinated, in 1968. ("I've seen the promised land. I might not get there with you...I'm not fearing *any* man. Mine eyes have seen the glory of the coming of the Lord!") It was a huge church without air-conditioning in a poor part of town with exposed rafters and a nearly all-black crowd in suits and dresses.

The President addressed the group's annual convention, and he absolutely lit it up: "What would Martin Luther King say if he were here today?... 'I did not live and die to have thirteen-year-old boys get automatic weapons and gun down nine-year-olds just for the kick of it!'" It was what has since come to be regarded as one of President Clinton's finest speeches.

The President stopped the motorcade shortly after departure and got out to shake hands in a housing project. Rain fell in a sudden downpour, and he got soaked. His suit clung to him, and his hair was slicked back. We stopped by Tennessee Democratic Congressman Harold Ford's town hall meeting at Olivet Baptist Church before heading back to the airport for a reception. Outside, John Gaughan (military office) watched the football game between Notre Dame and

Florida State (ranked first and second in the country, respectively) on a hand-held TV .

Inside, the usual assortment of middle-aged and older, prosperous white couples in business attire flocked to the President as soon as he entered the room, leaving open the food table. Director of Media Affairs Jeff Eller and I swooped in, scooping up ribs, barbecue sandwiches, baked beans and brownie pie with whipped cream. As I filled my plate, Eller sidled up to me. "Boy, you can sure tell who the staff is, can't you?" he said. "Forget the President—where's the food?"

Like King, President John F. Kennedy was a leader of the '60s who was assassinated while still in his forties. When we visited the JFK Library and Museum in Boston, it was a special treat for both President Clinton and his aides. For all of us on staff—whether we grew up as Massachusetts Democrats, like Kathy McKiernan (press assistant), or surrounded by Indiana Republicans, as I did—Kennedy had a special meaning for of us.

In the Boston Park Plaza Hotel's fifteenth-floor lounge serving as the traveling staff office, aides sat reading the news clips on a fall morning. Coffeepots, along with rolls and juice, were set on a nearby table.

Earlier that week, a memo went out from Patsy Thomasson (director of administration), saying that due to recent spills, all coffee cups in the West Wing had to have lids on them. The memo had been the subject of much joking in the morning communications meeting. So when a sign that said, "The lid rule remains in effect on the road—Patsy" was left near the coffee in the staff office that morning, we figured it had to be Director of Communications Mark Gearan's doing.

Gearan also had the largest family clutch I'd ever seen. (In staff terminology, a "clutch" was a moment with the President. Some people would literally try to clutch onto him. For aides, it was a chance to introduce family members to him and to get photos taken.) As some of us were headed down to the motorcade, the elevator opened, and Gearan exited with family members of all ages, all dressed up to meet the President. There must have been dozens of them.

The motorcade took us to the John F. Kennedy Library and Museum, an I.M. Pei-designed structure near the Columbia Point campus of the University of Massachusetts, overlooking the Old Harbor with boats and colorful trees on the opposite shore on a cloudy, windy day with temperatures in the fifties. When we walked up to the entrance, the smiling Kennedys were all lined up awaiting the President. Even from the motorcade, parked about 100 feet away, the scene looked like one huge row of gleaming teeth. Inside, we were all excited: "This is *so* cool. I can't believe we're here."

The President spoke at the dedication of the new museum wing, pressing for passage of the North American Free Trade Agreement and citing President Kennedy's legacy as an activist. Later, some of the staff thought it an inappropriate time and place for such comments. But my thinking was that he's always the President, and that was the event that would make the day's news. Massachusetts Congressman Joe Kennedy then made interesting remarks. He said that Ted Sorenson, Dave Powers and Pierre Salinger were to President Kennedy what people like Mack McLarty, George Stephanopoulos and Dee Dee Myers were to President Clinton, providing us perspective.

Then the traveling staff got a quick tour of the new wing before the President did. We were like little kids being whisked through Disney World without getting to stop at any of the attractions. After seeing displays of the 1960 Democratic National Convention and presidential campaign, we prepared to turn a corner. "Now this may look familiar to you," said Amy, our guide in black heels, black stockings and short black skirt. That's when we walked into what, for a brief moment, could've been the first floor of the executive mansion, or middle part, of the White House.

"Oh my gosh," I said, mouth agape. It was obviously a recreation meant to be more representative than exact, but at first sight it was like that "Star Trek" episode where the aliens confuse Captain Kirk by putting him aboard an exact duplicate they'd built of the USS *Enterprise*. "This must be weird for you guys," Amy said.

We wanted to linger, but with the President following, we had to hustle. The still and video photographers, prepositioned at two spots, got ready when they heard someone coming. "Oh, it's just you guys," they said. At the Oval Office mock-up, I said, "Now, that's not his desk. I *know* where his desk is." President Clinton, of course, used Kennedy's desk in the real Oval Office.

We ate lunch at a big reception downstairs in an area set up to look like the 1960 convention floor, complete with fallen confetti. We ate spinach fettucine, veal tortellini, Boston baked beans, breads and cookies, all of it delicious. The Kennedys don't do anything halfway.

On the way out, Paul Richard (deputy staff secretary) and I were standing next to Carter Wilkie, who'd written the President's speech. We were looking at some books in the gift shop when the President stopped on his way out. He thanked Wilkie and told him he'd done a good job. "That was your raise for next year," we later told Wilkie.

The President and Wilkie stood perusing the books on the shelves. "Have you read this one?" the President asked.

After the President, running late but seeming either to not know or not care, headed toward the door, Wendy Smith (trip director) angrily admonished us: "Guys, don't *do* that. We're *late*." We didn't try to explain. Later, Richard told her, "Hey, *he* came up and started talking to *us*." Sometimes we acted as if he were a child and you couldn't let him get distracted by toys in the store window. But Smith was right: we had to try to stay on schedule.

Aboard Air Force One on the way home, tired but upbeat, I ambled up to the front galley to see if I could get something to drink. But You Know Who was standing in front of the door, chatting with the crew. I figured I could wait.

One of Kennedy's legacies was space exploration. He challenged the country to land a man on the moon and safely return him by the end of the 1960s. In fact, a Mercury space suit is displayed in the JFK Library and Museum. When we visited Johnson Space Center and Space Center Houston, we got to see some of that Kennedy legacy.

The President's first event that day in Houston was a meet-and-greet with supporters downstairs in the Wyndham Warwick Hotel's Grand Ballroom.

At noon, the motorcade took us to the Hyatt Regency, where the President delivered a rambling speech to an unresponsive crowd of local business leaders. In the large holding room down the hall, I dialed in on one phone line while Bruce Lindsey (senior adviser) sat nearby talking to a reporter from *Time* magazine on another phone. "I told you that off the record," Lindsey said. "I *told* you I am not a tax lawyer. And listen to what you wrote...." Poor Bruce, I thought. Answering Whitewater questions couldn't be much fun. He did invaluable behind-the-scenes work that other people couldn't or wouldn't do.

Then it was on to Johnson Space Center. The four of us in the Staff 2 van—Carolyn Curiel (speechwriter), Debi Schiff (VIP receptionist), Paul Richard and I—instead toured Space Center Houston, the tourist area. Gwen, our guide, gave us a four-hour tour in twenty minutes. We saw the podium President Kennedy used in his famous speech at Houston's Rice University ("We choose to go to the moon in this decade and do the other things not because they are easy, but because they are hard."). We saw Mercury, Gemini, Apollo and Skylab spacecrafts and the lunar rover, in addition to moon rocks. Afterward, Gwen gave us T-shirts, books, videos and CDs from the souvenir shop.

In addition to rockets and space capsules, American technology in the '60s also produced new types of cars. One was the wildly popular Ford Mustang, which premiered at the 1964 New York World's Fair. Since President Clinton was a Mustang owner and aficionado, one sunny spring weekend we headed to the annual national Mustang convention.

I headed to the White House in a navy blazer, golf shirt and poplin slacks one Saturday for a two-day trip to Williamsburg, Virginia, and Charlotte, North Carolina. We motorcaded across the Potomac to the Pentagon and boarded three helicopters for a one-hour, five-minute flight to a Democratic Senate retreat in Williamsburg. The sun was slowly beginning to set on a comfortable late afternoon. Looking out the rear of the helicopter, we could see the monuments of the nation's capital as the sun began to sink below the horizon.

After landing, we rode to Kingsmill Resort, a sprawling complex of wealthy people and golf courses with seemingly not one blade of grass out of place. At the dinner site, Senate Majority Leader George Mitchell, wearing a V-neck sweater, warmly greeted the President, who was in casual slacks and shirt with a blazer. There was no staff hold at the dinner site, so we went to our rooms, which actually were more like condominiums or apartments, with fireplaces and views of the James River. The President and First Lady stayed in Anheuser-Busch Chairman August Busch's corporate condo.

The next morning, Jeff Eller and I borrowed a golf cart and drove around the expansive, well-tended complex. I watched the Sunday talk shows and ate doughnuts in the staff office, until the President finished his round of golf and we headed to the airport for the one-hour, fifteen-minute flight to Charlotte. Only about half a dozen aides, not counting military, medical and Secret Service, were aboard for our third trip to Charlotte in sixteen days. (We'd previously attended Arkansas' two NCAA Final Four basketball games there.)

It was a sunny, warm day as the motorcade took us to Charlotte Motor Speedway, forty minutes away in neighboring Conrad, for the annual Ford Mustang convention. We entered the track and took half a lap around on the twenty-three-degree banked turns, which looked especially steep from the apron, where we were driving.

The President cruised a couple hundred feet down pit row in his 1967 hornet-green convertible Mustang with the sticky left door, ever-present Secret Service agent Dave Carpenter in the passenger's seat. (The next day, when Carpenter walked into the Air Force One staff section, we all applauded and held up that day's major newspapers, which had front-page photos of the President and Carpenter in the Mustang. He laughed and waved us off.)

The President briefly spoke to the crowd, shook hands along a ropeline and then viewed the entrants' Mustangs in the infield. I dialed in on my laptop to check the news (Gorazde was under Serbian attack in Bosnia; the President had commented on it earlier to the press pool) and then walked around and saw some of the cars, getting a little sunburned. They were all shiny with spotless engines, their hoods and trunks open, with proud owners, mostly old, white couples, sitting nearby.

The President then conducted an interview with Phyllis George for her new television show before the motorcade pulled out. (George was the wife of former Kentucky Governor John Y. Brown, who was in office when Clinton was Governor of Arkansas.)

In the staff van back to the airport, Small Business Administration Director Erskine Bowles (who would begin Clinton's second term as White House Chief of Staff) said he and his wife were celebrating their twenty-third wedding anniversary that day. His wife joined him at the airport, and they sat in the guest section of the plane. The President came back and visited with them. He was still sitting there as we exited back at Andrews. His right leg was up on a table and he was wearing black slacks with a red and black golf shirt. And I noticed a couple of little things about our President: he has really long fingers, and he hardly has any hair on his arms. I have no idea why I noticed that.

▶

Traveling via helicopter was a highlight of early trips. Like everything else, it became routine after a couple dozen times. But especially at first, it was a thrill.

One autumn day, four enormous green Marine helicopters came swooping around the Washington Monument and landed on the Ellipse. Traffic on the Ellipse, a large grassy area encircled by parked cars and located between the White House and the Washington Monument, was blocked by Park Police. Fire trucks were on hand, and uniformed Secret Service kept the crowd at a safe distance. The view aboard Nighthawk 3, as it banked and flew in an arc toward Baltimore, was fantastic. We saw the White House and Constitution Avenue and the monuments and traffic from a new perspective on a partly cloudy day.

The President and First Lady spoke about health care at the Johns Hopkins University gymnasium at the Newton White, Jr., Athletic Center, and afterward conducted interviews with reporters from San Antonio, Miami, Pittsburgh and Columbus, Ohio. Afterward, he headed back to Andrews Air Force Base and she went to the White House. His staff surrounded him and her staff stood around her in a bare hallway as the two of them tried to say goodbye to each other. We tried to get out of the way as they briefly stepped around a corner for a modicum of privacy, and then the President walked past me on his way out. He and a phalanx of Secret Service agents headed down the stairs, and I followed, ever-present computer bags slung over each shoulder.

Due to the limited staff going back to Andrews, I got my first ride on Nighthawk 2, which is a white-top helicopter and is identical to Marine One. Nighthawk 2 is like a miniature Air Force One, with soft, fabric-covered, off-white, individual facing seats, a short couch, carpeting, no vibration, not much noise and little things like gum and candy trays, informational booklets, a sign listing the crew members, cloth curtains and headphones for communications. Also on board, as usual, were Secret Service agents and the White House Communications Agency and White House Military Office representatives on the trip.

(On Air Force One, there was always a tray of miniature candy bars, gum and mints, along with a basket of fruit, next to the couch near the front galley. If we missed lunch during our events on the ground, those candy bars wouldn't last long. The miniature Milky Ways and Three Musketeers would quickly disappear, but Dove bars were among the last taken. Fruit generally wasn't taken as quickly as candy. The crew had a whole closet full of treats for us.)

After landing at Andrews, we boarded Air Force One for the one-hour, five-minute flight to New York. We motorcaded to Electric Industries Hall in Flushing, where a packed gymnasium cheered wildly in the bright TV lights. Governor Mario Cuomo, Mayor David Dinkins and the President spoke at a Democratic unity rally. It was noisy and raucous. The staff stood off to the side in a doorway. Afterward, I stood outside by the motorcade with Paul Richard, who smoked a cigarette as we commiserated over the long hours on the road. "You know it's bad when you're beat at the end of the day and you're not even in the same *state* as your bed," I said.

Then we were whisked to the Waldorf-Astoria so the President could address *The Wall Street Journal* Second Annual Conference on the Americas. Much of the staff headed upstairs for dinner on the thirty-fifth floor. Everybody oohed and ahhed over the high-class cuisine, but personally I'd just as soon have had pizza. The room, Suite 35-H, was where President Johnson in 1965 met the first Pope ever to visit the United States. Then it was downstairs to the motorcade, past the ever-polite New York City cops: "Wha? Uh? Yo gotta pro'lem or wha? Aw, gowon, get outta heah."

Other times helicopters were used to transport us within a city. That was true when the President traveled to Chicago one Monday in late February.

The sun was just beginning to rise behind the Jefferson Memorial on a cold morning as the staff van took us to Andrews. As usual, Air Force One crew members stood at the bottom of the stairs, checking off our names on the manifest in their hands. One would stand in front of the stairs while the other looked for the name on his list. After a while, of course, they got to know me, so they'd just stand aside and politely nod: "Good morning, sir."

Once aboard, I was able to dial in to the White House's wire service computer system from my laptop computer. There was a small office aboard Air Force One, behind the staff section, that included four computers and two laser printers. I'd bring my laptop in there and plug a phone line into an empty jack. (The crew had removed a phone so I could have easier access.) I then would pick up a nearby white phone, and a voice in the upstairs crew area would answer.

"Yes, sir?"

"This is Ken Chitester. Could you give me dial tone on this line, please?"

"Coming right up, sir."

I'd plug into my built-in modem, access the wire service computer system in the Old Executive Office Building and produce a report of the latest news before takeoff, making copies for key aides on the machine around the corner.

I sat in the guest section with Chad Griffin and Jeremy Gaines (press assistants) and Barb Kinney (staff photographer) on the one-hour, forty-five-minute flight. Kinney went out in the cold to photograph the President's arrival aboard Marine One and returned just before we began to taxi. "Let's eat," she said, rubbing her gloved hands together. Breakfast was scrambled eggs, rolls, biscuits and gravy, melon slices and orange juice.

We rolled through Chicago's Interstate 90/94 in a fifteen-minute motorcade to Wright Community College, where there were huge piles of plowed snow in the parking lot. Inside, we used a small, temporarily vacated office as a staff hold. It was extremely crowded, with aides jammed in elbow to elbow. (On the wires, the big news story of the day was the shootdown of four Serbian planes by the North Atlantic Treaty Organization, using U.S. F-16 fighter planes, after the Serbs violated a United Nations resolution.)

At one point, Chief of Staff Mack McLarty looked over my shoulder: "What are you working on, Ken?"

"These are the Sunday talk show transcripts I'll e-mail to everybody, Mack," I said.

As I sat in the holding room, Mike Feldman, filling in as the President's personal aide in place of absent Andrew Friendly, looked in the President's thick black briefcase for an Olympic-related briefing paper.

"Is he doing something on the Olympics?"

"Yeah," Feldman said, "he's calling Nancy Kerrigan," who had won a silver medal in figure skating a few days ago. I looked in the President's briefing book in Feldman's hands, and there was the Presidential memorandum I'd written the day before on all the U.S. Olympic gold medal winners, and about how the medal count compared to other countries and to previous U.S. Olympic teams. I had written it and then faxed it to the Staff Secretary's office...all on my laptop, without ever leaving my living room, on a Sunday afternoon.

All staff correspondence for the President went through the Staff Secretary and ended up in an enormous briefing book (a three-ring notebook) issued daily to the President. It included his schedule and all the relevant background information imaginable. There were formats everyone was required to follow when submitting material. As a former newspaper sports writer/editor, I kind of took it upon myself to send sports-related information to him whenever appropriate.

After the President led a roundtable discussion on crime and health care and then spoke to students, we left Wright about 12:30 P.M. and helicoptered fifteen minutes to Hillsdale High School, just south of Chicago. Linda Moore (political), Pat Griffin (legislative affairs), Paul Toback (Chief of Staff's office) and I worked in the receptionist's area. At one point, Toback, unable to find McLarty, said in mock seriousness, "We have *lost* the Chief of Staff."

Another trip to Chicago a few months later was as hot as the previous trip had been cold. We went to the Robert Taylor Homes housing project on South Federal Street for the President's crime bill event. Temperatures outside were in the low nineties, but it felt even hotter inside the non-air-conditioned, windowless, virtually airless staff/President holding area next to a basketball court. I dialed in and downloaded stories, getting out of the way when the President came in.

The President spoke at the outdoor event about the need to pass the pending crime bill and for Americans to take personal responsibility in the fight against crime and violence. He then taped his weekly radio address before we motorcaded back to the Palmer House Hilton for lunch. He left quicker than we expected, and everyone going with him had to gobble their catered lunches of chicken, pasta, potatoes and RC Cola and dash after him for the five-minute motorcade to Soldier Field, site of the Brazil-Germany World Cup soccer opening game.

Checking the news after we returned home that evening, I found virtually every television station was carrying live coverage of O.J. Simpson fleeing police in his white Ford Bronco, finally stopping at his house, where he was arrested in connection with the murder of his ex-wife and her friend.

Other trips focused on economic issues, especially those with other countries. That was the highlight of a Group of Seven jobs summit with other countries' financial leaders in Detroit, which kicked off a three-day, four-state trip.

Because of the cabinet secretaries and their staffs manifested on Air Force One, I got bumped to the press plane. We left about 1:30 P.M. aboard an MGM Grand plane, where we were served boxed lunches. We found chilly, overcast weather upon landing at the Air National Guard base in Selfridge, Michigan, before riding the press bus forty-five minutes to Focus:Hope, a high-tech job training center. On the way, we passed General Motors headquarters, railroad tracks, abandoned factories, Tiger Stadium, Joe Louis Arena, Cobo Hall and the Detroit-Windsor bridge to Canada. Overall, it appeared to be a typical large Rust Belt city on a gray, late winter day.

At Focus:Hope, I caught up with the rest of the White House staff and worked in our holding area, which was a modern, spacious locker room, a few hundred feet from the event site. Father William Cunningham, the priest who ran the place (which was founded in 1968), and one of the students, both of whom were to speak at the event, waited in the holding area with us.

After the President spoke, we left the huge factorylike structure and boarded the motorcade, which took us downtown to the Westin Hotel, where the President attended a couple meet-and-greet events. I took the elevated crosswalk to the adjacent Omni Shoreham Hotel and worked in the staff office until midnight, downloading and compiling wire stories and transcripts and writing talking points on Arkansas' draw in that afternoon's NCAA Tournament pairings. Gene Sperling (economic policy), Michael Waldman (communications) and David Kusnet (speechwriting) also were there, working on the President's speech for the next day.

I was up at 4:30 A.M. the next day to produce the clips. Fortunately, I got a volunteer to make copies and deliver them to aides staying in the Westin while I delivered to those in the Omni. We brought a lot of staff for the event, and we were scattered all over the place.

Mack McLarty walked in to the staff office a little later.

"Ken, have you seen any coffee?"

"No, but Catherine…" I said, as Catherine Grunden, who advanced the hotel, walked in.

After McLarty left, Grunden said half-jokingly, *"Thanks,* Ken. Thanks for making me look good in front of the Chief of Staff." I laughed.

After a brief event at the Westin, the motorcade took us to the Fox Theater, through neighborhoods resembling a demilitarized zone and past a marquee with JOBS, the theme of the G-7 conference, repeated in several typefaces and colors. Inside, we found an ornate, refurbished old theater with several architectural styles and including guest boxes, a balcony and a high ceiling. It's often used for concerts, we were told. We sat in a box stage right as the President and Vice President spoke. I ate a sweet roll from a table set up for us and, with only four hours of sleep the previous night, tried to snooze in my seat without being noticed.

Next it was on to Detroit Diesel, a factory about twenty minutes away via motorcade. As usual, Bruce Lindsey and I were the only ones working in the staff hold. He told me CNN was carrying news of the resignation of Webb Hubbell, the number-three person at Treasury and a longtime Clinton friend. I found the story on the wire and let him read it on my computer screen.

Then a Detroit Diesel employee led us to the event site, where Michigan Democratic Senators Carl Levin and Don Riegle, United Auto Workers President Owen Bieber and then Roger Penske, who bought and saved Detroit Diesel, spoke. And the admiring crowd—all company employees—absolutely went nuts. Penske's never been cheered like that even at the Indianapolis 500, where cars he owns often win. I'd never seen anyone get a warmer reception than the President, but it happened that afternoon.

After the event, we were running behind schedule, and I dashed to the motorcade for the uneventful one-hour, fifty-minute flight aboard Air Force One to Boston. I sat in the guest section and munched a chili dog and chips, glad to be rid of the excess staff. The fewer aides I had to provide with clips and keep updated on breaking news, the less stressful my job was.

As we rolled down the tarmac after landing at Boston's Logan Airport, one of the local TV stations carried live coverage of our arrival. That always was a little odd, to see the plane turning on the on-board TV set while feeling it do the same under our feet as we stood, awaiting a full stop on the tarmac.

I then hopped into the Staff 2 van on the tarmac, squeezing in the back of a minivan in my long, heavy winter coat and two bulky shoulder bags, dodging the dangling seat belt strap on the way in. We took a two-minute ride to a nearby pier, where we boarded a boat for a cold, windy ride across Boston Harbor. Fortunately, there was inside seating, so several of us sat down and started working our cell phones as the President and Massachusetts Democratic Senators Ted Kennedy and John Kerry chatted in the front section. A press boat full of photographers sailed alongside us, as did a police boat and a firefighter boat spewing water. There was a huge crowd with signs awaiting us at Rowes Wharf: BOSTON WELCOMES PRESIDENT CLINTON.

Our hold was inside and upstairs, out of the cold, in a dark conference room. Bruce Lindsey, Don Steinberg (National Security Council), Dee Dee Myers, Paul Richard, Andrew Friendly and I discussed the FBI background checks done on each of us when we started working at the White House. (*The Washington Post* had reported that morning that Myers still hadn't done her paperwork and therefore hadn't been investigated and didn't have a permanent White House pass). Friendly said it cost $25,000 to $50,000 to perform a background check on *each* of us.

Then Marine Major Leo Mercado (military aide) told Lindsey that even though the President's back was hurting him and he wanted to skip the motorcade to New Hampshire, there weren't any Marine One pilots available there, the time savings would be minimal and that there were weather concerns. Mercado recommended sticking with the planned motorcade, and Lindsey agreed and said he'd tell the President.

After the speech, the motorcade took us to the Park Plaza Hotel for a Democratic fund-raiser. Paul Richard, Don Steinberg and I searched for our holding room and, more importantly, food. Downstairs, down the hall several hundred feet from the fund-raiser, we found a huge room with a couple tables and chairs and some pasta and vegetables, hot and delicious. I downloaded wire stories and printed them out on my portable plastic Diconix printer, page after page spitting out as Lindsey got down on his haunches and read.

Next door, Steinberg began playing the piano. I heard classical and other music before I finally stepped into the room as he played the Grateful Dead's "Uncle John's Band." Then Lindsey sat down to play. Richard, Ralph Alswang (staff photographer) and Linda Moore came by and we had some fun. "Play 'Misty' for me," Moore said, and Lindsey did. Steinberg playfully set up a tip jar as Lindsey performed, and Richard tried to convince Moore to sit atop the piano, but she declined because she was wearing a long skirt.

We finally headed down the hall to watch the President on a TV monitor in the hall outside the fund-raiser: "When I was a Democratic Governor, I never did to them the way they are doing to us in Washington, D.C." Later he pounded the podium and, imitating Republicans, said, "No, no, no...." a total of nine times. I was just kind of standing around waiting to go, but that sure caught my attention.

Then we headed downstairs, and Richard and I were the only aides who got in Staff 2. We were parked near the limo and saw the President walk outside and stand beside the open rear door about twenty feet away. Through our open window, we could hear him yelling at aides Andrew Friendly and Wendy Smith: "Where's my reading material? I *told* them...." He was cranky. It was getting late, his back was hurting and we still had an hour's ride ahead of us. I slept most of the way to Nashua, New Hampshire, which had several inches of snow on the ground.

At the hotel, I poked around the staff office to make sure the equipment worked. George Stephanopoulos (senior adviser) joined us at the hotel in Nashua. Stephanopoulos had accompanied then-Governor Clinton throughout the bruising 1992 New Hampshire primary and was a key reason for the candidate's success there.

"What's he doing here?" Lindsey asked, curious.

"Nostalgia?" I suggested.

"Because it's New Hampshire," Lindsey agreed.

Lindsey, in fact, was part of the reason when I discovered I'd just plain been on the road too long. Near the end of two years as a White House aide, I started having recurring dreams about traveling with the President.

The first was about Lindsey. One day when we were standing

around after yet another Presidential event awaiting yet another Presidential departure, I asked him, "Bruce, uh, can I ask you something? Have you been feeling all right?"

He looked at me sort of oddly. "Well, I've lost so much weight people keep asking if I have cancer or AIDS," he said. But he said that in fact he felt fine. "Why?"

"Well, 'cause I had a dream the other night," I said. I told him I'd dreamed that he wasn't with us on a trip, and that at every opportunity everyone on the traveling staff was madly dialing their cellular phones, calling Lindsey's assistant back in the West Wing to see if his lab results had come back yet. "We were all really concerned, and when I woke up I thought I'd better just, you know, check."

He chuckled and shook his head, thanking me for my concern.

Another time I dreamed the President was appearing as guest host on "Saturday Night Live." Except in my dream, the show aired on Fox, instead of NBC, and was produced in Los Angeles, instead of New York.

The President performed the traditional guest host's monologue as the setting sun streamed through large open studio doors behind the audience. I dreamed that traveling White House aides were included in skits. In one skit I had no lines and just stood in the background. But as my other appearance neared, I stood offstage in a dark blue suit, searching my trip book in vain to find my dialogue.

But another dream was stranger still. In this one, the traveling staff was with the Clintons back in Arkansas, in a grassy, empty area with a partially built house. And the President was pointing to the place where, he told us, they planned to live "after we leave public life." Even odder in this dream, the First Lady was pregnant. She was going to the doctor the next day to determine the baby's gender, but the President said he was sure it would be a boy.

But it got weirder. The next day, a tabloid reported the First Lady was pregnant. It was nonsense, of course, but I had *just* dreamed about that.

That's it, I thought. I've gotta get out of here. I'm starting to lose it.

12▶Have Passport, Will Travel

"YOU'RE IN TOKYO AND YOU ATE AT DENNY'S?" · SEOUL:
"AMERICAN! HOW 'BOUT NICE SUIT, YES?" · SUNBURNED
IN HAWAII · BRUSSELS' GRAND PLACE · PRAGUE:
"SMOKING CAUSES CANCER" · COMMIE PLUMBING IN THE
WORST MAJOR CITY IN THE INDUSTRIALIZED WORLD ·
SHOPPING IN MINSK · GENEVA: "WE HAVE TO GO IN
HERE"

WHEN I FOUND OUT I'D BE TRAVELING REGULARLY aboard Air Force One, one of my first questions was, "Does that include overseas?"

"Everywhere," was the answer.

As I'd anticipated, traveling abroad with the President became one of the highlights of my time at the White House. We visited Asia twice, Europe three times and the Middle East once.

The first trip began on the Fourth of July, with stops in Philadelphia, the Quad Cities and San Francisco (see "Introduction"). That first night at San Francisco's Fairmont Hotel (site of the United Nations charter meetings in 1945 and featured in the 1980s TV series "Hotel" with James Brolin and Connie Selleca), I only got two hours sleep, and that was interrupted by a phone call. I stumbled down the hall to the staff office and cranked out the daily clips. After delivering them to everybody's doors, I stood looking out the twenty-first-floor staff office window. It was a perfect sunny morning, and I could see Alcatraz Island. From the deserted, early-morning streets far below, I clearly heard a cable car bell.

That morning we took the motorcade to the Moscone Center, where the President addressed the National Education Association. In a large holding room nearby, I dialed in on my laptop. Strobe Talbott of the State Department worked the phones nearby. Just before leaving, I downloaded the latest wire stories onto a diskette and printed them on a nearby laser printer. The President and First Lady came into the room, greeting guests. Press Secretary Dee Dee Myers was there, too, and I tried to get the latest stories to her. I stared at the printer, imploring the pages to come out faster.

Then I looked up, and I was the only one in the room. I'd committed the fundamental mistake of getting behind the President. Once he reached the limousine, I knew, we'd take off. So I scurried through the crowd—where a Secret Service agent halted me before seeing my staff lapel pin—and finally got ahead of the President and First Lady, finding the staff van in the underground parking garage and climbing aboard just in time.

I had been issued a Secret Service pin (known as "hard pins" because they were permanent, as opposed to the temporary "tin pins" our advance teams wore) a few days before we left. The Secret Service office secretary on the Old Executive Office Building ground floor had said it wasn't to be worn around the White House normally, only when I'd be in close proximity to the President—like on trips. There were several similar styles and colors, denoting whether a staffer was a political appointee (White House staff), military, White House Communications Agency or Secret Service. There were similar pins for guests. And the colors were changed every once in a while to prevent counterfeiting.

We were at San Francisco International Airport by noon. I was on the backup plane, a specially configured 747 identical to Air Force One, only without the President. It had left Washington very early that morning and was full of sleepy-looking White House, State and National Security Council staffers. I found my seat in the back and relaxed, exhausted from my all-nighter, adrenaline ebbing and knowing we had a ten-and-one-half-hour flight to Tokyo ahead of us. At the last minute, a couple of staffers from the military White House Television Office scrambled aboard, having missed the motorcade leaving the Moscone Center as I almost had.

I took off my suit coat, tie and shoes (other folks changed clothes), easing back in the first-class blue seat and perusing a stack of briefing material from the State Department. Jeannie Bull of State brought me $600 in travelers' checks, temporary staff ID card and luggage tags. I watched three movies on the TV screen mounted above me.

Because of the long flight and the thirteen-hour time change, it was Tuesday afternoon local time when we landed in Tokyo. We rode a bus to the Hotel Okura and got settled in, going right to work.

I took a seat in the press advance office at a table overlooking the Tokyo skyline, a TV set tuned to CNN International audible from across the room, and tapped on my laptop, with a fax machine and phone at my elbow. I tried to monitor the wires but had difficulty dialing in. Nevertheless, I produced a set of news clips about 8:00 or 9:00 P.M., which, due to the time change, was also when they were being delivered around the White House.

I spent a good part of the day working with the White House Communications Agency team to figure out why I couldn't dial in properly. So they took me to their command center elsewhere in the hotel. Whoa! For a technical communications junkie, seeing that setup was like a weapons buff seeing the Secret Service vault. They had a huge switchboard with cables and wires running everywhere. Considering that it was both temporary and mobile, it was particularly impressive. After several experiments, they decided that insufficient bandwidth was the problem, and they solved it for me.

I took a look around the Hotel Okura, where rooms were normally $300 a night, and found it was huge. I worked on the twelfth floor of the south wing, but the press office (where I had to pick up Presidential transcripts on diskette) was in the basement of the main wing. It took fifteen or twenty minutes to get between the two. The lobby looked like an enormous version of George Jetson's living room. In fact, the decor in general was kind of like a 1960s version of what the future would look like. Tiny young women in traditional kimonos, speaking perfect English, operated the elevators.

I was up at 5:00 A.M. the next day to prepare materials for the staff meeting a couple doors down the hall from the office where I was working. I produced some wire reports for everybody to keep them updated on what was going on elsewhere, in addition to coverage of us there at the Group of Seven economic summit of the world's leading industrialized nations.

The rest of the morning I continued producing paper: copying magazine clips, downloading editions of "Hotline," compiling wire reports. At lunch, I strolled down the street. Having earlier converted my currency (108 yen = one dollar) in the State Department's control room, I walked a few blocks to the nearby U.S. Embassy, a large, clean-looking building constructed in the early 1970s. After I displayed my pass, the Marine guards buzzed me through and directed me to the cafeteria. I tried the pork curry, which wasn't bad, but it did cost about the equivalent of $15. I thought of that song by the Arc Angels: "I was down like the dollar comin' up against the yen / I was doin' pretty good for the shape I was in."

That night, after producing the clips, I went for a walk. I felt perfectly safe, but upon exiting the cocoon of the hotel, I became illiterate. I couldn't read any of the street signs. I realized if I got lost and did by some chance find someone who spoke English, they couldn't tell me which streets to take back to the hotel, because the street signs were in Japanese. I walked to a Denny's nearby, hoping to maybe try the Grand Slam breakfast, a taste of home. No chance. I pointed at a picture in the menu of linguini and seafood as the Beatles played over the speakers in the background.

The next day I again produced wire clips before the morning staff meeting. Afterward, Communications Director Mark Gearan looked at the table loaded with reports I'd been producing and had some positive comments, so that was encouraging. I'd been cranking out a ton of stuff, but sometimes it was hard to know if it was actually helping anybody.

I spent another morning overlooking Tokyo from the twelfth floor, occasionally dashing to the press office in the main wing basement to get Presidential transcripts on my diskette, then back upstairs to transmit them back to Washington. The White House Stenographers Office consisted of about a half dozen young women who taped everything the President said in public and then transcribed his remarks for distribution to the media. Part of my job was to electronically transmit the transcripts to USNewswire, a service which then fed them to newsrooms across the country. The transcripts also went to White House staff on my e-mail list.

On my way out the hotel's main entrance for lunch, I was momentarily held up by the President's arrival. That was the first time I'd seen him since we'd been there. When you're not part of it, the size of the President's entourage really is overwhelming.

After another afternoon of dialing in and scanning the wires, I called Jeff Eller (media affairs director) to check in. "How's the food?" he asked. I told him about my late dinner the previous night, and he was incredulous. "You're in Tokyo, and you ate at *Denny's?*"

That night the hotel graciously hosted a buffet dinner for us. One of the hotel's very polite managers chatted with me for a while, and his English was excellent. He gave me his business card, and having read my State briefing book, I knew to study it closely and then to put it away (not in a rear pocket, which would be an insult). The food was great, but I had to hustle back upstairs to crank out the clips for everybody.

By Friday I was into a regular routine, but that was our last full day in Tokyo. I was up at 5:00 A.M. again, checked the wires and produced the clips, attending the staff meeting at 7:00 A.M. I eventually got used to the thirteen-hour time change and the difference in U.S. news cycles compared to local time.

After lunch at the Embassy (steak and baked potato with Fanta orange soda, flown in from California), I stopped by the press office for more transcripts. In the basement, our press staff had no windows in its large room. "For all we've seen of Tokyo, we may as well have been in Cleveland," said Steve Cohen (press assistant).

That night I saw Japanese Prime Minister Kiichi Miyazawa (whom Dee Dee Myers privately referred to as "Yoda" because he looked so much like him) enter the hotel with his security personnel. The hotel staff was thrilled, just as Americans are to see our President. And yet I stood there thinking it was no big deal...just another country's leader.

Later I was on my way from the advance office back to the press office when Secretary of State Warren Christopher came walking toward me with his entourage of staff and Japanese security. One Japanese security guy walked right at me and wordlessly backed me into a glass wall of a hotel shop, literally getting in my face. I wanted to tell him, "Look, pal, if I wanted to do anything to the guy, I wouldn't have to come to Tokyo to do it." Our staff pins meant nothing there, except on our floor of the hotel, where Marine Embassy guards were posted. The only thing Japanese security cared about were the G-7 tags we were issued on the plane (which I was wearing).

That incident made me realize the Japanese I met were part of a society where individuality is surrendered for the sake of harmony. On an island so small, I guess that's important. They took their jobs—whether security guards protecting the Secretary of State or hotel maids making the beds—very seriously. P.J. O'Rourke once wrote that the Koreans are a nation of people who stayed home Friday nights and did their homework, and it probably describes the Japanese as well.

On Saturday morning, departure day from Tokyo, I went through what had become my regular routine, including tuning in Armed Forces Radio (which played the Proclaimers' "One Thousand Miles") while showering and dressing. Our Hotel Okura rooms featured nifty, if slightly outdated, electronic gadgets.

Then late that morning we rode buses back to the airport to board the two 747s for a two-hour, thirty-minute flight to Seoul, South Korea. We landed at K-16 airport (so named because it's 16 kilometers from Seoul), used for VIPs and military big shots. Mountains were in the background, and a sign saying "Welcome to Korea" was displayed beside a South Korean flag. Somehow it seemed as if the Cold War was still alive there, even though we weren't near the thirty-eighth parallel demilitarized zone dividing North and South Korea.

After a twenty-five-minute drive through Seoul, we arrived at our hilltop hotel, a huge complex called the Hotel Shilla, overlooking the city. I found work space upstairs in the advance office without air-conditioning and worked for a while. My hard drive crashed. I couldn't get my laptop even to boot up. I'd been carrying a backup laptop in another bag halfway around the world and suddenly realized why. Thank goodness.

The next day, the President headed to the demilitarized zone. But since there weren't any phone lines there and we could only take so many staff anyway, I didn't go. I was disappointed but unsurprised.

Instead, I went to Itaewon, a shopping district lining both sides of a busy four-lane street. A few fellow staffers and I rode a shuttle bus there and roamed the sidewalks all morning. There were tiny, hot stores in basements and attics where the smell of kimchi, a garlic and hot-pepper sauerkraut, permeated the humidity. Watches, purses, boots, leather jackets, sporting shoes…all the brand-name stuff one could imagine. I found a Gap shirt with a tag that said "Made in Korea" and realized why everything was so cheap. I found leather jackets and boots at one-third of their price in the States.

Of course, copyright infringement is rampant there, so $5 Chanel bags and $20 Nike shoes weren't necessarily the real thing. And every few steps some merchant would yell, "American! How 'bout nice suit, yes? You buy, you like!" or "Nike! Reebok! You want? We got!" or "You, sir—buy nice watchee?"

With my pasty white skin and navy blue suit, I was an easy mark. "American—you G.I.?" asked one group of young men. I shook my head. "USA? FBI?" And then they formed guns with their hands and rat-a-tat-tatted imaginary Tommy guns, like out of an old Edward G. Robinson film, laughing. I laughed and kept walking.

Later, a young man saw my lapel pin and asked if I was "an assistance of Bill Clinton" and offered me a seat. But after a morning of being hassled and harassed by overly anxious salesmen, I smelled a potential con. And I really didn't have the energy to fight through the language barrier. Later, I regretted not stopping. Overall, the whole humid flea market experience made me appreciate air-conditioned suburban shopping malls.

After a drenching mid-day rain, I got back to the hotel and had an Embassy car take me to the press hotel to pick up Presidential transcripts on diskette. My driver looked like a Korean Elvis Presley (circa *G.I. Blues*) with his shined black boots, baggy fatigues and short black hair. After I ducked inside the press hotel and dashed back out, he turned the key but got only a grinding noise. With about an hour until the buses left for the airport, I wasn't thrilled about getting stranded in Korea. Finally the engine turned over and we were on our way.

At K-16 airport, our busload of staff encountered a silly security hassle, having to stand in long lines for no apparent reason. When we walked across the tarmac, those two planes with "United States of America" and the U.S. flag on them, waiting to take us back to the States, were a welcome sight.

We were in Seoul just under twenty-four hours, but it seemed to me the Koreans I met were, generally, friendlier and more outgoing than the Japanese I'd met. The Koreans I encountered seemed like pretty nice folks.

Aboard the plane again, some staffers had a couple drinks with dinner and went to sleep for the all-night flight to Honolulu. I curled up with Norman Mailer's *Harlot's Ghost* and read for a while.

"Ken, you can get up and move around if you want," Wendy Smith said. "We're all up in the conference room." I told her I'd come up there later. Smith had a difficult job as trip director, but I appreciated her trying to make me feel at home as I attempted to figure out travel procedures on my first trip.

Smith was tall and dark-haired with brown eyes and high cheekbones, and looked a little like Sheryl Crow. She had a live-in boyfriend who worked at the State Department. A Texas native who moved to New York City, she started in the early days of the campaign, fighting the good fight in New Hampshire. She went on to become trip director during the 1992 campaign, meaning she was constantly at the candidate's side. The President obviously trusted her, meaning, for example, he wouldn't flinch or fidget if she adjusted his makeup just before a television camera came on. She bore the brunt of his temper tantrums, often caused by other people's mistakes. She was in charge of everything that happened on the road, from coordinating with the on-site advance teams to sometimes following the President as he worked ropelines, collecting items for him to autograph.

Later I fell asleep in my soft, wide seat. Sleeping on Air Force One—in a seat, in one's clothes and contact lenses—isn't as good as sleeping in a bed, but it sure beats the heck out of trying to sleep on a regular commercial flight, especially in coach. On Air Force One, there's plenty of room between the seats, which almost fully recline without bumping anyone.

When I awoke, I was confused. What? Sunday morning—again? Oh, I thought, crossing the international dateline is weird. It was like Bill Murray reliving the same day repeatedly in *Groundhog Day*. The digital clocks with three blue displays—telling us the time in Washington, our destination and where we were currently—had stopped meaning much.

I awoke to sunlight streaming into the cabin as fellow staffers awakened and lifted the window shades. I was snuggled under a fuzzy light blue blanket with the Seal of the President on it when Timmy, our steward in the staff section, asked, "Sir, are you ready for breakfast?" I was. He served French toast, fruit and orange juice. Breakfast in bed on Air Force One: This is the way to travel, I thought.

We landed at Honolulu's Hickam Air Force Base (elevation: three feet, according to the lettering on the operations building). Ukulele music played over the Staff 2 van's radio as we boarded the motorcade parked on the tarmac on a sunny, pleasant morning. We were driven to a naval base cafeteria so the President could eat breakfast with the enlisted men and women. The staff ate breakfast in the officers' mess. Afterward, we found that among those at the President's table was a young man from Little Rock. We joked about what a "coincidence" that was, and Bruce Lindsey (senior adviser) said, "The funny thing is, afterward he'll say, 'You'll never guess where the folks I sat with are from.'"

Next the motorcade took us to the USS *Arizona* Memorial. As we boarded small boats to ferry across Pearl Harbor, I said, "Am I the only one thinking 'Gilligan's Island' here?" Army Lieutenant Colonel Rusty Schorsch (military aide) reminded us all to turn off our pagers and cellular phones for the solemn ceremony. The President laid a wreath there in a short, moving event. Over the side, we could see oil in the water from the wreckage, over fifty years old. We were told that occasionally air bubbles surface from the battleship, which sank during the Japanese attack on December 7, 1941.

Then it was on to Camp H.M. Smith, a mountaintop Marine base which serves as Pacific Naval headquarters. The staff held in a lounge while the President was briefed by senior officers. CNN was on the TV as fewer than ten of us waited, watching baseball highlights. We were talking about a story in the news about a woman in Virginia who cut off her husband's penis. So John Gaughan (military office) called the National Security Council Situation Room at the White House and had the clipping from *The Washington Post* about Lorena and John Bobbitt faxed to us through Roadrunner, the fully equipped communications van parked outside. "This falls under the 'west of the Potomac' rule," Gaughan said, explaining, "Anything that happens (on trips) west of the Potomac isn't discussed east of the Potomac."

Later, Bruce Lindsey said Hawaii Governor John Waihee's staff wanted to host a dinner for us. It was a really nice gesture, but we were all exhausted from the trip. Lindsey canvassed us and the prevailing opinion was that we'd go if they'd gone to a lot of trouble already, but otherwise, unless they'd be offended, we'd just as soon have the evening off to rest.

That evening the President held a public event at the Hilton Hawaiian Village, speaking to the crowd and shaking hands. I stayed at our beachfront hotel, the Kahala Hilton, on the southeast shore of Oahu, not far from Diamond Head and Koko Head. I ate dinner in the hotel restaurant: a burger and fries with a Coke and a brownie with ice cream and hot fudge sauce. It was good to be back in the States.

The next day, I awoke before 6 A.M. to produce the clips, which was pretty easy since we were six hours behind Washington and the staff in my Old Executive Office Building office faxed everything to me.

After a buffet breakfast under a tent overlooking the beach, I headed out into the sun. I read and went swimming in the ocean, thoughts of Elvis in *Blue Hawaii* dancing in my head. Discovering lots of coral under the brilliant blue water, I also thought of Sean Connery as James Bond in *Dr. No*, when he discovers Ursula Andress on a Ja-maican beach. As I sat in the sun, several White House aides and Se-cret Service came by with their pagers and cell phones and notepads, holding outdoor meetings. If I were at this resort on vacation, I thought, I'd be annoyed by us.

The following day I was sunburned. I mean, I'd never been that sunburned. I was starting to get blisters in places, and I didn't feel so good. Some of us spent most of the day relaxing in the shade. I had lunch at a poolside table with some of our advance staff. Bev and Bruce Lindsey were there, too, and Bev was chiding a slightly sun-burned Bruce for not wearing sunscreen: "'I don't need sunscreen, I've got olive skin.'" Bruce chuckled.

It was decided to leave that night instead of the next morning so we could stop in Iowa, where the flooding had gotten worse in our ab-sence. I watched on the staff office TV a little of the tape-delayed baseball All-Star Game, which, ironically, was being played at Baltimore's Camden Yards, not far from Washington.

I paid my incidentals at the front desk and strolled outside to the motorcade, where a crowd of tourists in shorts waited behind a ropeline and popped camera flashbulbs, awaiting the President's de-parture on a pleasant, warm evening. We rolled through Honolulu's vowel-laden streets, blue police lights flashing in the island darkness, toward Hickam Air Force Base.

We flew overnight across the Pacific to the Midwest. After eating dinner and watching a movie, I felt jet-lagged, sunburned, sore and tired but still mentally exhilarated.

We landed the next morning in Des Moines, Iowa. Because of the flood, phone lines couldn't be installed at the event site. So I stayed on the plane for the five or six hours we were on the ground, watching all of the visit on live local television coverage. With my sunburn and exhaustion, that was fine with me.

The President, in jeans and a short-sleeved shirt, filled sand bags with local residents. As water covered 17 million acres across the Midwest, a small young woman cried to him, "We just can't take it anymore." The President hugged her and said, "Hang in there."

By late afternoon, everyone was back aboard, and we headed back to Washington. There was a tent on the South Lawn, so the President couldn't ride a helicopter back from Andrews Air Force Base. Instead, the motorcade took us to the South Lawn, pulling in the east side and parking under the familiar South Portico. It was evening, and most staff there were leaving for the day.

I headed back to my office in the Old Executive Office Building to drop off my computer bags and passed Jeff Eller in the hall. "Glad to have you back," he said, and that was nice to hear. I didn't stick around to wait for my luggage to show up and instead headed out. I arrived home to my rented condo in Arlington, Virginia, to find a happy dog and a stack of mail.

Whew…more than 18,000 miles, eleven days, thirteen time zones (twice each), two international dateline crossings and travel by foot, train, car, bus, van, plane, helicopter and boat. In terms of days, my first trip was the longest I took. I felt like Phileas Fogg.

The next month I got my first bill in inter-office mail from White House Airlift Operations, located on the fourth floor of the Old Executive Office Building. They kept tabs on who owed money for meals on Air Force One. We got per diem (about $30 a day), of course, but we also were billed for our meals on the plane. My first bill was $46.90 for the overseas trip and a weekend trip to St. Louis and Little Rock.

The State Department paid for meals on international legs of trips, and we had to pay for meals on domestic flights. The per diem on overseas trips, from State, could really add up, because the trips usually were long and included stays in expensive cities, like Tokyo.

On political trips, the Democratic National Committee (or sometimes other organizations like the Democratic Congressional Campaign Committee or the Democratic Senatorial Campaign Committee or state parties or even individual campaigns) would ultimately pick up the tab for the part of the trip that wasn't official business for the President.

In fact, the paperwork that went into traveling with the President was mind-numbing. For every trip, we had to fill out a travel authorization form before we left. Then, after the trip, a copy of that form would come back to us via inter-office mail, and we had to fill out a travel voucher and submit that. It was worth it, though. If we didn't fill out and sign the forms, we wouldn't get our per diem checks after the trips.

Our next overseas trip didn't cover as many miles, but it did kick off a busy period of international travel. We flew to Europe in January 1994, and returned to the continent twice in the next six months. In fact, after just one trip aboard in 1993, I accompanied the President on five overseas trips our second year.

Our first trip to Europe covered more than 11,000 miles, eight time zones and six countries in nine days, and the President met with two dozen heads of state or government. It began on a Saturday evening in early January. I drove to the White House about 8:00 P.M., bundled up in black wool overcoat, gloves, scarf and ear muffs, for the bus ride to Andrews Air Force Base. Some staffers were returning from the President's mother's funeral in Hot Springs, Arkansas, as we left.

We sat around the Distinguished Visitors Lounge at Andrews for what seemed like a long time. (Normally we would have immediately boarded the plane upon arrival, but we had to wait for the President.) Eventually we boarded the two identical blue-and-white 747s. The support plane was on the far side of the tarmac, next to Air Force One.

We boarded about 9:30 P.M. and were served dinner by 11:00 P.M. or so. All of us on the support plane (National Security Council, Department of State staffers and me) were seated in the guest section. I asked one of the stewards whom I knew if the conference room was available, and he said with a smile, "Sure. You know where it is." Indeed I did. So I grabbed a pillow and a blanket (knowing where those were stored) and made myself comfortable on the conference room couch. I slept reasonably well as the plane carried us more than seven hours over the Atlantic Ocean.

We reached Belgium's Zaventum National Airport about noon local time (6:00 A.M. Washington time) on Sunday. The President went directly to Brussels' Laeken Castle for a meeting with King Albert II. Those of us on the support plane boarded a bus and were driven to the Conrad Hotel. The hotel was beautiful, with perhaps the nicest bathrooms—with lots of gold fixtures and glass—of any place we stayed.

In the staff office, I immediately tried to dial in to the wires and did so successfully, catching up on overnight news. That never failed to amaze me, being able to dial in from anywhere around the world and see on my laptop computer exactly what was on the computer screen at my desk back in the Old Executive Office Building. News stories would appear on my computer screen halfway across the world at the same time they appeared in newsrooms back in the United States.

The President spent the rest of the day preparing for that night's speech. Late that afternoon we boarded a motorcade for the President's speech to a large crowd at Brussels' Grand Place. Our driver had a French accent but spoke English (sort of). He had been to California and had seen the Grand Canyon, and he told me of how Europeans had loved President Kennedy. Although it was obvious, for the first time it struck me that he—and other people I saw his age, and in fact everything I saw—fifty years ago had been under Nazi rule. To realize that upon seeing Europe for the first time was kind of unsettling.

At Grand Place, a large, historic and beautifully ornate plaza, the staff stood outside awaiting the President's speech on a cold evening. Don Steinberg (National Security Council) absentmindedly set down his briefcase and walked away. Soon at least a half dozen Belgian police, military and security officers surrounded it, talking excitedly to each other and into their two-way radios. Eventually the Secret Service got involved and helped confirm that it wasn't a bomb. Some of us ducked into quaint little shops nearby to get warm until the President came out to speak to the enthusiastic crowd.

On Monday, as usual, I was up early to produce and distribute the clips. The President went to North Atlantic Treaty Organization Headquarters to pitch his "Partnership for Peace" initiative, but since it would have been rude to our hosts to bring along a whole slew of staff, some of us stayed behind. The President had lunch with NATO heads of state and government at Laeken Castle and spent the afternoon in working sessions back at NATO Headquarters.

I worked all day in the staff office, downloading information from the wires and White House computer system. Then that evening (while the President attended a working dinner at Château Val Duchesse with other NATO heads of state), I roamed the area near our hotel on a pleasant January evening. Many stores still had Christmas decorations displayed. The city was sort of like Washington, actually. The intersection outside our hotel was kind of like 18th and K streets back in Washington—lots of traffic and office buildings, but little industry—except the signs were in French. (As Steve Martin once said, "Those French are amazing. It's as if they've got a different word for *everything*.")

As I walked the tiny, twisting streets and saw shops and cafés, I initially thought of the city as being Old World. But in fact it was much like any major East Coast U.S. city. Ultimately, though, what little I saw of Belgium struck me as being rather nondescript, half French and half Dutch. I mean, split up and join France and the Netherlands.

After I spent another early morning of cranking out the news clips at the hotel on Tuesday, the President spoke at an American business event downstairs in our hotel and then went to NATO Headquarters and to European Union events at Breydel Building. Those of us on the support plane left the Conrad Hotel about 12:30 P.M. to head for the airport and on to Prague.

As our twin 747s approached the Czech Republic, I couldn't help but think of a scene in *Stripes*, in which Bill Murray and Harold Ramis, both portraying U.S. soldiers, contemplate taking a heavily armored secret Army recreational vehicle into Czechoslovakia. Says Murray: "Come on, it's Czechoslovakia. We're not going to Moscow. We zip in, we zip out. It's Czechoslovakia. It's like going to Wisconsin."

We arrived at Ruzyne International Airport late afternoon, and during the motorcade it quickly became apparent we were behind what used to be the Iron Curtain. The city had old buildings, gray and drab. The apartments looked like the public housing projects I'd seen in Chicago.

The motorcade took us to Prague's Hotel Atrium, which was an adequate facility. The rooms, while small and sparsely furnished, included bowls of fruit and bottles of water (important, since we were advised not to drink the water outside of western Europe). The small staff office didn't have any windows, but it had the necessary phone lines, laser printer and copier. U.S. Embassy volunteers were on hand to help, as usual.

The President attended a few events, including a visit with Czech President Vaclav Havel at Prague Castle and a walk, surrounded by media, across the historic Charles Bridge.

Wednesday morning, after producing and delivering the clips, I headed downstairs to the press office in the hotel. I made my way through the crowded lobby, winding through a bunch of Lech Walesa-looking dudes dressed in several layers of winter clothes and smoking funky-smelling cigarettes. And I thought to myself, "You know, y'all want to join NATO and be part of the new world order. Here's a three-word idea: 'Smoking causes cancer.' You'll thank me later, I guarantee it.

The President attended a memorial event at the Old Jewish Cemetery, took part in bilateral meetings with leaders from Hungary, Poland and Slovakia, made a statement to the press with Czech President Vaclav Havel and spoke at a privatization/business event at a Kmart. We were only in the Czech Republic about twenty-four hours. I didn't even exchange my money.

That afternoon we flew one hour, forty minutes to Kiev, Ukraine, where the President met with Ukrainian leader Leonid Kravchuk. The stop was a last-minute addition to the schedule as a thank-you for Ukraine's decision to dismantle its nuclear missiles, left over from the Soviet regime, aimed at the United States. The President attended an official dinner at the airport (staffers who were there said much vodka was imbibed), but those of us not attending stayed on the plane as snow fell on the tarmac. I eased back into a soft leather swivel chair with armrests, ate dinner and watched a movie in the conference room. We were only in the Ukraine a few hours.

Then it was on to Russia. Even though it was late at night and I was exhausted from a long day, it was exciting to land in the former Soviet capital after our one-hour, twenty-minute flight. Air Force One landed first at Vnukovo II airport, so as we neared the ground, we were able to watch Russian television coverage of the President's airport arrival ceremony on board. Then on the windy, snowy, thirty-five-minute bus ride to our hotel, the radio on the bus played an Abba song. (In another flashback to the 1970s, Eastern Europe also calls its nightclubs "discos"—pronounced "*dees*-coze.") I noticed that an iron gate at the airport had the Aeroflot logo, including the Soviet hammer and sickle.

We arrived at the Slavyanska Radisson Hotel about 3:00 A.M. It was so late that some staffers just stayed up, pulling the old college all-nighter. I took a two-hour nap and awoke to produce and deliver the clips. Afterward, I took a look around the hotel, a joint U.S.-Russian venture. It was fine downstairs. But upstairs, where we stayed and worked, it was roughly the equivalent of a rundown Motel 6 in downtown Akron. It was hot, the air was stale and the bathrooms were straight out of the 1940s. ("Commie plumbing," I kept muttering to myself.) And keep in mind, I told myself, this is for the President of the United States and therefore probably the best Moscow has to offer.

But perhaps most strange—and maybe this is just because I grew up with Cold War horror stories—was the presence of Russian security personnel in cheap suits and bad haircuts, speaking Russian and hanging out on the President's hotel floor…especially when White House signs identified which rooms were "unsafe for production, discussion, and dissemination of classified material." I mean, what do you think those KGB goons did after the Cold War? You think they're all doing advertising and marketing for Coca-Cola? (Although somebody obviously was—red Coke bags with Coke towels, Coke T-shirts and Coke pins were left in our rooms for us.)

I also found myself thinking about the Russian people and what they'd gone through, especially the previous couple of years. When a nation-state dedicates its vast resources as a matter of policy, for decades on end, virtually all to guns and none to butter, the lasting effects on the people are overwhelming. In Washington, we'd toss around terms like Russia's "political instability" and "economic hard-ship," but it was daily, bitter reality for millions of people...people who seemed very warm and friendly despite it all. We may have ram-pant, unforgivable poverty in our rich country, I thought, but by com-parison we are nevertheless a spoiled, pampered nation of whiners.

The President attended bilateral discussions at the Kremlin and a reception at Spaso House on Thursday while I worked in the small staff office.

Friday was another stultifying day in the staff room, looking out the window at the bitter cold and slush that withered my sense of ad-venture and kept me from going out to explore the city. Moscow was the most depressing place I'd ever seen (barely beating out Danville, Illinois) and arguably the worst major city in all the industrialized world. Everything in Moscow was gray—the sky, the buildings, the cars, the snow, the food—everything but the people, who were Casper white, and the water, which was brown. In winter, at least, there's nothing to do, nothing to see, nowhere to go. There is sunlight maybe four hours a day and it's never sunny. It is just plain butt-ugly.

Lots of our staffers went shopping, especially for those thick fur hats Russians wear. I didn't get it. As Kathy Roth (scheduling and ad-vance) explained to me, "It's kind of a chick thing." I guess so. As far as I was concerned, Chuck Berry was right: "Anything you want, we got it right here in the USA."

Friday afternoon the President conducted a town hall meeting on live television to all of Russia, across nearly a dozen time zones, with citizens from around the country asking questions of the President via satellite. A half dozen aides sat in the holding room at Ostankino Tele-vision Center with Ted Koppel, whose "Nightline" crew was produc-ing daily shows on the President's trip. When a cherub-faced little boy asked a question and the President called him down front, Koppel jokingly accused us of staging the question. "Oh, geez—he's even got dimples," Koppel told Wendy Smith. "Wendy, you guys are shame-less."

In the motorcade back to the hotel, I noticed store signs. That goofy Cyrillic alphabet was weird. When we visited Japan and Korea, I knew at a glance I couldn't read anything. But in Russia, the letters were vaguely familiar enough to make me think I ought to be able to figure out the signs. Sometimes I could; often I couldn't.

The President had a busy day. He attended a wreath-laying ceremony at the tomb of the unknown soldier, conducted a news conference with President Boris Yeltsin, walked through the streets of Moscow, went to Kazansky Cathedral for a candle lighting and that night attended a state dinner at the Kremlin.

Meanwhile, I ordered room service. The bill: $68.88. Huh? This is one screwed-up economy, I thought. Less than two weeks before we arrived, transactions in foreign currency became illegal in Russia, even though some of the price tags were still in dollars. The ruble was virtually worthless.

Saturday morning I was up early again to produce and deliver the clips. We were all on the same hotel floor—even the President, which was unusual—so that helped my distribution. Then I sat around and awaited departure, watching American country music videos on TV in the staff office. I was ever-so-anxious to leave the former Evil Empire.

The two 747s took us to Minsk about 10:15 A.M. I was again on the backup plane, which staffer Kathy Roth nearly missed boarding. She was manifested on Air Force One, but overslept. In an incredible comeback, she got a U.S. Embassy car to dash her to the airport, somehow talked her way through the gate, past the KGB agents (who didn't speak English) and boarded the backup plane mere minutes before the doors were sealed. Hair frazzled, lacking makeup and breathing heavily for quite some time after collapsing into a seat in the conference room, she told us of her harrowing tale. (If left behind, she could've found another way to get home without flying commercial, like on the car plane, a cargo plane that transports the President's limousines. But who wants to be stuck in Moscow, of all places?)

After an uneventful, one-hour and forty-minute flight, we landed in Minsk, Belarus—like Ukraine, formerly a part of the Soviet Union. Several fellow aides and I went sightseeing with some kind U.S. Embassy staffers who served as our guides. When we visited, Belarus was perhaps the most Communist of the former Soviet states, and signs of that were apparent.

We visited a local market, where merchants sold anything they could get their hands on, like meat and bridal gowns in the same shop. Elderly women with wrinkled faces in scarves and heavy coats stood outside in the slush in lines, selling long sticks of what appeared to be sausage. One held a live chicken. Another place had a counter of items from the United States and western Europe, usually one of each, for sale in dollars (instead of rubles), what would've once been black-market goods.

We also ate lunch (sauerkraut, potatoes and rolls) at the U.S. Embassy. It was a small mansion formerly used by the Red Army general in charge of Belarus' occupation, located between the Russian and German embassies. Meanwhile, somewhere across town, the President held bilateral meetings with Belarussian leaders, attended a wreath laying at a World War I memorial, gave a speech at the Academy of Sciences and attended a ceremony at Kuropaty Memorial.

We were only in Minsk for about six hours. On the ensuing flight to Geneva, Switzerland, I met Juliann Bubolz, an advance staffer for the First Lady and live-in girlfriend of one of our top advance aides. We discovered that in college she dated one of my co-workers from the *Arkansas Gazette,* and we talked all the way to Geneva.

The motorcade in Geneva, near the Swiss-French border, took us from Cointrin Airport close to the Intercontinental Hotel, where our bus was scrutinized at a checkpoint. (European police and militia love to show off their weapons. These guys had semiautomatic weapons slung over their shoulders, in their hands and at the ready.)

In the hotel, my room was next to the staff office, which was convenient. Ashley Bell, one of my favorite advance staffers, said my enormous room—several times the size of everybody else's, I later learned—initially was reserved for the President, but he was moved so he wouldn't be disturbed by noise in the staff office. It always was nice, especially near the end of a long trip, when somebody on the advance team was looking out for me.

I sat at the desk in my room, laptop computer dialed in to the wire service system back home. I was finishing some work when Juliann Bubolz came by and stuck her head in the room: "You almost done? You want to go out to dinner?" Sounded good to me, especially since she spoke French and I didn't.

We caught one of the staff/press shuttle buses going downtown and roamed the winding, hilly, cobblestone streets on a chilly, dry Saturday night. We passed several restaurants and cafés before stopping at a small place with maybe ten tiny tables and cigarette smoke permeating everything. (Europeans really ought to read the 1964 Surgeon General's report.)

Looking through the window, we heard someone playing an acoustic guitar and others singing, in English, "Bad, Bad Leroy Brown." We looked at each other and said, "We *have* to go in here." We had a couple small bottles of wine, and a half dozen other staffers showed up later. The bartender took us all to two after-hours places, and we got back to the hotel about 3:00 A.M. It was the only actual fun (as opposed to parts of the job that were fun) I had on the trip.

But when I got up to shower, dress and produce the clips the next morning, it became apparent I'd messed up. I'd packed everything the night before so I could get a little more sleep by putting my luggage outside my door and therefore not have to get up for baggage call. Unfortunately, I hadn't left myself a shirt. (I probably deserved this for laughing at Chad Griffin of our press staff when he'd done it earlier on the trip.) So I put on my suit, wearing a white undershirt with it. I figured I'd be okay since all I had to do was get on the bus. Once on the plane, who'd care what I was wearing?

But I had to go downstairs to our press office to get presidential transcripts on diskette. On the elevator, I ran into Rita Braver, CBS' White House correspondent. We'd seen each other on trips and at the White House but never formally met. I ended up explaining my packing faux pas. "You mean that's not intentional?" she asked. "I thought it was kind of an Armani thing." Downstairs in the press office, Chad Griffin got a good laugh out of my misfortune.

After the President finished his bilateral meeting with Syrian President Hafez al-Assad, we took off for home Sunday afternoon. By that time, some of us had been sitting on the backup plane for about three hours before even beginning the eight-hour, thirty-minute flight. About a half dozen aides sat in the conference room and played perhaps the world's longest game of Trivial Pursuit (laughing ourselves silly throughout), watched two movies (both forgettable) and ate two meals (one particularly delicious). Air Force One has a cabinet full of board games for such occasions as long flights.

We got back to Andrews about 10:00 P.M. Washington time (4:00 A.M. European time), where it was twelve degrees, windy and bitter on the tarmac. We stood around waiting for our bags and finally returned to the friendly confines of the White House by 11:00 P.M.

After we returned, Washington endured a week of record sub-zero weather. Ice encased everything, the city was officially shut down and a power shortage closed the federal government. There was no heat one morning in our office, so I sat there at my desk in my coat, my fingers numbly typing. I'd started a mammoth project, analyzing all the news coverage of the President's trip to Europe. It was huge— an enormous stack of clips from more than a dozen newspapers, half a dozen wire services, three magazines and seven and a half hours of videotape spanning nine days. An intern from the communications research office was recruited to handle the television news while I focused on the newspapers, magazines and wire services. The two of us spent a combined seventy-nine hours on the project.

We produced charts showing numbers of stories by newspaper, topic and column inches; television stories by network, topic and air time; front-page stories, with headlines, by-lines and column inches; lead stories on the newscasts, with reporters' names and air time; photographs by newspaper and topic; and a list of key events during the trip. At more than nineteen single-spaced pages of analysis (plus eleven pages of charts), it showed that the six major newspapers ran 214 stories totaling 4,760 column inches, along with fifty photographs, on the President's trip. The weeknight television newscasts on the three major networks telecast 82 stories totaling 153 minutes and 25 seconds of air time. And the President's approval rating on foreign affairs climbed above fifty percent.

The President went to Camp David the weekend after we returned. So on Sunday morning I had the twenty-four-hour National Security Council Situation Room fax the news analysis report to him. I didn't check with anybody to get clearance or approval. I just figured by Sunday he was probably almost bored out there and might actually read it.

On Monday morning, David Dreyer (deputy communications director) and Bob Boorstin (communications) both mentioned to me that the President had received, read and commented on my news analysis of the European trip. They'd attended a meeting with him for the upcoming State of the Union speech the previous night, and apparently the President had good things to say about the report.

The next day I saw Gene Sperling (economic policy) on West Executive Drive, on my way to the morning communications meeting, and he, too, told me about the President's remarks about my report. He also said that, even though I'd put only "Produced by the Office of

News Analysis" on the cover, David Dreyer told the President that it was my work. "Your buddies took care of you," Sperling said.

That was nice to hear. And it was helpful to know somebody was on my side when we packed again for two more exhausting trips to Europe, less than a month apart.

13▶Across the Pond

EUROPE IS A POPULAR DESTINATION of American tourists for historical, cultural and geographical reasons. Whether it's foreign exchange high schoolers, backpacking college students, honeymooning couples seeing the sights or families visiting distant relatives, Americans flock to the Old World by the thousands. Among those Americans is the President.

Our second summer in Washington, President Clinton took two trips to Europe. The first, in June, commemorated the fiftieth anniversary of the Allied Forces' landing at Normandy in World War II. The second, in July, marked the annual Group of Seven economic summit of leading industrialized nations.

On a sunny weekday morning in June, we boarded both 747s at Andrews Air Force Base. We traveled all day across the Atlantic Ocean, and—with the time change—arrived at Rome's Ciampino Airport not long before midnight. Our hotel reminded me of the one the previous January in Prague—old, dark, outdated. The carpet was stained, the furniture was out of a 1950s rec room, the fixtures were antiquated, the air conditioning was iffy and the beds and bathtub were small. It wasn't fancy, but it was functional.

The next morning I began my routine, arising early to produce and distribute the news clips. The State Department had an office set up next to our press office downstairs in the hotel. They had several high-speed copiers, so cranking out the clips wasn't too stressful for a change.

As was typical on overseas trips, I stayed at the hotel during Presidential events and dialed in to monitor the wire services as reporters filed stories after each event. By checking for breaking news stories on my computer, I could keep senior aides abreast of news happening elsewhere and also inform them of the types of coverage our events were receiving, so we could formulate communications strategy.

I watched on CNN as the President met with the Pope at the Vatican and addressed the citizens of Rome at Piazza del Campidoglio. Some of the scheduling/advance staff and I watching on TV in the staff office thought having Office of Management and Budget Director Leon Panetta, who was of Italian descent, translate for part of the speech wasn't such a great idea, as it turned out. It had seemed like a good plan, but it killed the pace of the President's speech. Trip Director Wendy Smith said later that the President was upset afterward. But he looked as if he were enjoying it, we said—he said so at the event. "Well, of course he *said* that," Smith said.

During the day I got out briefly for a walk on a sunny, hot day. The area near our hotel was good for exploring the city. But my pager went off, and I was summoned to the press office to round up some wire stories.

After producing the clips the next morning, I downloaded and printed wire stories and had the White House Communications Agency communications center fax them to Dee Dee Myers (press secretary), who was with the President a helicopter flight away at Nettuno Beach, for ceremonies at a World War II U.S. cemetery. The "comm center" was a regular hotel room, but it was filled with more technical hardware than you can imagine. The door was locked, and there was a doorbell with dozens of wires running under, over and around the door into the room. "Could you send these to Dee Dee Myers via Roadrunner?" I asked. "Immediate precedence, unclassified. Thanks." Roadrunner was the communications van that followed the President on site. The fax cover sheets had blanks to indicate the priority and security status.

That afternoon I had a chance to do some sightseeing. I went out for lunch at a corner café, trying to avoid the motor scooters whizzing past on the narrow streets on the way. I sat at a sidewalk table in the shade, watching people and traffic. I was surprised that some of the Italian men really did wear their suitcoats draped over the shoulders, with wraparound sunglasses and dark, slicked-back hair. And many of the women wore miniskirts, had long legs, blond hair with dark roots, wrinkles around their eyes, suntans and long noses. Rome, I thought, is actually kind of like New Jersey. But I thought it would be a great place to visit on vacation—to dine late on seven-course dinners, sipping wine and staying out until dawn at nightspots, spending the days seeing ancient history and soaking up the sun.

On the way back to the hotel, I stopped at a fresh fruit stand, and everybody was very friendly. After a couple days, I was able to use a few Italian words—*buon giorno, ciao, grazie*—without sounding like a total rube. (At first I was saying "ban-*jer*-now" in my Arkansas accent). I found the language somewhat similar to the Spanish I studied for two years in college.

That night I roamed a little farther, past old, detailed architecture, mainly churches. I walked around a plaza early in the evening as the weather cooled a little. Lots of people, especially young folks, were out and about. And then I saw a McDonald's. While it drives people crazy ("You can do that at home!"), I know what I like. The Big Mac and fries, by the way, tasted the same as they do in Little Rock or any place else. The President and official party, meanwhile, attended a dinner with Italian President Scalfaro.

The next morning, we took a short flight, including a beautiful view over the French Alps, to RAF Brize Norton, a British air base. There the plane descended over the green, rolling English countryside and farmlands. We rode a bus two hours south to Portsmouth on a cloudy, cool, rainy day—just what I'd expected of English weather.

Our hotel was the Marriott, a modern American-looking hotel just off the highway exit. As Steve Bahar of the advance team said, "We're at a nicer Holiday Inn in Des Moines," and looking around—or even out the window—it was hard to see any difference. In our staff office, I had trouble connecting to the computer system on my phone line, and the White House Communications Agency's data technicians spent a couple hours correcting the problem. On TV in the background all afternoon were cricket and rugby. I think I understand rugby—it's not that different from football. But cricket? No way. Of course, non-Americans probably think baseball is weird.

During the day, the President gave a speech at the U.S. Cemetery at Cambridge and conducted a meeting with Prime Minister John Major at Chequers, Major's country home, which is sort of like Camp David.

That evening I wandered next door to a restaurant/bar for dinner and found Stephen Cavanah (doctor), Wendy Van Dyke (nurse) and Leo Mercado (military aide). I ate lasagna and drank a Heineken. Somebody made a crack about English food, but then Mercado noted, "Well, we *are* eating bar food." The bartendresses were big-eyed blondes with, of course, great accents. I wish we had had more time there. The lack of language barrier, the logical exchange rate, the friendly people—all made me want to come back.

The President, First Lady and a few key aides had dinner with Queen Elizabeth and then stayed aboard the HMS *Britannia* overnight.

Sunday morning everybody wanted to see clips from *The Washington Post*, which ran excerpts of Bob Woodward's behind-the scenes book about our first year in the White House. (My favorite excerpt was political consultant Paul Begala calling Leon Panetta "the poster boy for economic constipation.")

Staff buses later in the morning took us to big, green, double-propellered Navy helicopters that swooped in to land on a grassy field. We boarded them and were flown from Portsmouth to the nearby USS *George Washington,* where we landed on the flight deck. We could see other helicopters in the air and dozens of ships in the water below and were craning our necks toward the small, round windows like a bunch of kids on a field trip.

The *George Washington* was in the English Channel, having left the United States about a week before. (Our advance team sailed across the Atlantic with the crew, which was on its way to Bosnia for six months.)

Upon landing, we were ushered to Ward Room 1, where, we were told, we'd be eating our meals. We were given a brief orientation lecture and then stood in line to check in. A couple enlisted men sat behind a long table, handing out room keys and signing us in. It was sort of like orientation day at summer camp. A crew member was assigned to each of us and escorted us to our quarters. I shared a cabin with

Jeremy Gaines (press assistant). I think the room was normally used by a couple of lieutenants.

I then found our staff office, which was normally used as a classroom. Despite the low ceiling, there was room to move around, unlike most of the ship. But despite the White House Communications Agency's special setup, I could dial in on my laptop computer only infrequently and ineffectively.

Soon after we arrived, several senior aides wanted to get the latest news, since the President was going to conduct on-board interviews with all four television networks. Between what I was able to download and what Larry Sampas (news analysis) could fax me from Washington, I got them some stuff.

But delivering that material wasn't easy. It's not hard to get lost on a 6,200-man ship with 80 aircraft and a 4$\frac{1}{2}$-acre flight deck. And those knee knockers—cast iron around the doorways—are aptly named.

After the President spoke to the crew in one of the hangar bays, we got underway across the Channel to France. We were running late and so cruised along at twenty-eight knots, twice as fast as originally planned and almost as fast as she'll go. At that speed, even a ship that large will roll a little bit—not enough to make you seasick, but enough that you notice. Now I know what they mean by "getting your sea legs," I thought. Navy Captain Mark Rogers (White House Military Office) said that after sixteen years at sea, it still took him a day and a half to get used to it on each deployment.

Near sunset, a few of us on the White House staff went up to the flight deck, looking out over the water as we sailed along. We saw a helicopter land and watched the deck crew scramble around. We looked over the edge and saw the water rushing past the ship's hull.

We had dinner in the ward room, surrounded by officers. The food was kind of like cafeteria food—pretty good, and lots of it. In fact, Captain Rogers said, he used to have to be careful when he was on deployments or he'd end up "a little butterball." After some work in the staff office, I crawled into my tiny bunk and slept fitfully, hearing noises all around me and worrying about waking up on time.

Monday morning was D-Day, or at least it had been fifty years earlier. I got up painfully early once again (it always got tougher the longer a trip lasted) and headed down the hall to wait in line with the Secret Service agents for one of the three stainless steel showers. It was like being back in the college dorm.

I managed to get sets of clips produced, making copies in the ship's combat systems maintenance center, and scurried around, giving them to key staffers before they left with the President. He addressed a sunrise ceremony aboard the ship's deck, and I watched with the crew from far above.

Then much of the staff went with him aboard helicopters to Normandy. I was manifested to stay behind, and hung out all day with the advance team. From the flight deck, we could see the beaches where fifty years before Allied forces had stormed ashore in a long-anticipated invasion of Nazi-held France. There were all sorts of ships around us, some firing blanks. Some World War II-era planes flew overhead, a few trailing red, white and blue smoke. And we saw landing craft go ashore.

The helicopters that were supposed to pick us up and fly us to Paris, where the President would be heading at the end of the day, couldn't take off because of bad weather. So instead of leaving that morning, we waited around for six hours. We sat in a lounge and watched the same D-Day stories on CNN over and over, finally taking off late in the afternoon.

Arrival in Paris after the hour-long helicopter flight was uneventful. A small bus took us past the Eiffel Tower, the Arc de Triomphe, the Seine River and the National Assembly to our hotel. That evening I went for a long stroll and proceeded to get lost. I asked for directions but couldn't even pronounce the street names. "Rue de la Paix"—what is that, I thought. (I later found out it means "Avenue of Peace.") But the French I met were surprisingly pleasant and helpful, and after walking past the Louvre and the Royal Palace, I finally made it back to the hotel.

After the morning duty of getting the clips produced and distributed outside staffers' hotel room doors, I dialed in and monitored Tuesday's news and had key stories faxed to Dee Dee Myers with the President. He greeted U.S. Embassy staff, met with U.S. business leaders and met Paris Mayor Jacques Chirac and Prime Minister Eduard Balladur before addressing the National Assembly and appearing on TV with President François Mitterrand. The official party, mainly senior staff, attended a dinner with Mitterrand afterward.

I spent the evening roaming around Paris again. The sun didn't set until after 9:00 P.M. in "The City of Light." As in Rome, it was interesting to people-watch and guess who was French, who was from elsewhere in Europe and who was American. The latter were pretty easy to pick out. A family from South Dakota stopped me and asked if I could suggest a nearby place for dinner. (I couldn't.)

I roamed the streets, jammed with neon lights and corner cafes and people and shops. Too many bus fumes and too many people smoking, but otherwise a clean city. I ducked briefly into Harry's Bar, an historic site where F. Scott Fitzgerald and Ernest Hemingway used to hang out. It was striking how Americanized Paris is. No wonder the French whine about our "cultural imperialism."

After I cranked out one last set of clips Wednesday morning, the President and most of the staff boarded Air Force One to England, where the President received a degree at Oxford. The backup plane didn't leave until mid-afternoon, so I took the opportunity to see some more of Paris (and ate lunch at Pizza Hut…I know, I know.)

The backup 747 touched down at RAF Brize Norton for a couple hours. We hung out in a lounge and played billiards at the base, awaiting Air Force One's arrival. The two planes then took off and flew in tandem across the Atlantic.

During the long flight home, it occurred to me that visiting Europe is a bit like going to see your grandparents—it's a small-feeling place well rooted in history. From the point of view of a fast-paced American, whose job it is to be up to the moment and focused on current events, the Europeans I met seemed slow-moving and old-fashioned. Europe, I must admit, is a fascinating place to visit; it does represent the cultural past for most Americans, after all. But I couldn't help feeling relieved to be returning to America, coming back to the future.

Within a week of our return, one of my interns and I finished the news analysis of the eight-day, three-country, 9,700-mile trip. It was easier than the first time, but it was still a pain. The report compared coverage of the trip's events by the various media and assessed how our themes for the trip were reported, noting whether coverage was generally positive or negative.

It ended up being thirty pages, took seventy hours and included analysis of coverage from six major newspapers, about two dozen regional papers, nearly a dozen wire services, the three major weekly news magazines and four television networks. We found that the six major papers ran 94 stories totaling 2,295 column inches on the trip (including 25 front-page articles and 31 photos) and the three evening network newscasts aired 28 stories totaling 57 minutes. Polls showed the President's approval rating on foreign affairs rose seven points from the previous month, to 44 percent.

About the same time I was finishing the report, I received a memo addressed to "All staff who stayed on the USS *George Washington.*" It was from Isabelle Tapia and Mike Lufrano of the Office of Scheduling and Advance. It said that "a number of items were removed from staterooms on the ship during the White House visit." Someone had taken thirteen blue towels with the ship's logo, four "GW" bathrobes with insignia, twelve plain white robes and fifty-five white towels worth $562.

Later, Media Affairs Director Jeff Eller saw me with Ernie Gibble (media affairs), who worked on the advance team aboard the ship, in the hallway. "I better not see you two coming down the hall wiping yourselves off with those towels," he joked. I kiddingly said I'd already given away the bathrobes as gifts. But later that afternoon, the Associated Press ran a story about the memo, and another media frenzy began. We never did find out who took the towels and robes. For all we knew (and suspected) it could have been the press, who also stayed aboard.

When we returned to Europe the following month, I was beginning to burn out. I wasn't as excited before or during the eight-day, five-country, 11,600-mile trip as I had been the previous two visits there. It was still enjoyable and interesting, and parts of it were terrific. But I could sense faint indications within myself that perhaps the beginning of the end was at hand.

The day after Independence Day, we boarded a small bus for Andrews Air Force Base. I spent the night on the support plane, sleeping on the couch in the hallway near the forward galley as we flew eight hours to Latvia.

The support plane landed at Riga International Airport after the next morning's airport arrival ceremony, and the staff on Air Force One already had left in the Presidential motorcade. Kathy Roth (advance) met me on the tarmac and said George Stephanopoulos (senior adviser) had requested clips. She'd been instructed to bring me to him, so I crowded into a van with other staffers from the support plane, and we were driven to Riga Castle, where the President started the day with a bilateral meeting and signing ceremony with Latvian Prime Minister Birkavs.

It was 11:00 A.M. locally, and everyone wanted clips. But it was only 4:00 A.M. back in Washington, and few clips were available. Worse, the White House Communications Agency's phone lines and satellite setup prevented me from dialing in from my laptop to the computer system back at the Old Executive Office Building. The closest fax machine was three blocks away. And the only copier at the castle could only reproduce one page at a time.

Stephanopoulos sent Andrew Friendly (personal aide) in every few minutes to ask for all the latest news, but I had nothing to give him, through no fault of my own. Larry Sampas faxed some clips from Washington that April Mellody (press assistant) was kind enough to bring to me from our press office down the street. I finally got a couple of decent sets of information to Stephanopoulos and Dee Dee Myers so they could brief the President before his news conference, which I watched on TV upstairs with other staffers.

After a five-minute motorcade to the Latvian stock market building (where the President visited briefly with political, cultural and business leaders), I stood beside the motorcade in a large plaza in mid-afternoon. The curious crowd was kept behind barricades across the plaza. All offices were shut down for a national holiday declared in honor of the President's visit.

Then it was on to Freedom Plaza, where the President spoke to an enthusiastic crowd of 30,000 on a warm, comfortable afternoon. "Freedom!" he said in all three Baltic languages. (_"Briviba! Vabadus! Laisve!"_) I stood in the staff section, behind and to the side of the platform, in front of a band that played "Stars and Stripes Forever." A choir stood on the steps of the Freedom Monument, surrounded by green, leafy trees, and sang all four verses to "America" in flawless English on a sunny day. The President worked the crowd on his way to greet U.S. Embassy staff before getting in the motorcade.

Unlike the three former Soviet states we'd visited previously, Latvia didn't seem to be mired in depression and stagnation. Of course, it was summer as opposed to our previous visits in January.

But there were smiles, some of the people were surprisingly attractive, and while we were there only eight hours, it seemed an alive place.

We boarded the plane for a one-hour, five-minute flight to Warsaw, whereupon some aides were taken directly to the modern, forty-story Marriott Hotel. The President, meanwhile, attended an arrival ceremony at Poland's Presidential Palace. He then conducted a bilateral meeting with Polish President Lech Walesa and attended a state dinner.

After checking out the staff office (in the temporarily vacated Panorama Club, a two-level jazz club with a spiral staircase and a great view of Warsaw), I dialed in to make sure all the technical connections worked and to download stories on the day's events. Among the stories, Poland's biggest public opinion institution found that 75 percent of those polled had a favorable opinion of President Clinton, meaning Poles liked him better than any other foreign statesman.

The next morning I produced the clips and attended a staff meeting before going back to my room to order the "American Breakfast" from room service. I ate eggs, sausage, potatoes and rolls with juice and milk while watching Britain's Sky TV, the only English-speaking channel on the cable system beside CNN and MTV. Anna Walker and her male co-anchor said the top stories in England were a baby kidnapping and a couple of highway accidents. It was like watching local news back home.

In the afternoon, while the President attended wreath-laying ceremonies and meetings with Prime Minister Pawlak and legislative leaders, I went for a stroll through a crowded, tree-shaded area of office buildings and apartments near the hotel. Advertising signs, while not using the Cyrillic alphabet, nevertheless looked Russian to me.

It was on the way back that a Volkswagen Beetle painted with racing stripes and a circled "53," just like Herbie the Love Bug of 1970s Disney fame, turned a corner in front of me. Later, walking down a four- or six-lane street lined with shops, I noticed a little shack with "The Thrash Zone" painted on the side with heavy-metal lettering and apparently selling mosh paraphernalia. Posters around town advertised an upcoming Bob Dylan concert. On the other side of the street were stores selling U.S. products of various types, especially Gap-type clothing. A sports apparel store was heavily laden with NBA caps and shirts and posters. Kids on in-line skates rolled by on the sidewalk. Cars on the street were old, beat-up and Soviet-looking. They looked as if they were out of a scene from early 1960s Havana.

We left Warsaw that evening and flew two hours and twenty-five minutes to Naples, Italy, where the annual G-7 summit was being held. It was near midnight and hot when we landed at Capodichino Airport. I was manifested for the press hotel, not even within walking distance of the staff hotel. The hotel had tiny elevators, hot hallways and rooms with hard twin beds and no carpeting. I called an advance team member in the staff office to check it out by phone before setting up a wakeup call and an embassy car and driver so I could get to the office in the morning.

I found out the hard way the next morning that the White House Communications Agency didn't set up my specially-designed technical communications correctly, and I couldn't dial in. I had to create clip packages using only faxes from Washington, and therefore it took longer, and we missed a few stories in the clips. That drove me crazy. I mean, it's the same setup everywhere we go, I thought. Can't we get this stuff right?

The staff hotel, the Vesuvio, overlooked the Bay of Naples, with a little S.S. *Minnow*-type marina and Castel dell'Ovo, a twelfth-century castle, across the street. There were houses in the hills around the bay and a cloud-hazed view of Mount Vesuvius in the background. The staff office was on the fifth floor and consisted of four blank walls, a small window with a view of an old stone wall covered with weeds, no TV and a small table with bottles of carbonated water, a bucket of melting ice and no food.

At a meeting that morning in the staff office, senior aides discussed communications policy for the day, and I slipped relevant news clips and wire stories to Mark Gearan and Dee Dee Myers. David Gergen (counselor) kind of ran the meeting and dominated discussion.

Later, whenever I was creating any wire reports, Gergen wanted copies before anybody else. That got to be annoying. I mean, he could wait until I was done with everybody's copies, just like George Stephanopoulos and Gearan and Myers. He was no more important than they were. Besides, I thought, he's on his way to State. I'll admit I never did like the idea of a Republican in our midst, and since he was leaving, I was even less willing to go out of my way to help him.

At lunch I strolled a couple blocks with Jennifer Curley (State Department protocol), who I'd met on the flight from Washington. We ate thin, greasy pizza and drank small bottles of Coke with ice served in a bowl at a tiny, virtually empty pizzeria without air conditioning on a hot, sunny day. Throughout the day I produced wire reports and pulled wire stories for Mark Gearan for him to use in briefing the President for news conferences.

Saturday began with another early wake-up call and another embassy car pool vehicle and driver arriving at the press hotel to take me to the staff hotel. I dialed in about 5:30 A.M. local time and found an "Urgent" story that had moved a few minutes earlier: North Korean President Kim Il Sung had died. As I sat there trying to decide who I should awaken and tell, Neil Wolin (National Security Council) walked into the staff office in shorts and a T-shirt and started working on a related statement for the President. Dee Dee Myers soon joined him, and I printed wire stories for them as soon as the news appeared on my screen.

When the President left for G-7 meetings at nearby Palazzo Reale, I worked briefly in the staff office. But then I decided to see a little of Naples. The city had a reputation for being dirty and full of crime and corruption. But the so-called "red zone" created to surround the G-7 summit was cleared of everyone who didn't absolutely need to be there through a system of ID badges, with checkpoints manned by various types of *carabienza* (paramilitary) guards. I went for a walk and somehow ended up outside the red zone.

I found myself in an area of narrow cobblestone streets lined with small cars and scooters. There were tiny markets with open boxes of fruits and vegetables. Meat hung from hooks surrounded by flies, and fish lay in buckets of apparently lukewarm water on a warm Saturday morning. Balconies from the approximately eight-story buildings were covered with laundry drying on lines and hanging over railings. Here and there was the smell of garbage. Kids played soccer in the alley-like streets. Looking up at the people standing on their balconies, I thought of U.S. troops marching through Italian cities after ridding them of Nazi troops as crowds waved and cheered. What I saw could have been 1944 instead of 1994.

Walking back, the paramilitary guards wouldn't let me back

through the checkpoint, despite my ID tags. They spoke absolutely no English and since I speak no Italian, it was a little confusing. But they made it clear I had to find another way. Fortunately, it was a simple route back to a familiar area, and their hand gestures were sufficient.

I went to lunch again with Jennifer Curley at another nearby pizzeria and afterward worked on my laptop for a while, pulling wire stories in preparation for the President's pre-news conference staff briefing. Once that was over, early in the evening, I called for an embassy car to take me back to my hotel.

As I stood waiting on Via Santa Lucia, next to the staff hotel, I noticed a crowd of twenty-five to thirty people, mostly men, on a sidewalk across the street. They were straining to see inside a small bar. I walked over to check it out before I realized the World Cup quarterfinal game between Italy and Spain, being played in New Jersey, was in progress. I could barely see the big-screen TV as the crowd began to roar in anticipation. The game was 1-1 in the final two minutes as Italy approached the goal. The ball bounced in front of the Spanish goalie, and ponytailed Italian star Robert Baggio gathered it in, hitting an incredible shot, angling the ball low from right to left, past a defender, just inside the front far post and into the net.

In the street, the crowded roared, arms upraised. People jumped up and down and hugged. On the balconies above, Italians cheered and waved. A dog barked. A cannon boomed. Italian red, white and green flags were waved. A man on the sidewalk danced with a young woman who appeared to be his daughter. It was joyous bedlam, and I just stood there wide-eyed with a goofy grin on my face, soaking it all in. On the ride back to my hotel, fans on scooters carried large Italian flags that blew in the breeze, and drivers honked their horns. From my hotel room, I could still hear the blaring horns.

I went through the familiar routine our last morning in Naples to get to the staff hotel and crank out the clips. The President and his family toured nearby Mount Vesuvius, but I spent most of the day in the staff office. My job was such that most of the time I was invisible. But I couldn't afford to be away from my computer for too long, just in case some major story broke and I was needed to download and distribute it—immediately.

We watched the President's press statement with Russian President Boris Yeltsin on TV in the staff office. Then late in the afternoon we finally boarded the bus for a twenty-five-minute ride to the airport. After a departure ceremony on the tarmac, we loaded the two 747s for a two-hour flight to Bonn, Germany. Upon arrival, we rode through a lush, green area to a mountain where the hotel was located. Up, up, up the switchback roads we drove, past guards with semiautomatic weapons hanging around their necks, through a dark forest. At the top, the brightly-lit Petersberg Gastehaus (Guest House), with its quiet, elegant setting and armed German guards, reminded me of the mansion Lee Marvin's troops stormed in *The Dirty Dozen.*

When we entered, formally dressed staff offered us glasses of wine from silver trays. The Petersberg Gastehaus didn't have air conditioning, but fortunately the weather was mild enough that it wasn't necessary. There were signs on our room doors with our names, which was helpful but not unusual. Mine said, "Herr Chitester." My favorite, though, was chief speechwriter Don Baer's: "Herr Baer."

In the morning I produced and distributed the clips with some help from a U.S. Embassy volunteer. After the G-7 summit, some of the staff who had been receiving clips headed back to Washington. That made my job a little easier. Later, I strolled to the rear mountain-top stone terrace and thought of what Ed Harris, playing astronaut John Glenn, said in *The Right Stuff* when he first saw Earth from outer space: "Whoa! That view is tre*men*dous!" The Rhine River ran through the valley far below, with Bonn across the river, a collection of pleasant little houses surrounded by trees.

Late that afternoon, we headed back to the airport and boarded Air Force One for a forty-minute flight to Ramstein Air Base. In flight, I returned a message on my pager from Jeff Eller. But the only way the Air Force One crew could place my call was to use a secure phone line. So I picked up the beige phone (instead of the white one beside it), and experienced the disconcerting delay and echo typical of an encrypted call. He was seeking Presidential transcripts, and I said I'd e-mail them at my next opportunity.

At Ramstein, the staff room was hot and noisy and cramped. Some of us briefly toured the commissary, which was a tiny indoor mall and like being back in the States. We returned to watch the President address a crowd in a hangar and then shake hundreds of hands after accepting a leather flight jacket with his name on it. Then he sat in with the Air Force band and played "Night Train" on a saxophone. We finally took off for a one-hour, ten-minute flight to Berlin with the sun setting behind us. By the time we got to the Intercontinental Hotel in Berlin about midnight (much like its same-named sister hotels we'd visited around the world), I was exhausted, irritable and looking forward to the trip ending the next day.

After producing and distributing the clips, I went downstairs for breakfast at the L.A. Cafe, where a 1949 Harley-Davidson was on display. The cafe had another buffet of calorie-laden food, just as delicious as in Bonn. (I hadn't seen too many skinny Germans, and I was beginning to understand why.) Later that morning, a bus took a couple of dozen staffers to the President's speech at Brandenburg Gate.

It was a hot, sunny day, but much more comfortable than July in Washington. We arrived at the former site of the Berlin Wall. The Brandenburg Gate was an enormous, ornate, historic and imposing structure, but any remnants of the wall were long gone. In the five years since the wall had been torn down, everything apparently had returned to normal (although a State Department staffer pointed out a barren area in the distance she described as disputed territory that once included the U.S. Embassy, now in Bonn).

Even so, it was moving to stand on the east side of where the wall once stood, where people had died vying for freedom we take for granted, and to look out at the crowd of between 50,000 and 100,000 clutching their miniature U.S. and German flags. I thought, of course, of President Kennedy's famous 1963 speech here: "Freedom has many difficulties, and democracy is not perfect, but we have never had to put up a wall to keep our people in!"

We sat in the sun on small wooden chairs for an hour and a half (the crowd had been waiting much longer) before the President, Chancellor Kohl and their wives strolled through Brandenburg Gate, a scene which made for great video. And then the President spoke for about ten minutes, ending in German to huge cheers: _Nichts wird uns aufhalten. Alles ist möglich. Berlin ist frei!_ ("Nothing will stop us. Everything is possible. Berlin is free!")

Given the task of following Kennedy's _Ich bin ein Berliner_ and Reagan's "Mr. Gorbachev, tear down this wall," it was a great speech and a great event. I sat near National Security Council speechwriter Bob Boorstin, who worried throughout the speech. "Great job," I told

Boorstin afterward, patting him on the shoulder. "Thanks, Kenny," he said.

Back at the hotel, Jennifer Curley and I took a brief stroll before I knocked out one last wire report and boarded the bus for the airport. On the way, I thought to myself that Germany, like Great Britain, is a country I'd like to visit again. I sat on the support plane with the State Department's Mike McCurry and Mary Ellen Glynn, who were having a few drinks before our mid-afternoon takeoff.

"You know," I told them, "y'all are drinking at 10:00 A.M. Washington time."

"That's okay," McCurry said, "we do this back there, too."

I was going to say, "That would explain some of your briefings," but I didn't know McCurry that well and wasn't sure he'd know I was just kidding. (McCurry would later become White House press secretary, and Glynn would become one of his deputies.)

By the time I got back to the White House that evening, Larry Sampas had arrived with the early edition of *The Washington Post*. It was strange to see photos of an event I'd attended seemingly hours before, in another part of the world. But there it was in the next morning's newspaper, hours before it appeared on newsstands.

A week after returning, our office distributed the news analysis of the trip. It ended up being 32 pages (10,876 words) and took 67 hours to produce. The six major newspapers ran 137 stories totaling 3,109 column inches about the trip, and the three evening network newscasts aired 33 stories, totaling 44 minutes and 40 seconds.

We ended up taking two more overseas trips, but it was the last such report I produced. I just didn't have another one in me. In fact, I decided, I'd be glad just to physically, mentally and emotionally survive what I knew would be my last two, to the Mideast and Asia.

14▶Take the Long Way Home

CAIRO; "SADDAM" IN AMMAN · "WHEN I WAS IN DAMASCUS..." · "THE PARTRIDGE FAMILY" IN ISRAEL · WINDSHIELD TOUR OF KUWAIT CITY · TWENTY-EIGHT STRAIGHT HOURS ABOARD THE PLANE · MANILA: "BOHEMIAN RHAPSODY" FOR CHRISTMAS · JAKARTA: NEW YORK CITY IN THE TROPICS · "WHITE HOUSE BAG PEOPLE"

U_{SUALLY} *PRESIDENTIAL TRIPS WERE PLANNED* long in advance. That was especially true when the President traveled overseas. But one fall day we received word that Israel and Jordan had agreed on a peace treaty and would hold a signing ceremony in Aqaba, Jordan, to commemorate the event. It was decided the President would attend—in eight days. Our Mideast trip ended up being a whirlwind tour of five days, six countries and 16,000 miles.

The following month we traveled to Asia for the annual Asian Pacific Economic Cooperation summit. By that time I'd announced I was leaving the White House to return to the private sector in Arkansas. I was numb at that point, perhaps permanently jet-lagged.

We'd been on the road seven of the previous ten days before departing for the Mideast. We returned around 9:30 P.M. from a three-day trip to California, Washington State and Ohio, and I was back at the White House by 7:00 A.M. Tuesday to board a bus and head back out to Andrews for the ten-hour, thirty-minute flight to Egypt.

As usual, I flew on the support plane, boarding the farthest of two side-by-side 747s on the tarmac on a sunny morning with State Department and National Security Council staff. The rare sight of the two planes together—with their dark blue, light blue and white colors, "United States of America," U.S. flag and Seal of the President on the side—was majestic and impressive.

We arrived in Cairo well after midnight local time and headed immediately to the Semiramis Intercontinental Hotel. President Clinton's motorcade had stopped at Anwar Sadat's grave site, where he laid a wreath by the late Egyptian president's grave. The streets were dark and deserted on our way to the hotel. Cairo wasn't originally scheduled as an overnight stop, so the facilities we normally would have had weren't available. I couldn't dial in on my laptop computer, so I got some news clips faxed to me and went to bed about 3:00 A.M. for a couple hours. I found just going through the motions of getting under the covers, showering and changing clothes seemed to help, even if I didn't sleep much.

I was up at 6:00 A.M. to produce the clips to get them distributed before the President's departure for the Israel-Jordan peace signing ceremony.

We left our old, beat-up hotel in mid-afternoon, leaving behind a pretty view of the Nile River. But on the way to the airport, the rest of the city looked pretty drab: old and ugly. Although it's in Africa, Cairo is obviously more Mideastern than African. The weather was beautiful.

We arrived in Amman, Jordan, by early evening. White House Communications Agency personnel screwed up my phone/computer connections, so I had to work with them for two hours in the staff office to make it usable. The Marriott Hotel was a little bigger and in slightly better shape than the hotel in Cairo.

The next day I awoke at 3:30 A.M. to quickly produce the clips before our 5:30 A.M. departure for Damascus, Syria. Leaving the hotel that morning, I was literally taken aback as I walked out the front door. Granted, I was sleepy and preoccupied with delivering the clips, but still...for just a moment, I thought I saw Saddam Hussein. He was walking in the front door as I was walking out, and he was wearing military fatigues, short black hair and a bushy black mustache. But then, that describes millions of men in the Mideast. I guess I was taken aback because of lingering remnants in my mind of Desert Storm news coverage, when Saddam was on TV all the time.

There were more security forces on the Damascus tarmac after our fifty-five-minute flight than anywhere I'd seen, a reminder of the tensions in that part of the world. I was slightly jarred momentarily when troops gave a rifle salute to the President during an airport welcome ceremony. The blasts came from about a hundred yards behind us, and I didn't know the soldiers were even there.

The roads were deserted during our motorcade. We saw crowds—men, all with nearly identical hair, mustaches and clothes—jammed together on roofs of cube-shaped, adobe-like houses as the motorcade passed. I somehow felt less at ease in Syria than in any other country we visited.

At the hotel where we waited during the President's events, I dialed in and answered some e-mail from Washington. I'd explained to Jeff Eller (media affairs) in a previous message that I hadn't been able to see much so far on our whirlwind tour. Replied Eller: "Yeah, but you'll be able to say, 'When I was in Damascus....'"

A couple hours later we headed back to the airport and flew one hour and thirty-five minutes to Israel. I'd been looking forward to seeing Jerusalem for several reasons. Besides being our last overnight of the trip, Israel was a friend and an ally of the United States, not to mention its rich religious history, which I'd studied in one way or another since childhood.

Air Force One was gone by the time the support plane landed at Ben Gurion Airport in Tel Aviv. An old, underpowered bus—nicknamed "The Little Engine That Couldn't" by one State Department staffer—took us about an hour south to Jerusalem, along a highway similar to Interstate 95 between Baltimore and Washington.

We arrived at the King David Hotel, the most comfortable of the trip, early in the evening. We were issued triangle-shaped security tags, and security seemed especially tight there. I worked in the staff office, where, as usual, there weren't enough phones or work areas.

I would've liked to have roamed around, but it didn't seem like a good idea. A memorandum in our trip books in fact discouraged it. I'd never felt like that before in western Europe, eastern Europe or Asia. But there was no sense in taking a chance. I don't know...I guess that uneasy feeling was due to my earliest memories of the Mideast being those related to Iran's 1979 kidnapping of U.S. hostages at our Embassy in Tehran.

Jerusalem was the trip's only overnight site at which all of us stayed at the same hotel. So getting the clips distributed was pretty easy. I enjoyed rolls and juice in the staff lounge as daybreak streamed through the window and looked at an awesome view of the Old City, the golden dome of a famous mosque gleaming in the sunlight.

We rode to Tel Aviv, a beautiful drive on a picture-perfect Mediterranean morning with blue skies and huge mountain overlooks on the winding road. On the bus, an Israeli radio station played 1970s rock songs. In between the disc jockey's Hebrew patter, we heard Bob Seger's "Still the Same," Supertramp's "Take the Long Way Home" and Peter Frampton's "Feel Like I Do" back to back. A couple State staffers sang along, and one pointed out that we were riding in a bus, singing '70s songs and that our traveling staff was kind of a family. "This is like 'The Partridge Family,'" she said.

The flight to Kuwait City took three hours and fifteen minutes despite the short geographical distance because we had to fly via Cairo due to flight restrictions. As we neared Kuwait City, we saw flat, expansive desert with oil wells and huge water desalinization/hydroelectric plants. We could see sand for miles and miles.

Upon landing, I reminded one of my fellow staffers on the support plane to remove her Israeli security tag with Hebrew writing, lest we upset our Kuwaiti hosts. We were taken to the airport's distinguished visitors lounge, where non-pool press and some staffers watched live CNN coverage of the President's visit with U.S. troops in Kuwait.

The U.S. Embassy staff arranged a "windshield tour" of Kuwait City, driving us around with a Kuwaiti staffer. We saw downtown and rode a highway along the Persian Gulf, sort of like Route A1A in Fort Lauderdale, Florida—without the nightclubs, of course, since alcohol was forbidden in the Islamic country. And we saw the royal palace, the U.S. Embassy and American fast food restaurants like McDonald's and Fuddruckers.

Our Kuwaiti guide, dressed in flowing native garb, was a University of California-Irvine graduate who spoke unaccented English. He had served in the Gulf War and told of being under fire, hearing bullets whizzing by and seeing marks where they hit the sand beside him. We also saw a lone burned-out home, gutted and charred, left over from the Iraqi retreat near war's end. Otherwise, the rebuilding was remarkable. It was hard to tell the city had been looted and burned by rampaging Iraqi troops just a few short years previously.

We then flew fifty minutes to King Khalid Military City in Saudi Arabia, our last stop before home. Upon landing at an airport without lights after dark because we were behind schedule, the support plane blew out five tires. Air Force One, however, had no difficulty. I was among those scheduled to stay on the plane for the four or five hours the President attended official ceremonies.

But our tires—which actually overheated and then, by design, deflated when they got too hot—had to be replaced. Each plane carried two spare tires, so an additional one had to be flown to us via a C-5 cargo plane, we were told. Air Force One, scheduled to leave a few minutes ahead of us, instead took off hours before we did. Our four- or five-hour wait aboard the plane ended up exceeding thirteen hours.

The fourteen-hour flight home was about as far as the two planes used as Air Force One can go without refueling. The press plane, however, had to stop in Shannon, Ireland, to refuel en route to Washington. In fact, the 747s which usually serve as Air Force One have the capability for in-air refueling. But one of the military aides told me it can be a tricky procedure, and it isn't done.

So while we awaited delivery and installation of our tire, we relaxed in the conference room. The stewards, as always, were absolutely fantastic to us, bringing us plenty of food and drinks: "Can I get you anything, sir?" I settled into one of the big leather chairs at the conference table and read, wrote, watched movies and chatted with Ralph Alswang and Sharon Farmer (staff photographers).

Laura Bowen Wills of the State Department protocol office, a fellow Arkansan, showed us some of the gifts the President and First Lady had received. The Saudis gave the President a huge, heavy, gold medallion, the country's highest civilian honor, in an impressive green case. I set my watch to Washington time and finally snoozed on the conference room couch about midnight Eastern Daylight Time.

I awoke about 10:00 A.M. or so. Still on the plane? Where are we? A while after I awoke, I looked out a window and saw the New England coast. We could see sailboats in the water near Martha's Vineyard. A little further down the coast and we'd be home. We ate lunch (turkey and dressing with green beans) and landed an hour or two later.

The Andrews tarmac never looked so good. After nearly twenty-eight straight hours aboard the plane, it was exhilarating to breathe fresh air and soak in the sunshine of an East Coast autumn Saturday.

I got back to my office about 2:00 P.M. or so. I was checking my messages from mail, e-mail and voice mail when Rica Rodman (media affairs), who worked in the next office door, raced in.

"Did you just hear that?"

"What?"

"It sounded like firecrackers were going off out front, and one of the Secret Service guys at the gate said somebody was shooting at the White House."

Great, I thought. First we've got a plane crash landing on the South Lawn last month, and now this. The shots were fired from Pennsylvania Avenue, north of the Old Executive Office Building. My office faced the interior courtyard, so we couldn't have been hit. But my office was near the Pennsylvania Avenue end of the building, so shots at our building could have come near us. The press briefing room windows in the West Wing were hit by bullets. The President, having arrived home several hours before us, was upstairs watching a college football game on TV and reportedly never was in danger.

Our trip to Asia, just days before I left the White House, ended not with a bang but with a whimper. It was even more exhausting than the Mideast trip. After returning from the Mideast, we were in Washington for one day before heading out on the road for eight straight days, visiting twelve states and covering 8,900 miles. Then, after three days at the White House, we took off on a seven-day, two-country, 22,000-mile trip to Asia. In terms of miles, my final trip was the longest.

The seven-hour, ten-minute flight from Andrews Air Force Base took us toward our first stop, in Anchorage, Alaska, for refueling. We flew over the snow-capped Canadian Rockies before touching down at Elmendorf Air Force Base. Snow was falling upon our arrival, and there was a couple inches of accumulation while we were there.

Buses took us to an indoor rally on the base. As the planes were refueled, some of the staff went shopping at the base PX. I stayed in the staff hold (an officer's office) and dialed in to the wires. Then the President and First Lady attended a reception downtown, and most of us boarded buses back to the planes. There, we watched live coverage of their arrival and departure at the Anchorage Museum of Art and

History on the local TV news before takeoff. We were on the ground just a couple hours, leaving early in the evening.

On the eleven-hour flight to Manila, Philippines, we crossed the international dateline and lost a day. It was almost Sunday by the time we reached the Manila Hotel.

That morning I cranked out the clips as best I could with the screwy time change and limited dial-in capabilities overseas. Before boarding the motorcade, I noticed the Georgia-Auburn football game on ESPN and realized it was live coverage. Although it was Sunday morning in Manila, it was Saturday night back home.

We were driven to the Manila American Cemetery and Memorial, the largest American cemetery outside the United States, where 17,000 U.S. World War II veterans killed in the Philippines were buried. It was a sunny, windy, pleasantly warm mid-November day high on a hillside with palm trees swaying, overlooking mountains in the distance. In the summer-like setting, a Philippines military band played Christmas songs. (The Christmas season begins November 1 in the Philippines.)

The military band also played Queen's "Bohemian Rhapsody," and those of us on staff gave each other quizzical looks. (I thought of the scene in *Wayne's World,* with Mike Myers and Dana Carvey cruising Aurora, Illinois, and Queen's bombastic mid-1970s rock song blasting from their AMC Pacer's speakers.) Then the President and Philippines President Ramos arrived, walking through a long colonnade, where names of those missing in action were etched on the walls.

Back at the hotel later, I collected some wire stories and clips and sent them through the White House Communications Agency to Press Secretary Dee Dee Myers, who was with the President at Malacanang Palace for a news conference. She and others were able to brief the President, based partly on the latest news coverage I sent them.

That evening we left for Jakarta, Indonesia, arriving about midnight after a three-hour, thirty-five-minute flight. The next day I pulled whatever clips were available before the morning senior staff meeting, working in the Hilton Hotel's thirteenth-floor lounge, which overlooked a sports stadium and a vast parking lot.

That afternoon I assembled a collection of news clips and faxed them through the White House Communications Agency to George Stephanopoulos (senior adviser) at the U.S. ambassador's residence, where the President held a news conference. I also brought a set for Dee Dee Myers with me, a U.S. Embassy driver dropping me off at the residence. In the backyard, there were more staff than press at the outdoor news conference, held near a small swimming pool. Aides stood under a gazebo on a hot, humid day before hopping into the motorcade back to the hotel.

The next day I took a long walk in the afternoon, but most of what I saw was boring—highways and office buildings—although I did see a Planet Hollywood franchise. Indonesia is the world's fourth most populous nation, and Jakarta is unsurprisingly crowded: muddy, hot, humid, polluted, sticky and nasty...New York City in the tropics.

Late that afternoon I compiled clips on deadline for Bruce Lindsey (senior adviser), George Stephanopoulos, Dee Dee Myers and John Podesta (staff secretary) so they could brief the President before his live televised news conference at the convention center connected to the hotel.

There was no Presidential briefing the next day, so I just produced sets of clips to take to the plane that evening, so everybody could read them during the flight to Hawaii. Mike Lufrano (scheduling and advance) and I worked in the staff office while watching a movie on HBO. The President, First Lady and senior staff attended a state dinner as I packed my equipment and a filled a box with sets of clips before heading to the motorcade a little before 10:00 P.M. After a thirty-minute drive to the plane, I delivered the box to Air Force One before boarding the backup for the flight to Hawaii.

We ate a couple of meals and watched movies during the twelve-hour, thirty-minute flight to Honolulu. When we landed at Hickam Air Force Base, the weather was warm and humid but comfortable, and puddles from an earlier rain shower dotted the tarmac. Those of us on the backup plane walked to a nearby tarmac to await Air Force One's arrival. Sam Myers of the advance team put leis around everybody's necks and welcomed us to Hawaii.

A bus took us to the main terminal at the Honolulu airport, where we boarded a United Airlines' Flight 44 about 10:00 P.M. It was an eight-hour flight, and I had the middle seat in the middle section, three rows from the rear. At least the seat on my left was vacant, but it was a rude re-introduction to the real world of commercial air travel. Apparently the backup 747 stayed behind—along with Air Force One and the President—to bring home a large contingent of Secret Service agents.

The President's 747s were configured for 73 passengers. I looked around the United plane and realized there were probably closer to 350 people aboard. It was like a railroad cattle car. If I ever vacation in Hawaii, I thought, I'm stopping in Los Angeles or San Francisco on the way home.

I got about three hours sleep en route to the mainland. The only thing we had to eat was a so-called sandwich shortly after takeoff.

When we got to Chicago, it was the next morning local time. Who knows what time it was according to our body clocks. By then we traveling White House aides were all pretty disheveled. There were about two dozen of us, and the men all needed shaves. I was wearing sneakers, khakis and a baggy short-sleeved shirt, unshowered just like the rest of us. As we stood around O'Hare International Airport, John Podesta noted how well-dressed, well-made-up and generally fresh two of the female aides looked. Then he said, "The rest of us look like bag people." I looked around, and he was right: White House bag people.

After a two-hour layover, it was on to Washington National Airport. Our 737 arrived mid-afternoon on a cloudy, wet, cool day. White House drivers/baggage handlers were awaiting us with staff vans for the drive across the Potomac. I felt disoriented, jet-lagged and exhausted. Everybody else appeared to be in the same condition. We'd been on the road twenty-seven of the previous thirty-four days, and I felt like it.

My 200,000-mile odyssey as a White House aide was over. It was time to go home.

▶Epilogue

WHEN I ACCEPTED a position at the White House, I never intended to stay for an extended period. I didn't know for sure, of course, but I anticipated that I'd be there at least one year and no more than four. In any case, I knew I'd leave Washington after a short time and return to Little Rock.

After nearly two years, the unending, unrelenting series of Presidential trips—on top of my non-travel duties and without anyone to relieve me—was beginning to wear on me physically, mentally and emotionally. After the fiasco over my so-called promotion to Director of News Analysis, I started planning my departure from the White House.

The beginning of the end came one Thursday morning in early August 1994 when Director of Media Affairs Jeff Eller, who had hired me and assigned me to travel aboard Air Force One, stopped by my office.

"Talk to you for a minute?" he said.

"Sure."

We went out in the first-floor Old Executive Office Building hallway and stood next to a huge skid of copier paper, where he said he was going to Austin, Texas, to join a public policy firm by the end of the month. I wasn't surprised. And I was excited and happy for him. Then later, of course, I began to wonder what it would mean for me. Without Eller to run interference for me with both White House senior aides and government bean counters, I knew my job would become more difficult.

A few weeks later, Eller again stopped by my first-floor office, this time after a Presidential event on the South Lawn one Friday afternoon. He stood and I sat on my desk as we talked of unfinished projects, but we both knew he'd be gone in a week. And with me leaving for vacation the next day, we wouldn't see each other, at least as White House aides, again.

It was fellow Hoosier Eller who had hired me full-time at the campaign to come aboard and run the wire service news monitoring system. He was the one who put me on Air Force One and sent me traipsing after the President around the world. And now I was leaving on vacation, and he'd be gone by the time I got back.

"I…well, thanks for everything," I said, shaking his hand.

"Hey, thank *you*," he said, adding, "Don't worry. I won't fall far from the tree."

He promised to leave his new phone number and address, and he was gone.

By early October, I was having a hard time getting motivated, knowing that I'd already decided to go home to Arkansas after Thanksgiving. And I was getting downright cranky from repetition and laziness. I was exhausted mentally, physically and emotionally and was starting to snap at people around me. The poor interns and volunteers must have thought I was awful.

Trying to resign, in fact, eventually became an almost comical endeavor. One Friday in late October, more than four weeks before I would quit, I still hadn't been able to find anybody to tell I was leaving. I couldn't even get an appointment to see Mark Gearan, who last I knew was in charge of the Office of Communications. (With the recent reshuffling of top communications staff, I couldn't be sure.) I left voice mail for David Dreyer (deputy communications director) but he never returned my call. I had figured I could tell Press Secretary Dee Dee Myers on Air Force One during the previous weekend's trip, but she didn't go on the trip. And we didn't have a Media Affairs Director because Jeff Eller hadn't been replaced.

How screwed up is this place? I thought. I can't even find anybody to resign to. I felt like those weary Iraqi soldiers in the Persian Gulf War who, unable to find U.S. troops, surrendered to CNN camera crews. Maybe I should go out to the North Lawn and resign to Wolf Blitzer, I thought. I told Larry Sampas (news analysis) of my plight, and he said, "It's like 'Hotel California': 'You can check out any time you like, but you can never leave.'"

Finally, during our Mideast trip, I found both Mark Gearan and Dee Dee Myers on our floor of Jerusalem's King David Hotel and told them that I was leaving the White House to return to Little Rock. Gearan, to whom I'd talked about the problems my office had faced, was happy for me. Myers, to whom I hadn't talked about it, was surprised. But I told her I didn't have the salary, title, office space, staff or resources of my predecessor, and couldn't help adding, "all of which might sound a little familiar to you." She recently had received a high-profile promotion directly from the President after an Oval Office appeal following new Chief of Staff Leon Panetta's attempt to oust her.

On a Congressional campaign swing a few days later, I told Bruce Lindsey (deputy counsel) in a University of Michigan-Flint campus locker room serving as our staff hold that I was leaving the White House. I explained my burn-out and frustration, and he empathized. "I remember when we first got there how impressive it was when those gates would open and you'd drive through," he said. "Now you just want them to hurry up and open the gates so you can get to work."

During my last trip, to the Philippines and Indonesia, I said good-bye to other members of the traveling staff. After a morning staff meeting at the Jakarta Hilton, I told George Stephanopoulos (senior adviser) that I was on my last trip before going back to Arkansas. We shook hands, and he said, "You've done a great job." Even if he was just saying that, it was uplifting to hear from him. I'd worked indirectly for Stephanopoulos since the campaign. But during our first five months in Washington, when he was Communications Director, I sometimes felt in the morning meetings that I wasn't sharp enough for him. Of course, all of us were uncertain and even defensive back then as we adjusted to an unfamiliar, high-profile setting.

I'd open those meetings with a brief news summary. But too much of the time I was frustrated by never knowing what senior aides already knew. I came to realize it was a no-win situation. To be successful, I had to know exactly which stories each and every person attending already had read or seen, and tell them exactly what they didn't know. But since that was different for each person, I'd end up either telling some aides what they already knew, or leaving out what they didn't. And it was a moot point anyway, because of course I couldn't know what everyone else did or didn't already know.

Then on the way home from that trip, after a Presidential arrival ceremony at Honolulu's Hickam Air Force Base, I saw Army Lieutenant Colonel Rusty Schorsch (military aide). I told him I was going home to Little Rock. We only had a brief moment on the tarmac, but I was glad I got a chance to say goodbye to him.

▶

Shortly before I left the White House, I was handed a checkout list that required signatures from eighteen different departments so I could receive my final paycheck. (I didn't even know where some of these departments were located.) Oddly, I found I was actually quite excited about leaving the White House. As I scurried around the enormous Old Executive Office Building getting my checkout list completed, it sunk in that I was really leaving.

A highlight was returning my pager. I'm free! I thought. After never being without it—twenty-four hours a day, seven days a week, for two years—returning it was like removing a physical tether. Afterward I kept checking the spot on my belt just inside my right hip bone where it used to be and found myself being surprised when it wasn't there. It was as if I'd undergone an operation to have a part of my body removed.

When I turned in my permanent hard pass with blue trim and photo on my last day, it really hit home. After I removed the chain from around my neck, I felt like a visitor.

A few days later, during the two-day, 1,050-mile drive from Washington to Little Rock, my dog Camelot and I crossed the Mississippi River on Interstate 40, leaving Memphis behind on a rainy day. I looked up at a sign across the bridge that said, WELCOME TO ARKANSAS, THE NATURAL STATE, HOME OF PRESIDENT BILL CLINTON.

I was back home.

Do I miss the White House? Of course I do. I don't miss the hours, the pace, the stress or the wear and tear on my mind or body. But I do miss the sense of purpose, the people, the excitement, the feeling of being on the inside.

I don't follow the news nearly as closely anymore, certainly. But whenever the President or the White House are in the news, I pay special attention. Occasionally I see former co-workers on CNN or C-SPAN and think of them.

But for me, two years of Washington was enough.

▶Acknowledgments

NOT LONG AFTER LEAVING the White House, I was staying at a Holiday Inn on a business trip. As I walked into the hotel, bags slung over my shoulders, I had the feeling that something was missing. That's when I realized that there was no one there to greet me. I had to check in and carry my bags like a normal person.

That's just one of the adjustments I've had to make after leaving the White House. We had advance staffers all over the place whenever we traveled, and now it's just me.

During my more than 200,000 miles traveling with the President, among the people who made my life easier were the advance teams, especially the staffers who advanced the hotels. People like Catherine Grunden, Colleen McCarthy and Ashley Bell always made sure our rooms were ready, that we got our keys, that we knew what time baggage call was and that breakfast would be available in the staff room. Other aides on the advance teams—like the motorcade people—also had thankless tasks but handled them smoothly, an assistance to the traveling staff that can't be overestimated.

Since I went on virtually every trip, few staffers traveled as much as I did. Those who did included Bruce Lindsey, Wendy Smith, Andrew Friendly, Dr. Connie Mariano, Army Colonel Tom Hawes and Navy Captain Mark Rogers. Photographers Ralph Alswang, Sharon Farmer and Barb Kinney always made me laugh, no matter how tired I was. Press Assistants Jeremy Gaines, Kathy McKiernan, April Mellody, Dave Seldin, Dave Leavy, Steve Cohen and Chad Griffin were fellow former Clinton/Gore campaign staffers, and I especially enjoyed their company. Most of my fellow traveling staffers were under even more stress than me but outwardly bore it very well. Special thanks go to Trip Director Wendy Smith, who not only performed brilliantly in a difficult job for a long time, but when I was new to the routine went out of her way simply to be nice to me.

Other White House aides I want to thank are my fellow members of the Office of Communications. Most of those people and I went through the campaign together, and they were the folks I met with each morning and saw virtually every day. From George Stephan-opoulos and Mark Gearan to David Dreyer and Rahm Emanuel and Dee Dee Myers to Arthur Jones and Lorraine Voles and Ginny Terzano to the press office to media affairs to speechwriting to research to policy, these people provided a sense of teamwork and purpose.

A very special thanks goes to Jeff Eller, a visionary who first conceived the idea of a real-time wire service computer system in use both at the White House and on the road, and who wanted me to run the operation. I will be forever grateful for his confidence in me, beginning early in the campaign.

Similarly, the gifted, resourceful crew at Generation Technologies was instrumental to my job at the White House. Mike Bennett, Dave Cunningham and their team created software and modified it to our specifications, enabling me constantly to stay in touch with breaking news. They were terrific to work with and are great guys as well.

Likewise, the White House Communications Agency, especially its advance teams, simply made my job possible. Colonel Tom Hawes, Colonel J.D. Wells, Colonel Ken Campbell and their people didn't have an easy task, but they were always professional and generally resourceful.

Other military personnel who made a difficult job much easier were the officers who accompanied the President. The military aides really are our armed forces' best of the best. Lieutenant Colonel Rusty Schorsch (Army), Major Michelle Johnson (Air Force), Lieutenant Commander Bob Walters (Coast Guard), Lieutenant Commander Rich Fitzpatrick (Navy), Major Leo Mercado (Marines), Major Darren McDew (Air Force) and Lieutenant Commander Joe Walsh (Navy) helped us out repeatedly in a variety of ways, many of them outside their specific responsibilities.

The Air Force One crew retains a warm spot in my heart as well. The stewards—from Howie to Tim to Leah to Steve and everyone else—were gracious, classy and professional, and the flight crews were so effective I hardly noticed them carrying out their duties. The radio crew solved technical problems for me and helped me immeasurably.

Last but not least among White House personnel are the members of the Office of News Analysis. Keith Boykin, Larry Sampas and Julie Oppenheimer carried the load in my absence. In the latter months, Sampas did the work of several people, most of it thankless grunt work. He never sought to promote himself, and he never complained. He was the heart and soul of our office who never got the recognition he deserved. I couldn't have traveled as I did without his tireless, dedicated service, and I'll always be in his debt. Our dozens of News Analysis interns and volunteers—too numerous to list—also were invaluable to our operation. Without them, we simply wouldn't have been able to function.

Before going to Washington, I'd kept a journal for several years, for no particular purpose. But I knew when I started traveling for the White House that I'd want to have a record of my experiences. So that's how this started: just as a journal for myself. At some point I realized that perhaps these anecdotes would be interesting to others. My friends and co-workers often asked me to tell them stories from the road, and so the project eventually expanded.

When I wrote this book (over a period of about two years), I used my original journals to create the foundation and basic structure. I checked my office notepads, trip books, memos and newspaper clippings to verify facts and occasionally to supply missing details. It's important to remember that this book is merely a personal scrapbook of snapshots from my perspective, not a panoramic film of everything that happened.

In writing this book, I was assisted immeasurably throughout the process by several friends who took time to read early drafts and make comments. In Little Rock, some kind colleagues made early helpful suggestions, and others in Arkansas put me in touch with people in the publishing industry. Most importantly, Angela Lauria in Washington deserves more thanks than I can give for bringing her youthful expertise to this project. She gave excellent advice at several crucial junctures, and I am eternally grateful for her friendship and support.

I'm also grateful to the staff at Fithian Press, who were instrumental in bring this project to fruition. All first-time authors should be as fortunate as I was to work with such a good group.

And of course I owe a debt of gratitude to my co-workers at Wills Thompson Paschall in Little Rock, who indulged me in the final stages. They have made me glad I returned to Arkansas.

▶White House Travel Log

KEN CHITESTER, DIRECTOR OF NEWS ANALYSIS, 1993–1994

DATE	FROM	TO	AIR MILES
7/4/93	Washington, DC[9]	Philadelphia, PA	125
7/4	Philadelphia landing zone[9]	Philadelphia International Airport	10
7/4	Philadelphia, PA	Moline, IL/Davenport, IA/ Eldridge, IA/Moline, IL	800
7/4	Moline, IL	San Francisco, CA	1720
7/5	San Francisco, CA[3]	Tokyo, Japan	5135
7/10	Tokyo, Japan	Seoul, Republic of Korea	800
7/11	Seoul, Republic of Korea	Honolulu, HI	4680
7/14	Honolulu, HI	Des Moines, IA	3970
7/14	Des Moines, IA	Washington, DC	905
TOTAL			18145
7/17	Washington, DC	St. Louis/Arnold, MO	712
7/17	Arnold, MO[7]	St. Louis, MO	21
7/17	St. Louis, MO[4]	Little Rock, AR	305
7/18	Little Rock, AR[4]	Washington, DC	904
TOTAL			1942
7/26	Washington, DC[4]	Chicago, IL	597
7/26	Chicago, IL[10]	Washington, DC	597
TOTAL			1194
8/9	Washington, DC[4]	Charleston, WV	270
8/9	Charleston, WV[4]	Washington, DC	270
TOTAL			540
8/12	Washington, DC[4]	St. Louis, MO	712
8/12	St. Louis, MO[4]	Denver, CO	796
8/12	Denver, CO	Alameda/Oakland/Alameda, CA	941
8/13	Alameda, CA	Denver, CO	941
8/13	Denver, CO[3]	Washington, DC	1494
TOTAL			4884
9/9	Washington, DC	Cleveland, OH	306
9/9	Cleveland, OH	Washington, DC	306
TOTAL			612

9/10	Washington, DC	Mountain View/Sunnyvale/
		Mountain View, CA	2432
9/10	Mountain View, CA	Houston, TX	1645
9/11	Houston, TX[10]	Washington, DC	1220
TOTAL			5297

9/15	Washington, DC	Belle Chasse/New Orleans/B.C., LA	966
9/15	Belle Chasse, LA	Washington, DC	966
TOTAL			1932

9/23	Washington, DC	Tampa/St. Petersburg, FL	850
9/24	St. Petersburg, FL	Washington, DC	850
TOTAL			1700

9/26	Washington, DC	New York, NY	205
9/26	Wall Street landing zone[9]	JFK International Airport	15
9/27	New York, NY	Washington, DC	205
TOTAL			415

10/3	Washington, DC	Sacramento, CA	2440
10/3	Sacramento, CA[9]	San Francisco, CA	90
10/4	San Francisco, CA	Los Angeles/Culver City/Los Angeles, CA	347
10/5	Los Angeles, CA	Washington, DC	2300
TOTAL			5177

10/8	Washington, DC	Newark, NJ	210
10/8	Newark, NJ[9]	New Brunswick, NJ	25
10/8	New Brunswick, NJ[9]	Newark, NJ	25
10/8	Newark, NJ	Washington, DC	210
TOTAL			470

10/12	Washington, DC[10]	Raleigh-Durham/ChapelHill/
		Raleigh-Durham, NC	260
10/12	Raleigh-Durham, NC[10]	Washington, DC	260
TOTAL			520

10/28	Washington, DC (Ellipse)[9]	Baltimore, MD	36
10/28	Baltimore, MD[8]	Washington, DC	36
10/28	Washington, DC	New York, NY	205
10/28	New York, NY	Boston, MA	288
10/29	Boston, MA	Washington, DC	393
TOTAL			958

11/3	Washington, DC	Coraopolis/Ambridge/Coraopolis, PA	192
11/3	Coraopolis, PA	Washington, DC	192
TOTAL			384

11/4	Washington, DC	Lexington, KY	395
11/4	Lexington, KY	Washington, DC	395
TOTAL			790

11/13	Washington, DC	Memphis, TN	765
11/13	Memphis, TN	Washington, DC	765
TOTAL			1530

11/18	Washington, DC[5]	Seattle, WA	2329
11/20	Seattle, WA	San Francisco, CA	678
11/20	San Francisco, CA	Los Angeles/Pasadena/Los Angeles, CA	347
11/21	Los Angeles, CA	Washington, DC	2300
TOTAL			5344

12/3	Washington, DC	Albuquerque/Bernalillo/Albuq., NM	1710
12/3	Albuquerque, NM	Los Angeles, CA	590
12/5	Los Angeles, CA	Washington, DC	2300
TOTAL			4600

12/27	Washington, DC[1]	Hot Springs/Little Rock, AR	955
12/28	Little Rock, AR[10]	Fayetteville, AR	150
12/29	Fayetteville, AR[1]	Beaufort, SC	810
12/29	Beaufort, SC[9]	Hilton Head/Beaufort, SC	20
1/2/94	Beaufort, SC[10]	Washington, DC	520
TOTAL			2455

1/8	Washington, DC[3]	Brussels, Belgium	3850
1/11	Brussels, Belgium[3]	Prague, Czech Republic	500
1/12	Prague, Czech Republic[3]	Kiev, Ukraine	750
1/12	Kiev, Ukraine[3]	Moscow, Russia	510
1/15	Moscow, Russia[3]	Minsk, Belarus	418
1/15	Minsk, Belarus[3]	Geneva, Switzerland	1120
1/16	Geneva, Switzerland[3]	Washington, DC	4180
TOTAL			11328

2/6	Washington, DC	Houston, TX	1220
2/7	Houston, TX	Bossier City/Shreveport/Bossier, LA	230
2/8	Bossier City, LA	Washington, DC	1060
TOTAL			2510

2/15	Washington, DC	Columbus, OH	350
2/15	Columbus, OH[9]	London/Columbus, OH	30
2/15	Columbus, OH	Washington, DC	350
TOTAL			730
2/16	Washington, DC	Newark/Edison/Newark, NJ	210
2/16	Newark, NJ	Washington, DC	210
TOTAL			420

2/28	Washington, DC	Chicago, IL	597
2/28	Chicago, IL[9]	Country Club Hills, IL	20
2/28	Country Club Hills[9]	Chicago, IL	30
2/28	Chicago, IL	Coraopolis/Pittsburgh/Coraopolis, PA	405
2/28	Coraopolis, PA	Washington, DC	192
TOTAL			1244

3/10 Washington, DC	New York, NY	205
3/10 New York, NY	Washington, DC	205
TOTAL		410
3/13 Washington, DC[10]	Selfridge/Detroit/Selfridge, MI	396
3/14 Selfridge, MI	Boston, MA/Nashua, NH	613
3/15 Nashua, NH[10]	Fort Drum, NY	202
3/15 Fort Drum, NY[6]	Washington, DC	360
TOTAL		1571
3/20 Washington, DC	Miami/Bal Harbour/Deerfield Beach/	
	Bal Harbour/Miami, FL	923
3/21 Miami, FL	Washington, DC	923
TOTAL		1846
3/25 Washington, DC	Dallas, TX	1185
3/27 Dallas, TX	Coronado, CA	1200
4/2 Coronado, CA	Charlotte, NC	2120
4/2 Charlotte, NC	Washington, DC	382
TOTAL		4887
4/4 Washington, DC[6]	Cleveland, OH	306
4/4 Cleveland, OH[6]	Charlotte, NC/Troy, NC/	
	Ft. Mill, SC/Charlotte, NC	380
4/5 Charlotte, NC[6]	Washington, DC	382
TOTAL		1068
4/6 Washington, DC[1]	Bowling Green, KY	550
4/6 Bowling Green, KY[1]	Washington, DC	550
TOTAL		1100
4/7 Washington, DC	Topeka, KS	1020
4/7 Topeka, KS[9]	Kansas City, MO/Fairway, KS/	
	Kansas City, MO	55
4/7 Kansas City, MO	Minneapolis, MN	413
4/8 Minneapolis, MN	Washington, DC	934
TOTAL		2422
4/16 Wash., DC (Pentagon)[9]	Williamsburg/Newport News, VA	110
4/17 Newport News, VA	Charlotte/Conrad/Charlotte, NC	290
4/17 Charlotte, NC	Washington, DC	382
TOTAL		782
4/18 Washington, DC	Milwaukee, WI	680
4/18 Milwaukee, WI	Washington, DC	680
TOTAL		1360
4/27 Washington, DC[5]	Irvine/Yorba Linda/Irvine, CA	2250
4/28 Irvine, CA[5]	Washington, DC	2250
TOTAL		4500

5/3	Washington, DC	Marietta/Atlanta/Marietta, GA	600
5/3	Marietta, GA	Washington, DC	600
TOTAL			1200

5/9	Washington, DC	New York, NY	205
5/9	JFK International[9]	Wall Street landing zone	15
5/9	Wall St. landing zone[9]	JFK International Airport	15
5/9	New York, NY	Warwick/Cranston/Warwick, RI	150
5/9	Warwick, RI	Washington, DC	370
TOTAL			755

5/14	Washington, DC	Indianapolis, IN	494
5/14	Indianapolis, IN	Washington, DC	494
TOTAL			988

5/20	Washington, DC	San Bernardino, CA	2300
5/20	San Bernardino, CA[9]	Santa Monica/Los Angeles/	
		Santa Monica/Los Angeles, CA	50
5/21	Los Angeles, CA	Sacramento, CA	360
5/21	Sacramento, CA	Washington, DC	2440
TOTAL			5180

5/25	Wash., DC (Pentagon)[9]	Annapolis, MD	32
5/25	Annapolis, MD[9]	Washington, DC (Pentagon)	32
TOTAL			64

6/1	Washington, DC[3]	Rome, Italy	4690
6/4	Rome, Italy[3]	Brize Norton RAF/Portsmouth, England	900
6/5	Portsmouth, England[9]	USS *George Washington*	15
6/6	USS *George Washington*[9]	Paris, France	190
6/8	Paris, France[3]	Brize Norton RAF, England	250
6/8	Brize Norton, England[3]	Washington, DC	3700
TOTAL			9745

6/14	Washington, DC	Kansas City, MO	995
6/14	Kansas City, MO	Washington, DC	995
TOTAL			1990

6/16	Washington, DC	Chicago, IL	597
6/17	Chicago, IL	Washington, DC	597
TOTAL			1194

6/24	Washington, DC	St. Louis, MO	712
6/24	St. Louis, MO	Washington, DC	712
TOTAL			1424

7/5	Washington, DC[3]	Riga, Latvia	4600
7/6	Riga, Latvia[3]	Warsaw, Poland	360
7/6	Warsaw, Poland[3]	Naples, Italy	1090
7/10	Naples, Italy[3]	Bonn, Germany	820
7/11	Bonn, Germany[3]	Ramstein AFB, Germany	100
7/11	Ramstein AFB, Germany	Berlin, Germany	330
7/12	Berlin, Germany[3]	Washington, DC	4360
TOTAL			11660

7/15	Washington, DC[1]	Latrobe/Greensburg/Latrobe,PA	157
7/15	Latrobe, PA[6]	Philadelphia, PA	229
7/15	Philadelphia, PA[1]	Washington, DC	125
TOTAL			511

7/17	Washington, DC	Miami/Bal Harbour/Miami Beach/	
		Miami, FL	923
7/18	Miami, FL	Brunswick, ME	1390
7/18	Brunswick, ME[9]	Portland, ME	20
7/18	Portland, ME[9]	Brunswick, ME	20
7/18	Brunswick, ME	Boston, MA	130
7/19	Boston, MA	Washington, DC	393
TOTAL			2876

7/30	Washington, DC	Kansas City/Independence/K.C., MO	995
7/30	Kansas City, MO	Cleveland/Mayfield Heights/	
		Hunting Valley/Cleveland, OH	700
7/30	Cleveland, OH	Washington, DC	306
TOTAL			2001

8/1	Washington, DC	Newark/Jersey City/Newark, NJ	210
8/1	Newark, NJ	Washington, DC	210
TOTAL			420

8/12	Washington, DC	Minneapolis, MN	934
8/12	Minneapolis, MN	Washington, DC	934
TOTAL			1868

9/9	Washington, DC	Belle Chasse/New Orleans/	
		Belle Chasse, LA	966
9/9	Belle Chasse, LA	Washington, DC	966
TOTAL			1932

9/23	Washington, DC	Chicago, IL	597
9/24	Chicago, IL	Minneapolis, MN	355
9/24	Minneapolis, MN	Kansas City, MO	413
9/24	Kansas City, MO	New York, NY	1097
9/24	JFK International[9]	Wall Street landing zone	15
9/26	New York, NY	Washington, DC	205
TOTAL			2682

10/6	Washington, DC	Norfolk, VA	150
10/6	Norfolk, VA	Washington, DC	150
TOTAL			300

10/11	Washington, DC	Ypsilanti/Dearborn/Detroit/ Ypsilanti, MI	396
10/11	Ypsilanti, MI	Washington, DC	396
TOTAL			792

10/15	Washington, DC	Windsor Locks, CT	245
10/15	Windsor Locks, CT[9]	Stratford/Bridgeport/Stratford	45
10/15	Stratford, CT[9]	Windsor Locks, CT	45
10/15	Windsor Locks, CT	Miami, FL	1130
10/15	Miami, FL	Washington, DC	923
10/15	Andrews AFB, MD[8]	Reflecting pool (DC)	10
TOTAL			2398

10/17	Washington, DC	Albuquerque, NM	1710
10/17	Albuquerque, NM	Washington, DC	1710
TOTAL			2420

10/19	Washington, DC	New York, NY	205
10/19	JFK International[9]	Wall Street landing zone	15
10/19	Wall Street landing zone[9]	JFK International airport	15
10/19	New York, NY	Boston/Framingham/Boston, MA	288
10/20	Boston, MA	Washington, DC	393
TOTAL			916

10/22	Washington, DC	San Francisco/Belmont/S.F., CA	2530
10/22	San Francisco, CA	Seattle, WA	678
10/23	Seattle, WA	Cleveland/Akron, OH	2026
10/24	Akron, OH[2]	Washington, DC	271
TOTAL			5505

10/25	Washington, DC[3]	Cairo, Egypt	6090
10/26	Cairo, Egypt[3]	Amman, Jordan	270
10/27	Amman, Jordan[3]	Damascus, Syria	250
10/27	Damascus, Syria[3]	Tel Aviv/Jerusalem/Tel Aviv, Israel	540
10/28	Tel Aviv, Israel[3]	Kuwait City, Kuwait	1670
10/28	Kuwait City, Kuwait[3]	King Khalid Military City, Saudi Arabia	215
10/29	KKMC, Saudi Arabia[3]	Washington, DC	7090
TOTAL			16125

10/31	Washington, DC	Philadelphia, PA	125
10/31	Philadelphia, PA	Coraopolis/Pittsburgh/Coraopolis, PA	259
10/31	Coraopolis, PA	Washington, DC	192
TOTAL			576

11/1 Washington, DC	Ypsilanti/Dearborn/Detroit/	
	Ypsilanti, MI	396
11/1 Ypsilanti, MI	Cleveland, OH	125
11/1 Cleveland, OH	Washington, DC	306
TOTAL		827
11/2 Washington, DC	Providence/Pawtucket/Providence, RI	350
11/2 Providence, RI	Washington, DC	350
TOTAL		700
11/3 Washington, DC	Colonie/Albany/Colonie, NY	310
11/3 Colonie, NY	Des Moines, IA	1035
11/3 Des Moines, IA	Duluth, MN	360
11/4 Duluth, MN	Los Alamitos/Los Angeles/	
	Anaheim/Los Alamitos, CA	1617
11/5 Los Alamitos, CA	San Francisco, CA	347
11/6 San Francisco, CA	Seattle, WA	678
11/6 Seattle, WA	Minneapolis/Brooklyn Park/	
	Minneapolis, MN	1395
11/7 Minneapolis, MN	Flint, MI	493
11/7 Flint, MI	Wilmington, DE	485
11/7 Wilmington, DE	Washington, DC	95
TOTAL		6815
11/11 Washington, DC[3]	Anchorage, AK	3250
11/11 Anchorage, AK[3]	Manila, Philippines	5400
11/13 Manila, Philippines[3]	Jakarta, Indonesia	1760
11/16 Jakarta, Indonesia[3]	Honolulu, HI	6980
11/17 Honolulu, HI[11]	Chicago, IL	4297
11/18 Chicago, IL[11]	Washington, DC	597
TOTAL		22284

All flights on Air Force One (747) unless noted: [1]Air Force One (C-9). [2]Air Force One (707). [3]Support plane (747). [4]Support plane (C-9). [5]Support plane (707). [6]Support plane (C-20). [7]Marine One. [8]Nighthawk 2. [9]Nighthawk 3 or 4. [10]Press plane. [11]Commercial plane. Ground transportation indicated as (example): Newark/Edison/Newark, NJ.

All Washington, DC, departures and arrivals at Andrews Air Force Base, MD, unless noted.

Grand totals: 65 trips (162 days, 225 flights). 22 different countries (26 different cities). 36 different states (111 different cities). 201,197 statute miles.

Countries (listed in order visited, one visit each unless noted): Japan, South Korea, Belgium, Czech Republic, Ukraine, Russia, Belarus, Switzerland, Italy (2), Great Britain (2), France, Latvia, Poland, Germany, Egypt, Jordan, Syria, Israel, Kuwait, Saudi Arabia, Philippines, Indonesia.

States (in order visited, with number of visits): Pennsylvania (5), Iowa (3), California (11), Hawaii (2), Missouri (6), Arkansas (2), Illinois (5), West Virginia (1), Colorado (2), Ohio (6), Texas (3), Louisiana (3), Florida (4), New York (7), New Jersey (3), North Carolina (4), Maryland (2), Massachusetts (4), Kentucky (2), Tennessee (1), Washington (3), New Mexico (2), South Carolina (2), Michigan (4), New Hampshire (1), Kansas (1), Minnesota (5), Virginia (2), Wisconsin (1), Georgia (1), Rhode Island (2), Indiana (1), Maine (1), Connecticut (1), Delaware (1), Alaska (1).

Flights per plane: Air Force One (747)—133. Air Force One (C-9)—6. Air Force One (707)—1. Support plane (747)—32. Support plane (C-9)—7. Support plane (707)—3. Support plane (C-20)—5. Press plane—8. Commercial airplane—2. Marine One—1. Nighthawk 2—2. Nighthawk 3 or 4—26.

Types of planes: **747**: modified, military version of Boeing 747 (73 seats). **C-9:** modified, military version of Boeing DC-9 (42 seats). **707**: modified, military version of Boeing 707 (seating varies among four planes used). **C-20**: twin-engine jet (12 seats). **Press plane**: type and seating capacity vary. **Marine One**: 10-seat helicopter. **Nighthawk 2**: 10-seat Marine helicopter. **Nighthawk 3 or 4**: 20- or 34-seat Marine or Navy helicopter.

Modes of travel (9 types): Foot, car, van, bus, train, boat, ship, airplane, helicopter.

▶A Day in the Life

A lot of people used to ask me, What exactly do you do at the White House? Well, before I started traveling, that was kind of hard to answer. Basically, of course, I monitored the wire services and kept the White House staff abreast of coverage of the President. But for a specific look at what I did before being put on the Air Force One permanent manifest, here is a typical day. It was Thursday, June 10, 1993, but it could have been any day during that period.

5:30 A.M. Alarm goes off. Already? It's still dark outside. Groggily stumble through shower and into suit I've laid out the night before. Pull on a colorful tie. White House ID card on chain? Check. Beeper? Check. Metro ticket? Check.

6:05 A.M. Walk the dog. Down the asphalt path behind the condo and back, like every morning. He tries to chase a squirrel up a tree. How can anybody be so awake this early?

6:15 A.M. Depart Bedford Park condominiums en route to Clarendon Metro stop. Cut through quiet little middle-class neighborhood of nice, tiny houses in neat, tidy lawns and flat, straight sidewalks. Sunny morning. Warm already. Gonna get hot today.

6:35 A.M. Arrive Metro and board. Take one of last open seats. Most folks reading *The Washington Post.* Lots of blank stares, zombies en route to work in the District.

6:45 A.M. Four stops to Farragut West and then head up escalator into dawning sunlight of 17th Street.

6:50 A.M. Arrive Old Executive Office Building. Punch in personal access number and push through gray turnstile. Upstairs to Room 162. Click buttons on remote control to check morning network news shows. Log on to OASIS computer system. Scroll Generation wires. Print out daybooks and wire stories, preparing for communications meeting in Director Mark Gearan's office.

7:40 A.M. Finish highlighting printouts. Walk next door to White House West Wing, through lobby, stack of papers in hand.

7:45 A.M. Open meeting in Gearan's office with verbal briefing. Give highlights of today's late news and a couple overnight stories not in the morning papers. Deputy Communications Director David Dreyer gives background on President's event of day. Press Secretary Dee Dee Myers mentions possible questions we'll face. Gearan provides our position and leads discussion.

8:05 A.M. Return to OEOB 162, large and ornate office I share with Director of News Analysis Keith Boykin, a good guy to share an office with. Edit summary of last night's network newscasts written by volunteers and send on e-mail.

8:35 A.M. Arrive late for large 8:30 A.M. staff meeting down the hall in Room 180 (formerly Hubert Humphrey's and, later, George Bush's office). Find out what other departments have upcoming.

8:55 A.M. Return to OEOB 162. Read *The Washington Post.* (In Sports, Orioles win their seventh in a row.)

9:20 A.M. Downstairs to cafeteria to pick up breakfast.

9:30 A.M. Two muffins with margarine and orange juice for breakfast at my desk while reading *USA Today* and *The New York Times.*

10:10 A.M. Scroll wires, reading all sorts of stuff, some related to Administration, some not.

11:20 A.M. Call Dee Dee Myers' assistant, Dave Leavy, to give highlights of morning news in preparation for Myers' briefing. Deliver wire story printouts to Myers in her West Wing office.

12:00 P.M. Watch Myers' briefing on closed circuit TV while printing out wire stories. Reporters aren't too brutal today.

12:15 P.M. Take wire copy to West Wing basement and make copies. Rarely anybody down here, and the copiers even work.

12:25 P.M. Deliver 10 sets to senior staff throughout West Wing and Old Executive Office Building, past Secret Service agents in front of Oval Office. (Sometimes I catch a glimpse myself in the mirror, wearing a suit and a pager and a White House ID, and think to myself, "Who are you trying to kid?")

12:35 P.M. Send "Hotline," "Greenwire" and "Health Line" to Vice President's staff via e-mail. They're not on our mainframe, but we have an e-mail gateway.

12:50 P.M. Downstairs to cafeteria. Crowded, especially with 143 interns here for six weeks.

1:00 P.M. Lunch at my desk in Room 162. Sloppy Joe, fries, salad with French dressing, chocolate chip cookie and lemonade. Myers finishes briefing on TV as I eat and read the *Los Angeles Times*.

1:25 P.M. Get call from Julia Payne in Vice President's press office requesting Senator Bob Dole quotes from clips and wires in past couple days. (Veep being interviewed by Dan Rather tonight on CBS right after Dole).

1:30 P.M. Get call from Director of Media Affairs Jeff Eller requesting copies of wire stories filed after Myers' briefing.

1:35 P.M. To West Wing and back three times, taking relevant stories about Alan Greenspan's position on President's economic plan to Myers and Counselor David Gergen in Gearan's office. Remains of lunch get cold on my desk in my absence.

2:05 P.M. Office of the Press Secretary releases statement clarifying Clinton Administration's position on Federal Reserve chairman's role.

2:35 P.M. Take Dole research project upstairs to Vice President's Press Office. They're very grateful. Good group of folks.

2:55 P.M. Pick up pink paper phone messages from black plastic carousel on receptionist's desk.

3:00 P.M. Scroll wires and print out for mid-afternoon wire report. (Really give that HP II Laserjet a workout).

3:15 P.M. To West Wing basement and make copies.

3:25 P.M. Distribute wire reports in West Wing and Old Executive Office Building. Hang out briefly in lower press office. Good chance to see people around the 18 acres and keep in touch. After all, I've known some of them a year and a half now. Some folks sitting outside in sun on front steps of OEOB.

3:35 P.M. Return phone calls. Just routine stuff.

4:05 P.M. Send e-mail and write memo on status of wire system installation after speaking on phone with White House Communications Agency officer in charge of project.

4:30 P.M. Watch "Inside Politics" on CNN. Bernie Shaw talks to Wolf Blitzer on the White House front lawn, just outside our window, and Bob Franken on Capitol Hill about the status of the energy tax and the economic plan.

5:00 P.M. Scroll wires. Check Arkansas state wire for stories.

6:00 P.M. Print out wire stories. (Be glad when this all will be on diskette and can be e-mailed).

6:15 P.M. To West Wing basement and make copies.

6:25 P.M. Distribute last wire report of the day throughout West Wing and OEOB. Chat briefly with Tipper Gore's staff.

6:30 P.M. Back to Room 162. Feet up on my desk to watch "CBS Evening News" with Dan Rather and Connie Chung and flip through *The Wall Street Journal*. Gore does fine in interview from his West Wing office taped at 4:30 P.M.

7:00 P.M. Watch top stories on ABC and NBC on TV sets next door in "war room."

7:20 P.M. Say goodbye to volunteers monitoring evening news and head out Pennsylvania Avenue exit. Sunny, warm walk to Farragut West Metro stop as traffic bustles past.

7:25 P.M. Arrive Metro station and board. Lucky to get a seat.

7:45 P.M. Arrive Clarendon and emerge from escalator into setting sun. Stroll home on Washington Boulevard, jacket slung over my shoulder.

8:10 P.M. Arrive 150A North Bedford Street. My dog Camelot is glad to see me.

8:20 P.M. Check mail, change clothes, take dog for a walk. Legs tired from walking $2^{1}/_{2}$ miles total today in dress shoes.

8:40 P.M. Eat microwaveable frozen Salisbury steak dinner at kitchen table while reading *Rolling Stone.*

9:30 P.M. Into bed to get rested so I can get up at 5:30 A.M. and do it all over again. My mind races before I finally fall asleep.

▶*Where Are They Now?*

JODY POWELL, who was press secretary to President Carter, addressed our Office of Communications staff over lunch one day. He referred to working at the White House as "boot camp" that would pay off when we left. Some of my fellow White House aides have remained there, while many others have put that "boot camp" experience to use elsewhere. Among the fellow travelers mentioned in this journal, here's where some are now (or at least where they were, as of summer 1997):

Ralph Alswang, **Sharon Farmer**, **Barb Kinney** (Staff Photographers): All three are still at the White House, taking Presidential photos around the world.

Paul Begala (Political Consultant): He returned home to Austin, Texas, to teach a class on Presidents and the media at the University of Texas and to work for a public policy firm.

Keith Boykin (Media Affairs): He is now the executive director of the National Black Gay and Lesbian Leadership Forum and the author of "One More River to Cross."

Jeff Eller (Director of Media Affairs): He is working for Public Strategies Inc., a public policy firm, in Austin, Texas.

Mark Gearan (Director of Communications): After being nominated by the President and confirmed by the Senate, he is serving as director of the Peace Corps.

Arthur Jones (Deputy Press Secretary): He left the White House to work at the Department of Labor in Washington.

Bruce Lindsey (Deputy Counsel): He remains the President's loyal companion, traveling across the country at his side.

Dr. Connie Mariano (Presidential Physician): She is still attending to the world's most powerful patient.

Mack McLarty (Counsel to the President): He continues to assist the President on outreach to the business community and in other areas, including Latin America.

Dee Dee Myers (Press Secretary): The former co-host of "Equal Time" for cable channel CNBC, she is now married and living in Los

Angeles. She also is a contributing editor for *Vanity Fair.*

Larry Sampas (Deputy Director of News Analysis): He left the White House in January 1995 and is still living in Maryland.

Lieutenant Colonel Rusty Schorsch (Military Aide): Last I heard, he was headed to Fort Benning, Georgia, for his next assignment.

Matt Smith (Campaign Staff): He is working as director of public affairs for Chicago's Department of Planning and Development.

Wendy Smith (Trip Director): After leaving the White House in mid-1997, she joined *The New Yorker* to work directly for publisher Tina Brown.

George Stephanopoulos (Senior Adviser): He left the White House after the 1996 election for a two-year stint as a visiting professor of political science at Columba University, his alma mater. He also is a contributing correspondent for ABC News.

David Wilhelm (Democratic National Committee Chairman): He is in Chicago, working as senior managing director of investment banking for Kemper Securities, Inc.

Index

ABOUT THE AUTHOR

Ken Chitester is the former White House Director of the Office of News Analysis (1993–1994) for President Bill Clinton. In that role, he traveled more than 200,000 miles aboard Air Force One to 22 countries, 36 states and 137 cities. He managed more than 35 staffers, interns and volunteers, supervising production of nearly 40 news reports weekly (a total of 5.7 million pages annually). He also administered the White House's $1.5-million-plus wire service computer system.

Before joining the Clinton for President Committee in 1992, he was an award-winning six-year veteran of daily newspapers. He has received national first place "Best of Gannett" honors for writing a week-long series of newspaper articles. He also has won third place from the Illinois Press Association for original column writing and was cited by contest judges for "excellent writing and style." His work has appeared in *USA Today* and in newspapers across the country through Gannett News Service.

He is a graduate of Indiana University with a bachelor's degree in journalism, and currently lives in Little Rock, Arkansas.